COBALT
RED

ALSO BY SIDDHARTH KARA

Modern Slavery: A Global Perspective
Bonded Labor: Tackling the System of Slavery in South Asia
Sex Trafficking: Inside the Business of Modern Slavery

COBALT
RED

HOW THE BLOOD OF
THE CONGO POWERS
OUR LIVES

SIDDHARTH KARA

ST. MARTIN'S PRESS
NEW YORK

First published in the United States by St. Martin's Press,
an imprint of St. Martin's Publishing Group

COBALT RED. Copyright © 2023 by Siddharth Kara. All rights reserved. Printed
in the United States of America. For information, address St. Martin's Publishing
Group, 120 Broadway, New York, NY 10271.

www.stmartins.com

The Library of Congress Cataloging-in-Publication Data
is available upon request.

ISBN 978-1-250-28430-3 (hardcover)
ISBN 978-1-250-28429-7 (ebook)

Our books may be purchased in bulk for promotional, educational, or
business use. Please contact your local bookseller or the Macmillan Corporate and
Premium Sales Department at 1-800-221-7945, extension 5442, or by email at
MacmillanSpecialMarkets@macmillan.com.

First Edition: 2023

10 9 8 7 6 5 4

For my daughter

Contents

List of Acronyms

CDM   Congo DongFang Mining

CMKK   Coopérative Minière Maadini kwa Kilimo

CMOC   China Molybdenum Company

COMAKAT   Coopérative Minière et Artisanale du Katanga

COMIAKOL   Coopérative Minière Artisanale de Kolwezi

COMIKU   Coopérative Minière KUPANGA

COMMUS   La Compagnie Minière de Musonoie Global SAS

FARDC   Forces Armées de la République Démocratique du Congo

Gécamines   La Générale des Carrières et des Mines

IDAK   Investissements Durables au Katanga

KCC   Kamoto Copper Company

KICO   Kipushi Corporation

MIKAS   La Minière de Kasombo

MUMI   Mutanda Mining Sarl

SAESSCAM   Service d'Assistance et d'Encadrement du Small-Scale
    Mining

SAEMAPE   Service d'Assistance et d'Encadrement de l'Exploitation
    Minière Artisanale et à Petite Echelle

SICOMINES   Sino-Congolaise des Mines

TFM   Tenke Fungurume Mining

UMHK   Union Minière du Haut-Katanga

ZEA   Zone d'Exploitation Artisanale

Nyama tembo kula hawezi kumaliza.
("You never finish eating the meat of an elephant.")

—Congolese saying

COBALT
RED

Introduction

Such then was the main task: to convince the world that this Congo horror was not only and unquestionably a fact; but that it was not accidental or temporary, or capable of internal cure . . . To demonstrate that it was at once a survival and a revival of the slave-mind at work, of the slave-trade in being.
— E. D. Morel, *History of the Congo Reform Movement*, 1914

THE SOLDIERS ARE WILD and wide-eyed as they point their weapons at the villagers trying to enter the mining area at Kamilombe. Although they are desperate to reach their loved ones just a stone's throw away, the villagers are denied access. What has happened here must not be seen. There can be no record or evidence, only the haunting memories of those who stood at this place where hope was lost. My guide urges me to stay at the periphery; the situation is too unpredictable. From the fringes, it is difficult to see the details of the accident. The craterous landscape is obscured by a leaden haze that refuses the entry of light. Distant hills appear only as the vague silhouette of a lumbering beast.

I move closer to investigate, treading carefully into the boiling crowd. I catch sight of a body in the dirt. It is a child, lying motionless within a storm of dust and despair. I try to make out the features of his face, but they elude me. Around the lifeless body, the ocher gravel has been stained in dark shades of red, like burnt umber or rusted metal. Until this moment, I thought that the ground in the Congo took its vermillion hue from the copper in the dirt, but now I cannot help but wonder whether the earth here is red because of all the blood that has spilled upon it.

I inch toward the cordon to see the child more clearly. Tensions between the soldiers and villagers escalate to the brink of riot. A soldier shouts angrily and waves his gun at me. I've drifted too close and lingered too long. I take one final look toward the child. I can see his face now, locked in a terminal expression of dread. That is the lasting image I take from the Congo—the heart of Africa reduced to the bloodstained corpse of a child, who died solely because he was digging for cobalt.

◎ ◎ ◎

There is a frenzy taking place in the Democratic Republic of the Congo, a manic race to extract as much cobalt as quickly as possible. This rare, silvery metal is an essential component to almost every lithium-ion rechargeable battery made today. It is also used in a wide array of emerging low-carbon innovations that are critical to the achievement of climate sustainability goals. The Katanga region in the southeastern corner of the Congo holds more reserves of cobalt than the rest of the planet combined. The region is also brimming with other valuable metals, including copper, iron, zinc, tin, nickel, manganese, germanium, tantalum, tungsten, uranium, gold, silver, and lithium. The deposits were always there, resting dormant for eons before foreign economies made the dirt valuable. Industrial innovations sparked demand for one metal after another, and somehow they all happened to be in Katanga. The remainder of the Congo is similarly bursting with natural resources. Foreign powers have penetrated every inch of this nation to extract its rich supplies of ivory, palm oil, diamonds, timber, rubber . . . and to make slaves of its people. Few nations are blessed with a more diverse abundance of resource riches than the Congo. No country in the world has been more severely exploited.

The scramble for cobalt is reminiscent of King Leopold II's infamous plunder of the Congo's ivory and rubber during his brutal reign as king sovereign of the Congo Free State from 1885 to 1908. Those familiar with Leopold's regime may reasonably point out that there is little equivalency between the atrocities that took place during his time and the harms taking place today. To be sure, the loss of life during Leopold's control of the Congo is estimated to be as high as thirteen million people, a sum equal to half the population of the colony at the time. Today, the loss of life caused either directly by mining accidents or indirectly by toxic exposure and environmental contamination in the mining provinces would likely be a few thousand per year. One must acknowledge, however, the following crucial fact—for centuries, enslaving Africans was the nature of colonialism. In the modern era, slavery has been universally rejected and basic human rights are deemed *erga omnes* and *jus cogens* in international law. The ongoing exploitation of the poorest people of the Congo by the rich and powerful invalidates the purported moral foundation of contemporary civilization and drags humanity back to a time when the people of Africa were valued only by their replacement cost. The implications of this moral reversion, which is itself a form of violence, stretch far beyond central Africa across the entire global south, where a vast subclass of humanity continues to eke out a subhuman existence in slave-like conditions at the bottom of the global economic order. Less has changed since colonial times than we might care to admit.

The harsh realities of cobalt mining in the Congo are an inconvenience to every stakeholder in the chain. No company wants to concede that the rechargeable batteries used to power smartphones, tablets, laptops, and electric vehicles contain cobalt mined by peasants and children in hazardous conditions. In public disclosures and press releases, the corporations perched atop the cobalt chain typically cite their commitments to international human rights norms, zero-tolerance policies on child labor, and adherence to the highest standards of supply chain due diligence. Here are a few examples:[1]

> Apple works to protect the environment and to safeguard the well-being of the millions of people touched by our supply chain, from the mining level to the facilities where products are assembled . . . As of December 31, 2021, we found that all identified smelters and refiners in our supply

chain participated in or completed a third party audit that met Apple's requirements for the responsible sourcing of minerals.

Samsung has a zero-tolerance policy against child labor as prohibited by international standards and relevant national laws and regulations in all stages of its global operations.

While Tesla's responsible sourcing practices apply to all materials and supply chain partners, we recognize the conditions associated with select artisanal mining (ASM) of cobalt in the DRC. To assure the cobalt in Tesla's supply chain is ethically sourced, we have implemented targeted due diligence procedures for cobalt sourcing.

For Daimler, respect for human rights is a fundamental aspect of responsible corporate governance . . . We want our products to contain only raw materials and other materials that have been mined and produced without violating human rights and environmental standards.

Glencore plc is committed to preventing the occurrence of modern slavery and human trafficking in our operations and supply chains . . . We do not tolerate child labour, any form of forced, compulsory or bonded labour, human trafficking or any other form of slavery and actively seek to identify and eliminate them from our supply chains.

As scrutiny over the conditions under which cobalt is mined has increased, stakeholders have formulated international coalitions to help ensure that their supply chains are clean. The two leading coalitions are the Responsible Minerals Initiative (RMI) and the Global Battery Alliance (GBA). The RMI promotes the responsible sourcing of minerals in accordance with the UN Guiding Principles for Business and Human Rights. Part of the RMI's platform includes a Responsible Minerals Assurance Process that purports to support independent, third-party assessments of cobalt supply chains and to monitor cobalt mining sites in the DRC for child labor. The GBA promotes safe working conditions in the mining of raw materials for rechargeable batteries. The GBA has developed a Cobalt Action Partnership to "immediately and urgently eliminate child and forced labour from the cobalt value chain"[2] through on-ground monitoring and third-party assessments.

In all my time in the Congo, I never saw or heard of any activities linked to either of these coalitions, let alone anything that resembled corporate commitments to international human rights standards, third-party audits, or zero-tolerance policies on forced and child labor. On the contrary, across twenty-one years of research into slavery and child labor, I have never seen more extreme predation for profit than I witnessed at the bottom of global cobalt supply chains. The titanic companies that sell products containing Congolese cobalt are worth trillions, yet the people who dig their cobalt out of the ground eke out a base existence characterized by extreme poverty and immense suffering. They exist at the edge of human life in an environment that is treated like a toxic dumping ground by foreign mining companies. Millions of trees have been clear-cut, dozens of villages razed, rivers and air polluted, and arable land destroyed. Our daily lives are powered by a human and environmental catastrophe in the Congo.

Although the scale of destruction caused by cobalt mining in the name of renewable energy is without contemporary parallel, the contradictory nature of mining is nothing new. Some of the most transformative advancements in human civilization would not have been possible without gouging the earth for minerals and metals. The revolution began around seven thousand years ago when people first applied fire to mined materials. Metals were melted and formed into objects used for commerce, adornment, and weapons. Tin was discovered five thousand years ago and mixed with copper to make bronze, the first alloy harder than its constituent metals. The Bronze Age was born, and the advent of metalworking sparked rapid advancements in human civilization. Bronze was used to fashion weapons, agricultural tools, and coins. The first forms of writing developed, the wheel was invented, and urban civilization evolved. It was also during the Bronze Age that cobalt was first used to color pottery. During the Iron Age, iron ore was mined and smelted into steel, which was used to fashion more powerful tools and weapons. Armies were built and empires were forged. During the early Middle Ages, Europeans created the first mining concessions. Governments offered commercial entities the rights to mine minerals from a parcel of land in exchange for a portion of revenues, a system that continues to this day.

Mining technology leaped forward during the late Middle Ages when miners started using black powder from China to blow up large rocks. The influx of mineral wealth from the New World, especially gold, financed much of the Renaissance, leading to the Industrial Revolution, which gave birth to the modern mining industry. Coal mining powered industrialization, and with it came a troubled history of environmental contamination, degradation of air quality, and exacerbation of climate change. The Industrial Revolution spurred further improvements in mining equipment—mechanical drills increased the efficiency of mining hard rock, and manual loading and hauling were replaced by electric conveyors, mine cars, and heavy-duty vehicles. These and other technological advancements allowed mining companies to dig deeper and more extensively than ever before.

By the late twentieth century, mining contributed to almost every aspect of modern life. Steel was used for buildings, homes, bridges, ships, trains, vehicles, and planes. Aluminum, tin, nickel, and other metals were used in thousands of industrial and consumer applications. Copper was used for electrical wiring and circuitry, military ordnance, and industrial machinery. Petroleum derivatives gave us plastics. Advancements in agricultural productivity would not have been possible without machinery from mined materials. Although today's trillion-dollar global mining industry is dominated by coal, iron, bauxite, phosphate, gypsum, and copper, the so-called strategic and rare earth elements used in modern technology devices and renewable forms of energy are rapidly growing in economic and geopolitical importance. Many of these strategic minerals can be found in central Africa, chief among them cobalt.

Throughout much of history, mining operations relied on the exploitation of slaves and poor laborers to excavate ore from dirt. The downtrodden were forced to dig in hazardous conditions with little regard to their safety and for little to no compensation. Today, these laborers are assigned the quaint term *artisanal miners,* and they toil in a shadowy substrate of the global mining industry called *artisanal and small-scale mining* (ASM). Do not be fooled by the word *artisanal* into thinking that ASM involves pleasant mining activities conducted by skilled artisans. Artisanal miners use rudimentary tools and work in hazardous conditions to extract dozens of minerals and precious stones in more than eighty countries across the global south. Because ASM is almost entirely informal, artisanal miners rarely have formal agreements for wages and working conditions. There are usually no avenues to seek assistance for injuries or redress for abuse. Artisanal miners are almost always paid paltry wages on a piece-rate basis and must assume all risks of injury, illness, or death.

Although ASM is fraught with hazardous conditions, the sector has been growing rapidly. There are roughly forty-five million people around the world directly involved in ASM, which represents an astonishing 90 percent of the world's total mining workforce. Despite the many advancements in machinery and techniques, the formal mining industry relies heavily on the hard labor of artisanal miners to boost production at minimal expense. The contributions from ASM are substantial, including 26 percent of the global supply of tantalum, 25 percent of tin and gold, 20 percent of diamonds, 80 percent of sapphires, and up to 30 percent of cobalt.[3]

To uncover the realities of cobalt mining in the Congo, I journeyed into the heart of the country's two mining provinces—Haut-Katanga and Lualaba. I formed well-reasoned plans on how I would conduct my investigations, but few plans survive first contact with the Congo. Conditions were adversarial at every turn, including aggressive security forces, intense surveillance, the remoteness of many mining areas, distrust of outsiders, and the sheer scale of hundreds of thousands of people engaged in the feverish excavation of cobalt in medieval conditions. The journey into the mining provinces was at times a jarring time warp. The most advanced consumer electronic devices and electric vehicles in the world rely on a substance that is excavated by the blistered hands of peasants using picks, shovels, and rebar. Labor is valued by the penny, life hardly at all. There are many episodes in the history of the Congo that are bloodier than what is happening in the mining sector today, but none of these episodes ever involved so much suffering for so much profit linked so indispensably to the lives of billions of people around the world.

The field research for this book was conducted during trips to the Congo's mining provinces in 2018, 2019, and 2021. Travel during 2020 was not possible due to the COVID-19 pandemic. As the pandemic wreaked havoc across the globe, its impact on the destitute people mining for cobalt remains largely unassessed. When industrial mines went into lockdown for extended periods during 2020 and 2021, demand for cobalt did not graciously hibernate. It only grew as people across the world relied more than ever on their rechargeable devices to continue working or attending school from home. The increased demand for cobalt pressured hundreds of thousands of Congolese peasants who could not survive without the dollar or two they earned each day to clamber into the ditches and tunnels, unprotected, to keep the cobalt flowing. COVID-19 spread rapidly in the artisanal mines of the Congo, where mask wearing and social distancing were impossible. The sick and dead infected by the disease were never counted, adding an unknown number to the industry's bleak tally.

To obtain the testimonies included in this book, I devoted as much time as possible listening to the stories of those living and working in the mining provinces. Some spoke for themselves; others spoke for the dead. I followed institutional review board (IRB) protocols for human subject research during all my interviews with artisanal miners and other informants. These protocols are designed to protect sources from negative consequences for participating in research and include securing informed consent prior to conducting an interview, not recording any personal identifying information, and ensuring that any written or typed notes always remained in my possession. These procedures are especially important in the Congo, where the dangers of speaking to outsiders cannot be overstated. Most artisanal miners and their family members did not want to speak with me for fear of violent reprisals.

My investigations in the DRC were only made possible with the assistance of several guides and translators who were trusted in local communities. These guides assisted me in gaining access to scores of mining sites, as well as the people who toiled at them. Every one of the guides who worked with me did so at considerable personal risk. The Congolese government has historically gone to great lengths to obscure conditions in the mining provinces. Anyone seeking to expose the realities, such as journalists, NGO workers, researchers, or foreign news media, is heavily monitored during their stay. The Congolese military and other security forces are omnipresent in mining areas, making access to mining sites dangerous and at times impossible. Perceived troublemakers can be arrested, tortured, or worse. Out of an abundance of caution, I have used pseudonyms for my guides and the brave individuals whose testimonies are included in this book. I have also limited any personal descriptions or information that could be used to identify these individuals, as such information would place them and their families in jeopardy.

The severity of harm being caused by cobalt mining is sadly not a new experience for the people of the Congo. Centuries of European slave trading beginning in the early 1500s caused irreparable injury to the native population, culminating in colonization by King Leopold II, who set the table for the exploitation that continues to this day. The descriptions of Leopold's regime remain disturbingly applicable to the modern Congo.

Joseph Conrad immortalized the evil of Leopold's Congo Free State in *Heart of Darkness* (1899) with four words—"The horror! The horror!" He subsequently described the Congo Free State as the "vilest scramble for loot that ever disfigured the history of human conscience" and a land in which "ruthless, systematic cruelty towards the blacks is the basis of administration." The year after *Heart of Darkness* was published, the first known person to walk the length of Africa from the Cape to Cairo, E. S. Grogan, described Leopold's territory as a "vampire growth." In

The Casement Report (1904), Roger Casement, British consul to the Congo Free State, described the colony as a "veritable hell on earth." Casement's indefatigable ally in bringing an end to Leopold's regime, E. D. Morel, wrote that the Congo Free State was "a perfected system of oppression, accompanied by unimaginable barbarities and responsible for the vast destruction of human life."[4]

Every one of these descriptions equally conveys conditions in the cobalt mining provinces today. Spend a short time watching the filth-caked children of the Katanga region scrounge at the earth for cobalt, and you would be unable to determine whether they were working for the benefit of Leopold or a tech company.

Although the people of the Congo have suffered through centuries of exploitation, there was a moment—a fleeting flash of light at the dawn of independence in 1960—when the direction of the nation could have drastically shifted. The country's first democratically elected prime minister, Patrice Lumumba, offered the nation a glimpse of a future in which the Congolese people could determine their own fates, use the nation's resources for the benefit of the masses, and reject the interference of foreign powers that sought to continue exploiting the country's resources. It was a bold, anti-colonial vision that could have altered the course of history in the Congo and across Africa. In short order, Belgium, the United Nations, the United States, and the neocolonial interests they represented rejected Lumumba's vision, conspired to assassinate him, and propped up a violent dictator, Joseph Mobutu, in his place. For thirty-two years, Mobutu supported the Western agenda, kept Katanga's minerals flowing in their direction, and enriched himself just as egregiously as the colonizers who came before him.

Of all the tragedies that have afflicted the Congo, perhaps the greatest of all is the fact that the suffering taking place in the mining provinces today is entirely preventable. But why fix a problem if no one thinks it exists? Most people do not know what is happening in the cobalt mines of the Congo, because the realities are hidden behind numerous layers of multinational supply chains that serve to erode accountability. By the time one traces the chain from the child slogging in the cobalt mine to the rechargeable gadgets and cars sold to consumers around the world, the links have been misdirected beyond recognition, like a con man running a shell game.

This system of obfuscating the severity of exploitation of poor people of color at the bottom of global supply chains goes back centuries. Few people sitting for breakfast in England in the 1700s knew that their tea was sweetened by sugar harvested under brutal conditions by African slaves toiling in the West Indies. The slaves remained far removed from the British breakfast table until a band of abolitionists placed the true picture of slavery directly in front of the English people. Stakeholders fought to maintain the system. They told the British public not to trust what they were told. They espoused the great humanity of the slave trade—Africans were not suffering, they were being "saved" from the savagery of the dark continent. They argued that Africans worked in pleasing conditions on the islands. When those arguments failed, the slavers claimed they made changes that remedied the offenses taking place on the plantations. After all, who was going to go all the way to the West Indies and prove otherwise, and even if they did, who would believe them?

The truth, however, was this—but for the demand for sugar and the immense profits accrued through the sale of it, the entire slavery-for-sugar economy would not have existed. Furthermore, the inevitable outcome of stripping humans of their dignity, security, wages, and freedom can only be a system that results in the complete dehumanization of the people exploited at the bottom of the chain.

Today's tech barons will tell you a similar tale about cobalt. They will tell you that they uphold international human rights norms and that *their* particular supply chains are clean. They will assure you that conditions are not as bad as they seem and that they are bringing commerce, wages, education, and development to the poorest people of Africa ("saving" them). They will also assure you that they have implemented changes to remedy the problems on the ground, at least at the mines from which they say they buy cobalt. After all, who is going to go all the way to the Congo and prove otherwise, and even if they did, who would believe them?

The truth, however, is this—but for their demand for cobalt and the immense profits they accrue through the sale of smartphones, tablets, laptops, and electric vehicles, the entire blood-for-cobalt economy would not exist. Furthermore, the inevitable outcome of a lawless scramble for cobalt in an impoverished and war-torn country can only be the complete dehumanization of the people exploited at the bottom of the chain.

So much time has passed; so little has changed.

Although conditions for the Congo's cobalt miners remain exceedingly bleak, there is nevertheless cause to be hopeful. Awareness of their plight is growing and, with it, hope that their voices will no longer call out into an abyss but into the hearts of the people at the other end of the chain, who are able to see at last that the blood-caked corpse of that child lying in the dirt is one of their own.

1

"Unspeakable Richness"

It is in every aspect an enormous and atrocious lie in action. If it were not rather appalling the cool completeness would be amusing.
—Joseph Conrad, letter to Roger Casement, December 17, 1903

W E ARE ALL AWARE of just how much today's world depends on fossil fuels. Oil, coal, and natural gas are extracted in every corner of the globe, beneath oceans, deserts, mountains, and land. Imagine for a moment if almost three-fourths of all fossil fuel beneath the earth's surface was instead extracted from a single patch of earth roughly four hundred by one hundred kilometers in size. Imagine that within this patch of earth, approximately half the oil was located in and around a single city and that the deposits were shallow enough for anyone to access with a shovel. This would surely be the most indispensable city in the world. Massive drilling companies would flock to it to stake their claims on the riches. So too would the local population from miles around. Violence would erupt to secure control of valuable territory. Preservation of the environment would become an afterthought. Regional governance would be marred by corruption. Profits would be asymmetrically distributed, with powerful stakeholders at the top of the chain accruing the most benefit while the local inhabitants languished. This is the exact situation taking place today with a crucial mineral that will be as important to our future as fossil fuels have been to our past. The mineral is cobalt, and the city is Kolwezi.

Kolwezi is tucked in the hazy hills of the southeastern corner of the Democratic Republic of the Congo. Although most people have never heard of Kolwezi, billions of people could not conduct their daily lives without this city. The batteries in almost every smartphone, tablet, laptop, and electric vehicle made today cannot recharge without Kolwezi. The cobalt found in the dirt here provides maximum stability and energy density to rechargeable batteries, allowing them to hold more charge and operate safely for longer periods. Remove cobalt from the battery, and you will have to plug in your smartphone or electric vehicle much more often, and before long, the batteries may very well catch on fire. There is no known deposit of cobalt-containing ore anywhere in the world that is larger, more accessible, and higher grade than the cobalt under Kolwezi.

Cobalt is typically found in nature bound to copper, and the copper-cobalt deposits in the Congo stretch in varying degrees of density and grade along a four-hundred-kilometer crescent from Kolwezi to northern Zambia, forming an area called the Central African Copper Belt. The Copper Belt is a metallogenic wonder that contains vast mineral riches, including 10 percent of the world's copper and about half the world's cobalt reserves. In 2021, a total of 111,750 tons of cobalt representing 72 percent of the global supply was mined in the DRC, a contribution that is expected to increase as demand from consumer-facing technology companies and electric vehicle manufacturers grows each year.[1] One might reasonably expect Kolwezi to be a boom town in which fortunes are made by intrepid prospectors. Nothing could be further from the truth. Kolwezi, like the rest of the Congolese Copper Belt, is a land scarred by the mad scramble to feed cobalt up the chain into the hands of consumers across the globe. The scale of destruction is enormous, and the magnitude of suffering is incalculable. Kolwezi is the new heart of darkness, a tormented heir to those Congolese atrocities that came before—colonization, wars, and generations of slavery.

The first European to cross the heart of the African continent in a single trip from east to west, British lieutenant Verney Lovett Cameron, ominously wrote this about the Congo in *The Times* on January 7, 1876:

The interior is mostly a magnificent and healthy country of unspeakable richness. I have a small specimen of good coal; other minerals such as gold, copper, iron and silver are abundant, and I am confident that with a wise and liberal (not lavish) expenditure of capital, one of the greatest systems of inland navigation in the world might be utilized, and from 30 months to 36 months begin to repay any enterprising capitalist that might take the matter in hand.[2]

Within a decade of Cameron's missive, "enterprising capitalists" began pillaging the "unspeakable richness" of the Congo. The great Congo River and its capillary-like tributaries provided a built-in system of navigation for Europeans making their way into the heart of Africa, as well as a means by which to transport valuable resources from the interior back to the Atlantic coast. No one knew at the outset that the Congo would prove to be home to some of the largest supplies of almost every resource the world desired, often at the time of new inventions or industrial developments—ivory for piano keys, crucifixes, false teeth, and carvings (1880s), rubber for car and bicycle tires (1890s), palm oil for soap (1900s+), copper, tin, zinc, silver, and nickel for industrialization (1910+), diamonds and gold for riches (always), uranium for nuclear bombs (1945), tantalum and tungsten for microprocessors (2000s+), and cobalt for rechargeable batteries (2012+). The developments that sparked demand for each resource attracted a new wave of treasure seekers. At no point in their history have the Congolese people benefited in any meaningful way from the monetization of their country's resources. Rather, they have often served as a slave labor force for the extraction of those resources at minimum cost and maximum suffering.

The rapacious appetite for cobalt is a direct result of today's device-driven economy combined with the global transition from fossil fuels to renewable sources of energy. Automakers are rapidly increasing production of electric vehicles in tandem with governmental efforts to reduce carbon emissions emerging from the Paris Agreement on climate change in 2015. These commitments were amplified during the COP26 meetings in 2021. The battery packs in electric vehicles require up to ten kilograms of refined cobalt each, more than one thousand times the amount required for a smartphone battery. As a result, demand for cobalt is expected to grow by almost 500 percent from 2018 to 2050,[3] and there is no known place on earth to find that amount of cobalt other than the DRC.

Cobalt mining in towns like Kolwezi takes place at the bottom of complex supply chains that unfurl like a kraken into some of the richest and most powerful companies in the world. Apple, Samsung, Google, Microsoft, Dell, LTC, Huawei, Tesla, Ford, General Motors, BMW, and Daimler-Chrysler are just some of the companies that buy some, most, or all their cobalt from the DRC, by way of battery manufacturers and cobalt refiners based in China, Japan, South Korea, Finland, and Belgium. None of these companies claims to tolerate the hostile conditions under which cobalt is mined in the Congo, but neither they nor anyone else are undertaking sufficient efforts to ameliorate these conditions. In fact, no one seems to accept responsibility at all for the negative consequences of cobalt mining in the Congo—not the Congolese government, not foreign mining companies, not battery manufacturers, and certainly not megacap tech and car companies. Accountability vanishes like morning mist in the Katangan hills as it travels through the opaque supply chains that connect stone to phone and car.

The flow of minerals and money is further obscured by a web of shady connections between foreign mining companies and Congolese political leaders, some of whom have become scandalously rich auctioning the country's mining concessions while tens of millions of Congolese people suffer extreme poverty, food insecurity, and civil strife. There was not a single peaceful transfer of power in the Congo from 1960, when Patrice Lumumba was elected to be the nation's first prime minister, until 2019, when Félix Tshisekedi was elected. In the interim, the country was subjected to one violent coup after another, first with Joseph Mobutu, who ruled the Congo from 1965 to 1997, followed by Laurent-Désiré Kabila's reign from 1997 to 2001, followed by his son Joseph Kabila from 2001 to 2019. I use the words *rule* and *reign* because Mobutu and the Kabilas ran the country like despots, enriching themselves on the nation's mineral resources while leaving their people to languish.

As of 2022, there is no such thing as a clean supply chain of cobalt from the Congo. All cobalt sourced from the DRC is tainted by various degrees of abuse, including slavery, child labor, forced labor, debt bondage, human trafficking, hazardous and toxic working conditions, pathetic wages, injury and death, and incalculable environmental harm. Although there are bad actors at every link in the chain, the chain would not exist were it not for the substantial demand for cobalt created by the companies at the top. It is there, and only there, where solutions must begin. Those solutions will only have meaning if the fictions promulgated by corporate stakeholders about the conditions under which cobalt is mined in the Congo are replaced by the realities experienced by the miners themselves.

To understand these realities, we must first lay a bit of groundwork in this chapter on the Congo and the cobalt mining supply chain. Our journey will then begin in an old colonial mining town called Lubumbashi. From there, a single road traverses the mining provinces deeper into the heart of cobalt territory. As we follow this road, the conditions of cobalt mining will be revealed with each passing mile through the firsthand accounts of the children, women, and men who dig for cobalt, as well as my own reporting on the mineral traders, government officials, multinational corporations, and other stakeholders that profit from their work. Nearing the center of cobalt mining in Kolwezi, we will encounter testimonies of a darker truth, one that cannot be fathomed. I saw it for myself on September 21, 2019, at a place called Kamilombe. I will take you there, just as I took the journey, down the only road that leads to the truth.

THE HEART OF AFRICA

Occupying the entire heart of the African continent, the Democratic Republic of the Congo is an extraordinary land teeming with nature. Wild forests, rugged mountains, broad savannas, and raging rivers fill the land. The nation is bordered to the north by the Central African Republic, to the northeast by South Sudan, to the east by Uganda, Rwanda, Burundi, and Tanzania, to the south and southeast by Zambia, to the southwest by Angola, and to the west by the Republic of the Congo and a sliver of coastline where the Congo River empties into the Atlantic. Imagine a giant ball of clay pinched at two ends—southwest from Kinshasa to the ocean, and southeast in a terrestrial peninsula that traces the Copper Belt. The upper two-thirds of the country is dressed in tropical rain forest, second in size only to the Amazon and home to the largest population of great apes in the world. South of the forest, plateaus slope downward into sprawling savannas. The rugged peaks of the Rwenzori Range stand guard along the northeastern border adjacent to the Rift Valley and the great lakes of Africa. The equator transects the top third of the Congo, and when it is the rainy season on one side of the equator, it is the dry season on the other. As a result, it is always raining somewhere in the Congo, and the country has the highest frequency of thunderstorms in the world.

The major cities of the DRC include the frenetic capital, Kinshasa, located near the southwestern edge of the country along the banks of the Congo River. It is one of Africa's fastest-growing megacities and home to more than seventeen million "Kinois." Mbuji-Mayi is capital of Kasai-Orientale Province, situated in the south-central part of the country and home to the largest diamond deposit in the world. The capital of Tshopo Province, Kisangani, is located near numerous gold mines and serves as a trading hub in the heart of the Congo River. Perched at the southern end of Lake Kivu, Goma is the main city on the dangerous border with Rwanda, where coffee, tea, and other agricultural products are grown. Roughly 2,300 kilometers southeast of Kinshasa at the opposite end of the country is Lubumbashi, capital of Haut-Katanga Province and administrative head of the mining provinces. Kolwezi is the capital of the adjacent province of Lualaba at the other end of the Copper Belt. Aside from Lubumbashi and Kolwezi, none of the aforementioned cities are connected by road or rail.

The soul of the Congo is its extraordinary river. It is the deepest river in the world, and through its system of tributaries, it drains a region the size of India. The crescent shape of the Congo River makes it the only one in the world that crosses the equator twice. By the time the river reaches the Atlantic, it empties with so much force that it clouds the ocean with sediment for a hundred kilometers offshore. The source of the Congo River was the final great mystery of African geography, and the drive by European explorers to solve this mystery tragically altered the fate of the Congo and made possible all the suffering taking place in the mining provinces today.

For most of its history, the southeastern corner of the DRC was called Katanga. The region was annexed into the Congo Free State by King Leopold in 1891 before its vast mineral riches were fully evident. Katanga has always been an outlier in the DRC. The people in Katanga largely see themselves as Katangans first and Congolese second. Crucially, Katangan leaders never fully subscribed to the premise that their mineral riches should be shared with the nation. Prior to Congolese independence, the Belgians established extensive mining operations in Katanga, and they also made every effort to keep control of the region after independence by orchestrating the secession of the province followed by the assassination of Prime Minister Lumumba. With so much money at stake, control of Katanga has always been a bloody affair.

Although the copious mineral riches of Katanga could easily fund numerous programs to improve child education, alleviate child mortality, upgrade sanitation and public health, and expand electrification for the Congolese people, most of the mineral wealth flows out of the country. Despite being home to trillions of dollars in untapped mineral deposits, the DRC's entire national budget in 2021 was a scant $7.2 billion, similar to the state of Idaho, which has one-fiftieth the population. The DRC ranks 175 out of 189 on the United Nations Human Development Index. More than three-fourths of the population live below the poverty line, one-third suffer from food insecurity, life expectancy is only 60.7 years, child mortality ranks eleventh worst in the world, access to clean drinking water is only 26 percent, and electrification is only 9 percent. Education is supposed to be funded by the state until eighteen years of age, but schools and teachers are under-supported and forced to charge fees of five or six dollars per month to cover expenses, a sum that millions of people in the DRC cannot afford. Consequently, countless children are compelled to work to support their families, especially in the mining provinces. Despite helping to generate untold riches for major technology and car companies, most artisanal cobalt miners earn paltry incomes between one or two dollars per day.

FROM TOXIC PIT TO SHINY SHOWROOM

The global cobalt supply chain is the mechanism that transforms the dollar-a-day wages of the Congo's artisanal miners into multibillion-dollar quarterly profits at the top of the chain. Although the two ends of the chain could not be more disconnected in terms of human and economic valuation, they are nevertheless linked through a complicated set of formal and informal relationships. The nexus of these links resides in a shadow economy at the bottom of the mining industry that flows inevitably into the formal supply chain. This merging of informal with formal, artisanal with industrial, is the most important aspect of the cobalt supply chain to understand. It is, despite claims to the contrary, all but impossible to isolate artisanal cobalt from industrial production.

Opposite is a rough sketch of what the global cobalt supply chain looks like. The links inside the box indicate points in which cobalt from various sources can be mixed.

Artisanal miners occupy the base of the chain. Known locally as *creuseurs* ("diggers"), they use rudimentary tools to dig in pits, trenches, and tunnels to find an ore called heterogenite, which contains copper, nickel, cobalt, and sometimes uranium. The Congo's artisanal mining sector is regulated by a government agency called SAEMAPE, which until 2017 was called SAESSCAM.[4] SAEMAPE has designated fewer than one hundred sites across the Copper Belt in which artisanal mining is authorized to take place, called Zones d'Exploitation Artisanale (ZEAs). The small

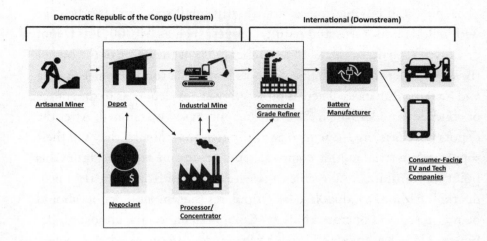

number of ZEAs is woefully insufficient to accommodate the hundreds of thousands of people who try to earn a living by digging for cobalt. As a result, artisanal miners dig in hundreds of unauthorized mining areas spread across the Copper Belt. Many of these sites are located right next to industrial mining operations since the diggers know there is likely to be valuable ore under the ground. Artisanal mining also takes place directly on many industrial mining sites, even though it is forbidden under Congolese law.

Artisanal cobalt feeds into the formal supply chain via an informal ecosystem of *négociants* (traders) and *comptoirs* (depots), also known as *maisons d'achat* (buying houses). These are the fuzzy linkages that serve to launder minerals from artisanal sources into the formal supply chain. *Négociants* are independent operators who work in and around artisanal sites to purchase cobalt from artisanal miners. They are almost all young Congolese males, and they either pay a fixed price per sack or offer a split of the sales price to the depots. Once the *négociants* have loaded their hauls onto motorbikes and pickup trucks, they transport the ore to the depots for sale. In some of the larger artisanal mining areas, there are depots located on-site, in which case artisanal miners can sell directly to them.

Depots and buying houses are usually small shacks that advertise with telltale pink tarps and painted names, such as $1,000,000 Depot or Cuivre-Cobalt, or just with a number (555) or the name of the owner (Boss Xi). There are hundreds of depots scattered around Haut-Katanga and Lualaba Provinces. There is no scrutiny at any depots as to the source or conditions under which the ore being purchased was mined. After the depots purchase ore from *négociants* or artisanal miners, they sell their supply to industrial mining companies and processing facilities. From this point forward, it is impossible to isolate artisanal from industrial production. Although Congolese law stipulates that mineral depots should be registered and operated only by Congolese nationals, almost all depots in Haut-Katanga and Lualaba Provinces are operated by Chinese buyers. Artisanal production accounts for up to 30 percent of all cobalt mined in the DRC, although the number could be even higher, as there is no accurate way to disaggregate artisanal from industrial production.

The formal segment of the supply chain begins with the massive industrial copper-cobalt mines that span the Copper Belt. Some of the mines, such as Tenke Fungurume and Mutanda, are as big as a European capital. The industrial mining operations in the DRC are typically structured as joint ventures between the state-owned mining company, Gécamines, and a foreign mining company. As of my last ground count in November 2021, there were nineteen major industrial copper-cobalt mining complexes operating in Haut-Katanga and Lualaba Provinces, fifteen of which were owned or financed by Chinese mining companies. Most of the Chinese-owned mining sites I visited were secured either by a military force called the FARDC or the elite Republican Guard. Other industrial sites and many informal mining areas are guarded by any array of armed units, including the Congolese National Police, the mining police, private military contractors, and informal militias. These armed security forces are devoted to two tasks: keep prying eyes out, and keep minerals secure.

Prior to export from the DRC, cobalt-containing ores must undergo a preliminary processing stage during which the cobalt is separated from other metals in the ore. Some of this processing takes place at industrial sites, and some of it takes place at dedicated processors in Kolwezi, Likasi, and Lubumbashi. The preliminary processing typically yields either crude cobalt hydroxide or cobalt concentrate. These semi-refined forms of cobalt are loaded onto trucks and driven to seaports in Dar es Salaam and Durban for export to commercial-grade refiners, most of which are in China. In 2021, China produced 75 percent of the world's refined cobalt. The largest single refiner was Huayou Cobalt with a market share of 22 percent.[5] Huayou owns Congo DongFang Mining, one of the largest copper-cobalt mining companies operating in the DRC. The vertical integration of Chinese companies across the cobalt supply chain has accelerated in recent years, solidifying the country's dominance over the rechargeable battery industry. Although it would seem advantageous for the DRC to refine cobalt to commercial-grade form and control more of the value chain, a senior official at Gécamines explained, "In Congo, we do not have sufficient electricity capacity to refine cobalt."

Fully refined cobalt is combined with other metals to make cathodes— the positively charged part of a battery. The largest lithium-ion battery manufacturers in the world are CATL and BYD in China; LG Energy Solution, Samsung SDI, and SK Innovation in South Korea; and Panasonic in Japan. In 2021, these six companies produced 86 percent of the world's lithium-ion rechargeable batteries, with CATL alone holding a one-third global share.[6] Most of the cobalt in these batteries originated in the Congo.

COBALT AND THE COPPER BELT

For much of human history, cobalt was little more than a color. As far back as the Persian Empire and the Ming dynasty, cobalt was used to create blue pigments in art and pottery. In the modern era, the element has accrued a range of industrial functions. Cobalt is used in the manufacture of superalloys for turbines and jet engines; as a catalyst for cleaner fuels; in carbides used to make cutting tools; in materials used for dental and bone surgeries; in chemotherapies; and in the cathodes of rechargeable batteries. Given its wide range of uses, the European Union has designated cobalt to be one of twenty "critical" metals and minerals, and the United States has designated cobalt to be a "strategic mineral." Initiatives to secure reliable supplies of refined cobalt that bypass China's current monopoly have become matters of considerable geopolitical importance to the U.S. and the EU.

By virtue of geographic fluke, the Central African Copper Belt holds roughly half of the world's cobalt reserves at an estimated 3.5 million tons.[7] Although geographic fluke may be responsible for the massive reserves of cobalt in the Copper Belt, the artisanal mining crisis in the DRC would not be possible unless there were substantial deposits of cobalt at depths shallow enough to be accessible by a shovel. According to Central African geology expert Murray Hitzman, the reason the copper-cobalt deposits in the Copper Belt are so shallow is because they are uniquely found in "sediment hosted stratiform deposits." This type of deposit indicates that the cobalt-containing ores occur in discrete layers of sedimentary rocks that were initially laid down in water. Such deposits are the only ones with the potential to be pushed upward to the surface by tectonic activity, thereby making them accessible to artisanal miners. The Central African Copper Belt happens to be located on the western shoulder of one of the most spectacular examples in the world of this tectonic activity—the East African Rift.

The East African Rift is a 6,500-kilometer fracture in the earth's surface that stretches from Jordan to Mozambique; it is caused by three plates pulling apart from each other—the Nubian plate, the Somalian plate, and the Arabian plate. Beginning around 800 million years ago, tectonic activity in the rift caused ocean water to enter an enclosed basin in the Copper Belt region. Most of the ocean water evaporated, but some of the saline fluids circulated into the sediments within the basin and stripped metals from them, including copper and cobalt. At some point between 650 and 500 million years ago, the salt layers began to move upward due to tectonic action, forming salt diapirs—domed rock formations in which a core of rock moves upward by several kilometers to pierce the earth's surface. A similar process took place along the Gulf Coast of the United States, which made numerous oil and gas fields accessible to drilling.

As a result of the ocean water deposits and subsequent tectonic action, copper-cobalt ores across the Copper Belt are found both at great depths and near the surface. At depths below the level of a fluctuating water table, the copper and cobalt are combined with sulfur in the mineral carrollite, which is the primary source of industrially mined cobalt in the Congo. Closer to the surface, water combines with sulfur to create sulfuric acid, causing ores to "rust." This weathering turns a sulfide into an oxide. Oxidized cobalt forms cobalt hydroxide in the mineral heterogenite. According to Hitzman, "The cobalt-hydroxide ore bodies in Katanga are unique. They form blocks that can be tens of meters to several kilometers in length floating like raisins in a cake." Artisanal miners dig tunnels up to sixty meters deep to find these "raisins" of heterogenite. One of the largest known deposits of cobalt raisins is beneath a neighborhood of Kolwezi called Kasulo, a madhouse of tunnel digging that is unlike any place on earth.

DARK SIDE OF THE EV REVOLUTION

That cobalt is found in massive, shallow, high-grade deposits in the DRC illuminates the supply side of the equation playing out in the country's mining provinces. The demand side is driven by the fact that cobalt is used in almost every lithium-ion rechargeable battery in the world. Development of lithium-ion batteries dates to the 1970s at Exxon, during the time of the OPEC oil embargo, when alternate energy sources were being explored. Sony produced the first commercial-scale lithium-ion batteries in the early 1990s, at which time they were used primarily for small-scale consumer electronics. The lithium-ion battery market received its first upward demand shock with the smartphone and tablet revolutions. Apple introduced the iPhone in 2007, and Android smartphones were launched in 2008. Since that time, billions of smartphones have been sold, and each one of them requires a few grams of refined cobalt in their batteries. A similar eruption of gadgets took place in the tablet market. Apple launched the iPad in 2010, followed soon after by Samsung's Galaxy Tab. Billions of tablets have since been sold, each of which requires up to thirty grams of cobalt in the battery. Add in laptops, e-scooters, e-bikes, and other rechargeable consumer electronic devices, and the aggregate amount of cobalt needed from all devices, save those with four or more tires, adds up to tens of thousands of tons each year.

The EV market, however, is where cobalt demand has really exploded. The first rechargeable electric vehicle was invented in 1880s, but it was not until the early 1900s that electric vehicles were being produced on a commercial scale. By 1910, around 30 percent of vehicles in the United States were propelled by electric engines. Had the trend continued, we would all be living on a cleaner, cooler planet. Instead, internal combustion engines came to dominate the next century of the automobile industry. There are several developments cited for the shift to gasoline-powered vehicles. First, the U.S. government invested heavily to expand road infrastructure beginning with the Federal Aid Road Act of 1916. Driving across the nation required greater ranges than could be achieved by EV technology at the time. In addition, the discovery of large oil reserves in Texas, California, and Oklahoma made internal combustion–powered cars much cheaper to operate.

Electric vehicles were relegated to a niche market until the push for renewable sources of energy beginning in 2010 led to an electric vehicle renaissance. This renaissance shifted into overdrive after the Paris Agreement in 2015, in which 195 nations agreed to a shared goal of keeping the increase in global average temperatures to less than 2°C from preindustrial levels. To achieve this goal, CO_2 emissions must be reduced by at least 40 percent below 2015 levels by 2040. Since about one-fourth of CO_2 emissions are created by vehicles with internal combustion engines, the expansion of battery-powered transportation provides the only solution.

In 2010, there were only 17,000 electric vehicles on the road in the entire world. By 2021, that number had skyrocketed to 16 million. Meeting the ambitions of the Paris Agreement would require at least 100 million total electric vehicles in use by 2030. An even more ambitious EV30@30 Campaign was launched in 2017 with the goal of accelerating the deployment of electric vehicles, targeting a 30 percent market share for electric vehicles sales by 2030. The EV30@30 target would require a global stock of 230 million EVs by 2030, a fourteen-fold increase over 2021 numbers.[8] EV sales could end up being even greater, as twenty-four nations pledged at COP26 to eliminate the sale of gas-powered vehicles entirely by 2040. Millions of tons of cobalt will be needed, which will continue to push hundreds of thousands of Congolese women, men, and children into hazardous pits and tunnels to help meet demand.

WHY DO LITHIUM-ION BATTERIES NEED COBALT?

To achieve mass adoption of electric vehicles at the levels projected will require that EV batteries become cheaper and are able to achieve longer ranges between charges. Prices of lithium-ion battery packs have steadily decreased as EV manufacturers seek to achieve cost parity with internal combustion vehicles. Measured in price per kilowatt-hour, the production cost of lithium-ion battery packs has fallen 89 percent from $1,200/kWh in 2010 to $132/kWh in 2021. Production costs are projected to reach the all-important mark of $100/kWh by 2024, at which point EVs will achieve cost parity with gas-powered cars.[9] Equally important to cost in accelerating EV adoption is the range the car can travel between charges. To increase range, batteries require higher energy densities, and only lithium-ion chemistries using cobalt cathodes are currently able to deliver maximum energy density while maintaining thermal stability. To understand why requires a brief review of how batteries work.

Batteries provide portable sources of electrical energy by rebalancing a chemical imbalance between a cathode (positive electrode) and an anode (negative electrode). The cathode and anode are separated by a chemical barrier called an electrolyte. When the cathode and anode are connected to a device, this creates a circuit, which results in a chemical reaction that generates positive ions and negative electrons at the anode. An opposite reaction takes place at the cathode. Nature always seeks balance, so the positive ions and negative electrons in the anode travel to the cathode, but they take different paths to reach their destinations. The ions flow directly through the electrolyte to the cathode, whereas the electrons flow through the external circuit to the cathode. The electrons are unable to travel through the electrolyte because its chemical nature acts as a barrier and forces them to pass through the outer circuit / device. This flow of electrons creates the energy that powers the device. As a battery generates electrical power, the chemicals inside it are gradually "used up." A rechargeable battery, on the other hand, is one that allows a change in the direction of flow of electrons and ions using another power source that pushes everything back to the starting point. Different materials have different abilities to release, attract, and store electrons and ions, and this is where lithium and cobalt enter the picture.

Lithium-based chemistries became the dominant form for rechargeable batteries because lithium is the lightest metal in the world, which has obvious benefits for consumer technology and electric vehicle applications. Cobalt is used in the cathodes of lithium-ion batteries because it possesses a unique electron configuration that allows the battery to remain stable at higher energy densities throughout repeated charge-discharge cycles. Higher energy density means the battery can hold more charge, which is critical to maximize the driving range of an electric vehicle between charges.

The three primary types of lithium-ion rechargeable batteries used today are lithium cobalt oxide (LCO), lithium nickel manganese cobalt oxide (L-NMC), and lithium nickel cobalt aluminum oxide (L-NCA). Lithium accounts for only 7 percent of the materials used in each type of battery, whereas cobalt can be as high as 60 percent.[10] Each battery chemistry has its strengths and weaknesses.

LCO batteries provide high energy density, which allows them to store more power per weight of battery. This quality makes them ideal for use in consumer electronic devices such as mobile phones, tablets, and laptops. The tradeoff is that LCO batteries have shorter life spans and deliver a lower amount of power, qualities that make them unsuitable for use in electric vehicles.

L-NMC batteries are used in most electric vehicles, except for Tesla, which uses L-NCA batteries. Since 2015, the trend with these batteries has been to reduce cobalt reliance by moving toward higher ratios of nickel.[11] Nickel has lower thermal stability than cobalt, so the higher the ratio of nickel used, the lower the battery's stability and safety.

The limited supply and high cost of cobalt has not gone unnoticed by the EV industry. Battery researchers are working on alternative designs that can minimize or eliminate reliance on cobalt. At present, most cobalt-free alternatives have significant disadvantages relating to energy density, thermal stability, manufacturing costs, and longevity. Many of them are also a decade or more away from commercial-scale production.

For the foreseeable future, there will be no avoiding cobalt from the Congo, which means there will be no avoiding the devastation that cobalt mining causes the people and environment of the mining provinces of the DRC. Even after battery designers find a way to eliminate cobalt from rechargeable batteries without sacrificing performance or safety, the misery of the Congolese people will not end. There will surely be another prize slumbering in the dirt that will be made valuable by the global economy. Such has been the curse of the Congo for generations. Unspeakable riches have brought the people of the Congo little other than unspeakable pain.

More than a century ago, E. D. Morel described the Congo Free State as "a gigantic slave-farm reeking with cruelty."[12] Cobalt mining is the slave farm perfected—the cost of labor has been nullified through the degradation of Africans at the bottom of an economic chain that purports to exonerate all participants of accountability through a shrewd scheme of obfuscation adorned with hypocritical proclamations about the preservation of human rights. It is a system of absolute exploitation for absolute profit. Cobalt mining is the latest in a long history of "enormous and atrocious" lies that have tormented the people of the Congo.

The truth, as ever, waits to be revealed.

2

"Here It Is Better Not to Be Born"

Lubumbashi and Kipushi

Of all the shameful and infamous expedients whereby man has preyed upon man . . . this vile thing dares to call itself commerce.
  —Roger Casement, letter to the Foreign Office, September 6, 1903

LUBUMBASHI ANNOUNCES ITSELF CLEARLY the moment you arrive. There is a giant open-air copper-cobalt pit mine called Ruashi located next to the airport.

"You will fly right over it when you land in Lubumbashi," my local guide, Philippe, said prior to my first trip.

The mine was impossible to miss. It was an enormous hollowing of the earth consisting of three behemoth pits, each of which was several hundred meters in diameter. Heavy-duty excavators drove along the terraced edges of the craters like little yellow ants. Next to the pits, there was a mineral-processing facility with numerous chemical storage vats and rectangular pools of water. Toxic waste from the processing plant was discarded into a large, square-shaped depository roughly one square kilometer in size. The entire complex was more than ten square kilometers, much smaller than some of the colossal industrial sites we will encounter on the road to Kolwezi, but nevertheless a sight to behold.

From the tarmac, the dirt wall of the Ruashi mine dominated the horizon like a khaki-colored Uluru. Thousands of brick huts in various shades of red and brown were crammed next to the concession and spread for many kilometers to the west. The Belgians founded a mining town here called Élisabethville in 1910 to exploit their very first mine in Katanga, Étoile du Congo ("Star of the Congo"), which is just south of Ruashi. Excavations at Ruashi followed in 1919. The original settlement contained white-owned businesses surrounded by tree-lined streets where the Europeans lived. Mine-worker compounds for African laborers were erected in patchwork plots near Étoile and Ruashi. Both mines still operate today, and for many people in nearby communities, the working and living conditions have changed very little since the Belgians first arrived.

Although time moves slowly in the Congo, names change with every new regime. When the Congo Free State passed in ownership from King Leopold II to the Belgian government, the colony was renamed the Belgian Congo. At independence in 1960, the nation was renamed Republic of Congo. In the early 1970s, Joseph Mobutu commenced an "Africanization" campaign in which all colonial names were replaced with African ones—Élisabethville became Lubumbashi, Léopoldville became Kinshasa, Katanga became Shaba, and Republic of Congo became Zaire. In 1997, Laurent Kabila invaded the country, took control from Mobutu, and renamed it to the Democratic Republic of the Congo. Being a Katangan by birth, he renamed Shaba back to Katanga. After Laurent Kabila was assassinated in 2001, his son Joseph took power and later subdivided the existing eleven provinces of the country into twenty-six. Katanga was broken into four provinces. The two in the bottom half—Haut-Katanga and Lualaba—encapsulate all the nation's copper-cobalt mines.

The name *Katanga* originally comes from a village located not far from where the Belgians first founded Élisabethville. Native Katangans had been mining copper from the region's copious deposits long before Europeans arrived. Katangan copper first made its way to Europe via Portuguese slave traders as early as the sixteenth century. In 1859, the Scottish explorer David Livingstone arrived on a trek from South Africa into Katanga and noted large pieces of copper "in the shape of a St.

Andrew's cross" that were used as a form of payment.[1] In the same trip, Livingstone became the first European to encounter a warlord named Mwenda Msiri Ngelengwa Shitambi. Msiri traded copper for firearms with Europeans, amassing an imposing military force. He had a reputation for violence and was infamous for his collection of gleaming white human skulls, which may have provided inspiration for Kurtz's collection of skulls in *Heart of Darkness*.

In the summer of 1867, Livingstone returned to Katanga in search of the source of the Nile River. He wrote about natives who melted malachite to produce large copper ingots in the shape of a capital *I*, some of which weighed more than fifty kilograms. Verney Lovett Cameron was the next European to mention Katanga when he began his transcontinental trek in 1874. He too noted large copper ingots and the sale of slaves to Msiri in exchange for Katangan copper. A Scottish missionary, Frederick Stanley Arnot, arrived next in 1886 in the hopes of bringing Christianity to the natives of Katanga. He described the local method of mining copper, which is remarkably similar to the technique used by artisanal miners to dig for cobalt today:

> The malachite from which the copper is extracted is found in large quantities on the tops of certain bare, rugged hills. In their search for it, the natives dig little round shafts seldom deeper than 15 or 20 feet. They have no lateral workings, but when one shaft becomes too deep for them, they leave it and open another.[2]

Arnot's descriptions in 1886 caught the attention of British imperialist Cecil Rhodes, founder of the prestigious Rhodes Scholarship. Rhodes ventured north from his eponymous Rhodesia (Zambia) into Katanga to meet with Msiri in the hopes of signing a treaty that would place Katanga under British dominion. Msiri sent Rhodes packing without a treaty. Hearing of Rhodes's efforts in Katanga, King Leopold, who had just secured his Congo Free State in 1885, immediately dispatched three teams to secure a treaty with Msiri. A campaign led by the Belgian explorer Alexandre Delcommune arrived first on October 6, 1891, and met with

Msiri. Like Rhodes, Delcommune was rebuffed. A second campaign of
Zanzibari mercenaries led by the British turncoat William Grant Stairs
arrived on December 20, 1891. Stairs met with Msiri, but the next day,
Msiri left for a neighboring village. Stairs sent his two most trusted men
to reason with Msiri, but after three days of failed negotiations, the Europeans shot Msiri, decapitated him, and stuck his head on a pole for
all to see the consequences of standing against Leopold and his Congo
Free State.[3] Blood had been spilled for control of Katanga's riches. There
was no turning back.

The third team dispatched by Leopold arrived on January 30, 1892,
to see the flag of the Congo Free State already flying in the city. The team
happened to include a Belgian geologist, Jules Cornet. Cornet surveyed
the territory from August 8 to September 12, 1892, cataloging the region's mineral deposits, which he described as a "veritable geological
scandal." Cornet was the first European to document the extensive copper deposits in what would turn out to be the Central African Copper
Belt. He even had a local stone named after him, cornetite. Additional
prospecting on behalf of the Belgians in 1902 led by an American mining
expert, John R. Farrell, made more detailed assessments of the copper
deposits. Farrell stated in his report to King Leopold:

> It will be utterly impossible to exhaust your bodies of oxidized ores
> during this century . . . The quantity of copper you can thus produce is
> entirely a question of demand—the mines can supply any amount. You
> can make more copper and make it much cheaper than any mines now
> working. I believe your mines will be the source of the world's future
> supply of copper.[4]

Almost all that copper had cobalt attached to it, although it would
take another 110 years before the rechargeable battery revolution would
make the cobalt ten times more valuable than the copper.

In securing Katanga, Leopold had literally struck pay dirt, and the
Belgians moved quickly into exploitation mode. On October 18, 1906,
the Belgians created Union Minière du Haut-Katanga (UMHK) to exploit

the copper deposits across the Katanga region. The Belgian state granted UMHK extensive parastatal powers, including the ability to build and manage urban centers with African laborers to be used in the exploitation of mining assets. Élisabethville grew rapidly around Étoile and Ruashi and soon had hotels, a British consulate, sports clubs, bars, and a golf course next to Lake Kipopo that still exists today. Katanga's native population proved insufficient to meet the labor requirements of UMHK's fast-growing mining operations, so the company recruited thousands of workers and purchased slaves to work in the mines. African laborers were crammed into ramshackle barracks and exploited in a forced labor regime reminiscent of some of the harshest systems of African slavery. Profits soared, especially after the start of World War I, during which time millions of bullets fired by British and American forces were made with Katangan copper.[5]

As UMHK expanded its mining footprint across the Copper Belt, Europeans flocked to Élisabethville in search of opportunity. Some worked for UMHK, others started businesses, and others came to teach European children in newly founded schools. The son of one such teacher, David Franco, now a Hollywood music composer living in Los Angeles, spent the first twenty years of his life in Élisabethville from 1940 to 1960:

Every aspect of our lives in Elizabethville was centered around UMHK . . . Despite the distances from the mother country, Belgium also ran an active cultural life of art and music throughout its colony by bringing major talent, both local and from Europe. One such example I can never erase from my memory is, when I was nine years old, attending a recital together with my parents by world-famous violinist Yehudi Menuhin. At that time, [he was] the biggest name in the classical music field. Can you imagine? I was mesmerized by his performance. That was the day I decided to be a musician.

During World War II, Katanga again proved indispensable to the Allied war effort, providing gold, tin, tungsten, cobalt, and more than eight hundred thousand tons of copper for the manufacture of ordnance. The governor-general of the Belgian Congo, Pierre Ryckmans, declared in June 1940: "The Belgian Congo, in the present war, is the most important asset of Belgium. It is entirely at the service of the Allies, and through them of the motherland. If she needs men, it will give them; if she needs work, it will work for her."[6] Tens of thousands of Congolese people were worked to the bone in copper mines and sent to the war to die for the benefit of Belgium and its European allies.

At independence on June 30, 1960, the formal economy of the Congo was based almost entirely on the extraction of minerals from Katanga Province. Most of this extraction was controlled by UMHK, which had no interest in parting with its highly profitable mining operations. UMHK and the Belgian military backed a Katangan politician, Moise Tshombe, in declaring Katanga's secession from the Republic of Congo eleven days after the nation's independence.

"I remember when I woke up in the middle of the night to the sound of metal rattling to the concrete of the road," recalls Franco. "I peeked through the curtains to see tanks going through the streets . . . I woke my parents up and told them 'we have to get out of here!' We went to one of the high schools where people were taking refuge. After a few days we drove south and made our way to the Rhodesian border. We left everything behind."

It was another coup for control of Katanga's mineral riches. More blood would be spilled, reaching all the way to the secretary-general of the United Nations.

If the mining sector makes itself known upon arrival at the Lubumbashi airport, so too does the police state. Stern-faced soldiers wielding Kalashnikovs scrutinize passengers on the tarmac, and another batch of soldiers waits in the compact arrival hall to direct select passengers to a secondary screening room behind a locked door. Secondary screening, for which I was almost always selected, involved having to answer several questions about the purpose of my trip, where I would be staying, and to fill out various forms. Only after completing the secondary screening process was I allowed to cross the hall to retrieve my luggage.

The luggage room at Lubumbashi's airport is about as big as a school classroom. Luggage arrives in metal crates being dragged by a farm tractor. A single luggage handler unloads suitcases onto a single luggage belt, one bag at a time. The luggage room is manned by a third batch of soldiers who rummage through the suitcases of foreign passengers for items that might indicate the person has an interest in prying into matters they should not, like the mining sector. A fourth squad of soldiers patrols the exit of the terminal, which consists of a handful of taxi drivers standing next to rusted sedans and a billboard that says WELCOME TO LUBUMBASHI. There are also soldiers at checkpoints leaving the airport and all around Lubumbashi that make random searches and ask to verify the travel paperwork of foreign visitors. The process repeats itself at every one of the five *péage* (toll) checkpoints on the road between Lubumbashi and Kolwezi. Even with pristine paperwork, harassment by soldiers at the checkpoints is common.

Most of my trips to the DRC took place during the dry season to avoid flooded roads and landslides, which make passage into many of the mining areas impossible. The trade-off to travel during the dry season is that the mining provinces are oppressed by a plague of dust and grit. Buildings, homes, roads, people, and animals are draped in dirt. Land and sky blend together into a vague coppery palette. Trees are reduced to brittle sticks. Small lakes and tributaries are transformed into fields of rust. The heat is also more intense during the dry season, although it is a dry heat since the Copper Belt sits at an altitude of 1,500–2,000 meters. Only one of my trips to the Congo reached into the rainy season. When the storms finally arrived, they erupted with biblical fury, and the parched land was transformed overnight. Green exploded upon the barren hills, trees proudly displayed their newborn plumage, the air was crisp and cool, and the great blue sky returned from exile.

No one knows how many people live in Lubumbashi—or in any other

Congolese city, for that matter—because the last census conducted by
the government was in 1984. Local estimates put Lubumbashi's population at more than two million, making it the second-largest city in
the country behind Kinshasa. The main arterial road of Lubumbashi
is called 30 June 1960 Street, the day of Congolese independence. Motorbikes and generally well-maintained vehicles speed along the road.
Yellow minibuses jammed with passengers, including a few hanging off
the back bumper, start and stop every fifty meters to let people on and
off. Billboards advertise banking and mobile phone services. Uniformed
children walk home from school past boom boxes that blare the latest
rap or dance songs outside local markets. Most adults dress in a vibrant
style called *liputa,* an explosion of rich colors and bold motifs. On more
formal occasions, women wear the resplendent *pagne,* a three-piece out-
fit of matching skirt, blouse, and headscarf drenched in brilliant hues
and eye-catching designs. There are numerous places of worship on 30
June 1960 Street, including a synagogue, mosque, and several churches.
Half of the Congolese population is Catholic, and about one-fourth of
the country is Protestant.

The main roads of Lubumbashi are crammed with a plethora of small
businesses, such as hair salons, vehicle repair shops, mobile phone top-up
kiosks, bakeries, restaurants, cafés, and grocery stalls. Most shops are
small, single-room concrete structures with hand-painted names along
the front walls that either refer to God, like Alimentation Don de Dieu,
or to the name of the proprietor, like Julia Shopping or Beatrice Boucherie.
I found that the best market for stocking up on supplies before heading
into rural areas was Jambo Mart. It was always filled with a wide array
of goods, almost all of which were imported from South Africa, China,
and India.

There is a sizable Indian population in the Congo, which assisted
greatly with my ability to move around the mining provinces without
drawing too much attention. Indians own or manage many of the hotels in
cities like Lubumbashi and Kolwezi, and large numbers of Indians have
migrated to the Congo to work as laborers and traders. Being Indian al-

lowed me to have a range of cover stories as I traveled deeper into the
Copper Belt. Sometimes I was a businessman looking to import goods
or invest in a hotel; other times I was a mineral trader looking to understand the cobalt trade. With government officials, I was always myself—a
researcher from America who wanted to learn more about conditions in
the cobalt mining sector. My first meeting with a government official in
the Congo took place the day after I arrived.

I met Mpanga Wa Lukalaba, director of cabinet of the governor of
the province of Haut-Katanga at the headquarters of the provincial government in Lubumbashi, to secure his support for my journeys into the
mining areas. I was advised that I would not get very far into the mines
of Haut-Katanga Province without his approval. My goals for the meeting with Director Lukalaba were twofold: do not set off any alarm bells
that might stymie my ability to venture into the mining areas, and secure
his personal stamp and signature on my *engagement de prise en charge*
("commitment to support") documentation that accompanied my visa.
Should mining police or a militia commando seek to detain me, I could
show them Director Lukalaba's stamp to verify that I had the support of
the office of the governor to move about in mining areas.

I was prepared for a lengthy interrogation about my intentions, but
Director Lukalaba welcomed me warmly and asked only one question—
Why did I wish to spend my time in the unpleasant mining areas, as
opposed to some of the nicer parts of the province? I explained that it
was my understanding that too little of the value of the Congo's minerals was retained by artisanal miners, and I hoped that if more people
understood the conditions under which they worked, it might inspire
efforts to address that disparity. I was careful not to talk about issues
such as child labor or to point a finger at the Congolese government for
bearing its share of responsibility in depriving its people of an equitable share in the country's mineral resources. After a pleasant conversation about Director Lukalaba's graduate studies in the United States,
he pulled out his personal stamp from a drawer in his desk, pressed it
onto the bottom of my *prise en charge* documentation, and signed his

name. Little did I know at the time that this stamp and signature would probably save my life.

Although Lubumbashi is the administrative capital of the DRC's mining sector, there is very little mining that takes place in the city outside of Ruashi and Étoile, which combined to produce about 8,500 tons of cobalt in 2021.[7] Both mines passed from UMHK to Gécamines on the first day of 1967 after Mobutu nationalized the country's mining sector. Production under Gécamines was inconsistent and eventually abandoned after the company's financial collapse in the early 1990s. The rights to Ruashi were acquired in 2012 by the state-owned Chinese mining giant Jinchuan Group. The rights to Étoile were acquired in 2003 by Chemicals of Africa (CHEMAF), a copper-cobalt mining company owned by Dubai-based Shalina Resources. CHEMAF is also one of the major players in the DRC's artisanal mining sector. The company operates a "model mine" for artisanal miners in Kolwezi in conjunction with a U.S.-based NGO, Pact. At least it did, until it became clear that all was not what it seemed.

Étoile is noteworthy not only because it was the first mine the Belgians started exploiting in the Congo in 1911 but also because it was the first industrial mine in the Congo at which artisanal miners were formally encouraged to work, beginning in the late 1990s. Soon after seizing the country in a military coup in 1997, Laurent Kabila promoted artisanal mining at Étoile to generate desperately needed revenue for his fledgling government. Although local villagers were promised improved incomes and living conditions, their labor was instead used to restart production at Étoile for paltry wages. Artisanal miners continue to work at Étoile to this day, helping to boost production for the same meager incomes.

"They pay us so little," said Makaza, a man from the nearby village of Mukwemba. "They take all our minerals, but they do not support the communities who live here."

Sitting on a plastic chair next to his thatched hut in the shade of a tall avocado tree, Makaza explained that he and his sons worked as artisanal miners at Étoile, as did many of the male inhabitants in the village.

Makaza said that he typically produced between forty and fifty kilograms of heterogenite each day by digging in the large pits or along the pit walls, for which he was paid 2,000–2,500 Congolese francs (CF) (about $1.10–$1.40). I asked who exactly paid him, and Makaza said, "The men from CHEMAF." Makaza lamented that the paltry income was insufficient to meet his family's needs. He also expressed displeasure that CHEMAF did little to support nearby villages. He took me on a tour of his village, and the conditions were bleak. There was no electricity or sanitation. Water came from narrow wells ringed at the top by old jeep tires. The villagers subsisted on vegetables grown in a few sallow fields. The closest medical clinic was five kilometers away, and the closest school was seven.

Makaza's family used to live in a nicer village much closer to basic amenities, but that village was demolished during one of Étoile's expansions. Like most of the industrial mines in the Congo, Étoile's concession has grown across the years, displacing thousands of local inhabitants. Displacement of the native population due to mine expansion is a major crisis in the mining provinces. As the living conditions of displaced people worsen, their desperation increases, and that desperation is precisely what drives thousands of local inhabitants to scrounge for cobalt in hazardous conditions on the land they once occupied. Makaza said he lived in constant fear of being displaced the next time the mine expanded, or when some new mine was built.

"Eventually, there will be no place left in Congo for Congolese people," he said.

I explored a few villages near Étoile, and they were similar to Mukwemba. It appeared that a substantial number of men and boys, perhaps in the thousands, were digging for cobalt inside the mine for a dollar or two a day. I tried to investigate Étoile directly, but my first effort had to be aborted, as there was a flare-up in militia violence in the area. The militia, called Mai-Mai Bakata Katanga, was an especially violent group that occasionally seized control of villages and mineral territory with the purported mission of seceding Katanga Province from the country. It was not the only time my movements in mining areas would be thwarted by local militias. My second effort to inspect Étoile met with a denial of entry by CHEMAF security at the main entrance to the mine. It was not the only time that would happen either.

Although I was unable to investigate inside the Étoile concession, this much seemed clear—the inhabitants of the villages near the mine lived in itinerant, Stone Age conditions similar to those endured by the African laborers UMHK first brought to Élisabethville to work at Étoile in the early 1900s.

Most of the Congo's major artisanal mining sites are located far to the west of Lubumbashi between the cities of Likasi and Kolwezi. Before departing for these mining areas, I met with a group of three vivacious students at the University of Lubumbashi who were organizing efforts to help support artisanal mining communities. Gloria, Joseph, and Reine treated me to a lunch of ugali, a traditional Congolese dish that consists of a boiled ball of maize flour served with stew. It looked very similar to one of my favorite South Indian dishes, idli and sambar, except idli is made with rice. The students were natives of Lubumbashi and planned on applying to graduate programs in Europe and Canada. They were aware of how fortunate they were relative to most of the people in their country and especially those in mining communities. From their perspective, the problems started at the top.

"In Congo, the government is weak. Our state institutions are impotent. They are kept this way so they can be manipulated by the president to suit his ambitions," Reine said.

"Congo is only a bank account for the president," Gloria added.

When I asked about their impressions of artisanal mining, they did not mince their words.

"Kabila allows the foreigners to steal the country's resources, and the artisanal miners suffer because of this. He takes bribes and closes his eyes while the *creuseurs* are made like animals," Joseph explained.

"Kabila sold the mines to the Chinese," Reine added. "All they care about is cobalt, cobalt, cobalt . . . They treat the Congolese people like slaves."

"It is not only the Chinese. All the mining companies treat the Congolese people like slaves," Gloria said. "They think because our people are poor, they can be humiliated."

"All Africans are poor in their eyes. They steal our resources to keep us poor!" Joseph exclaimed.

"When you see what the mining companies have done to our forests and rivers, your heart will cry," Reine added.

Gloria reinforced Reine's concerns over environmental damage caused by mining companies. She then laid out an even greater concern:

> Let me tell you the most important thing that no one is discussing. The mineral reserves in Congo will last another forty years, maybe fifty? During that time, the population of Congo will double. If our resources are sold to foreigners for the benefit of the political elite, instead of investing in education and development for our people, in two generations, we will have two hundred million people who are poor, uneducated, and have nothing left of value. This is what is happening, and if it does not stop, it will be a disaster.

Gloria's prognosis was grim. I could not help but wonder whether the nation's leadership understood the long-term consequences of allowing the DRC to be drained of its resources by foreign interests with little benefit to its people. My meeting with the three students took place in August of 2018 while Joseph Kabila was still in power. Elections were scheduled for December 30, 2018, after more than two years of delays. Kabila was termed out of running again, which meant that there was bound to be a head of state not named Kabila for the first time in twenty-two years. I asked the students whether they thought conditions might improve after the elections.

"Kabila has already arranged for [Félix] Tshisekedi to win," Joseph responded. "He will be Kabila's puppet. Everyone knows this."

Tshisekedi indeed won the election, but in the early months of his term, something unexpected happened—he began to wage an anti-corruption campaign that included scrutiny of some of Kabila's dealings in the mining sector. I spoke with Mike Hammer, the hard-nosed U.S. ambassador to the DRC, a few months after the elections.

"When I first arrived in the Congo when Kabila was in power, I could not talk about corruption or risk being expelled for 'interference,'" he explained. "Under President Tshisekedi, there is a changing mentality on corruption. We can talk about it now. It is recognized as a serious problem and as a priority."

A power struggle has since ensued between Tshisekedi and Kabila. Tshisekedi is perceived as trying to align the country closer to the U.S., whereas Kabila is fighting to maintain links to China.

"Tshisekedi's vision for the country clashes with Kabila's vision," Hammer said. "Tshisekedi is looking for American investment because it brings better jobs, delivers for local communities, and respects the environment."

Tshisekedi expanded his efforts to challenge Chinese hegemony over the country's mining sector with the bold announcement in May 2021 that he would renegotiate contracts with Chinese mining companies that were signed under Joseph Kabila. A senior member of President Tshisekedi's administration, Sylvestre, spoke to me on condition of anonymity in August 2021 and described the administration's reasoning:

> Let's say in eighty-five percent of the major mining contracts you will always find a Chinese company behind the deal. Most of these deals lacked transparency. Their modus operandi was to ensure that nothing would be published in terms of these contracts. There were a lot of bribes going around in the last regime to make this happen. We want to publish the details of these agreements so we can hold the Chinese companies accountable.

As the power struggle between Tshisekedi and Kabila continues, a fateful decision with considerable geopolitical and economic implications will be made as to whether the country will align more with China or the U.S. Whether this decision will lead to any improvements in the lives of the nation's artisanal miners remains to be seen.

Before departing Lubumbashi to journey into the mining areas, I visited an abandoned Gécamines mining site near the outskirts of the city called Gécamines Sud ("Gécamines South"). The mine was once the pride of Lubumbashi and a symbol of its economic strength. At its peak, Gécamines Sud employed thousands of citizens and produced tens of thousands of tons of copper annually. Operations at the mine ceased in the early 1990s, and the site has been dormant ever since. Inside the derelict concession, a one-hundred-meter mountain of slag and rubble sat next to the towering chimney of the mineral-processing facility. Tangles of metal lay rusting across wide fields of dirt. All was ashen and pale under the hazy radiance of the sun.

Gécamines Sud was a picture of what mining had done to the Congo—a once great land reduced to ruin. From the ruins, a new breed of mining was born, one that was more violent and voracious than ever. As we will discover with each passing mile on the road to Kolwezi, the rechargeable battery revolution has unleashed a malevolent force upon the Congo that tramples all in its path in a merciless hunt for cobalt.

KIPUSHI

We will travel northwest on the road from Lubumbashi to Kolwezi to uncover the realities of cobalt mining in the DRC; first, however, we must take a short detour to a town called Kipushi. Kipushi is located about forty kilometers southwest of Lubumbashi right at the Zambian border. Like most cities in the Copper Belt, Kipushi was founded as a mining town. It is home to the immense Kipushi Mine, which was originally called the Prince Leopold Mine when the Belgians established it in 1924. At that time, the mine had the largest known deposits of copper and zinc in the world. UMHK exploited the mine until it was nationalized by Mobutu under Gécamines. Gécamines operated the mine for almost three decades, after which operations ceased around the same time as they did at Gécamines Sud. Canada-based Ivanhoe Mines resuscitated the mine in 2011 through a 68–32 joint venture with Gécamines called Kipushi Corporation (KICO). Ivanhoe also shares rights with China-based Zijin Mining to a second concession located at the opposite end of the Copper Belt—the giant Kamoa-Kakula copper mine west of Kolwezi. The site contains the largest undeveloped high-grade copper deposit in the world.

The road from Lubumbashi to Kipushi is the primary route of export for cobalt and other minerals from the DRC. The road was in good condition until 1997 when Laurent Kabila and his Rwanda-Uganda-backed army, the AFDL, invaded the country. The AFDL shelled the road to cut off reinforcements from Zambia, which was allied with Joseph Mobutu. In 2010, a Chinese consortium called SICOMINES repaved the road as part of an agreement brokered by Joseph Kabila, through which China managed to corner most of the global cobalt market before anyone knew what happened. It was one of many infrastructure-for-resources agreements that China has negotiated across the African continent.

The foundation for China's dominance in Africa was established in 2000 when President Jiang Zemin proposed the creation of the Forum on China-Africa Cooperation to facilitate Chinese investments in African countries. The relationship was billed as a win-win: the Chinese would build much-needed roads, dams, airports, bridges, mobile networks, and power plants across Africa, and in exchange, China would secure access to vital resources to support its growing economy. In 2006, President Hu Jintao deepened the economic ties with a Sino-African summit in Beijing that was attended by forty-eight African heads of state. A deal was struck between SICOMINES and Joseph Kabila in which SICOMINES agreed to provide $6 billion toward construction of roads and $3 billion toward upgrading mining infrastructure in Katanga. The money was to be repaid through the value of copper-cobalt deposits excavated by SICOMINES. If the deposits proved insufficient, the DRC agreed to repay the loans through "other means."

There was considerable controversy with the SICOMINES agreement the moment the ink dried. The International Monetary Fund (IMF) and World Bank, both major creditors to the DRC, were not pleased with the new debt load on the Congo and the "other means" clause in the agreement, particularly if it led to the loss of collateralized mining assets on their loans. The IMF and World Bank pressured Kabila to renegotiate terms. In December 2009, the "other means" clause of the agreement was removed, and the total loan amount was reduced from $9 billion to $6 billion. Under the new terms, SICOMINES agreed to pave 6,600 kilometers of road and to build two hospitals and two universities in Katanga, in exchange for mining rights to two concessions near Kolwezi: Dikuluwe and Mashamba West.

President Kabila hailed the SICOMINES agreement as the "deal of the century" and moved quickly to profit from it. Kabila established a private firm called Strategic Projects and Investments (SPI), which received money from a range of Chinese projects, including the tolls paid by trucks that crossed the border at Kipushi after the new road was built. An investigation by Bloomberg revealed that SPI collected tolls of $302 million between 2010 and 2020, and that this was just one of the many Chinese deals through which Kabila and his family profited.[8] The nation, however, has seen little profit from the SICOMINES agreement. Infrastructure projects have been delayed, road quality has been poor, and there has been little by way of environmental or social impact considerations in the construction and mining operations of SICOMINES. Crucially, the SICOMINES deal is exempt from taxes until infrastructure and mining loans are fully repaid, which means that the DRC will not receive meaningful income from the deal for many years to come.

I drove from Lubumbashi to Kipushi with my trusted guide, Philippe. His depth of knowledge about artisanal mining made him the best companion for my early explorations in the Congo's mining sector. The drive took us through several villages that hugged the arterial road. The huts in these villages were the only ones I saw in the mining provinces that were not rust-hued but were more of a tan or khaki color. The dirt at the southeastern corner of the Copper Belt is less dense with copper and iron oxide, so the mud-brick huts look more like regular mud. Many of the huts were built on platforms raised by chopped tree branches to protect from floods during the rainy season. Most huts were topped either by thatched roofs or sheet metal held in place by large stones. In the distance, scores of large mounds and towers of dirt were scattered across the landscape, some of which were more than five meters in height and had trees growing on top of them.

"Those are termite hills," Philippe explained. "The termites are drawn to copper in the dirt. They build the hills at that location. *Creuseurs* sometimes dig under them because they know there will be copper and cobalt there."

As we drove closer to the border, eighteen-wheelers loaded with minerals coughed and careened down the narrow highway, befouling everything in their wake. Every hut, tree, villager, and child was draped in a blanket of grit. Shortly after we passed a weathered green-and-white arc over the road that read BIENVENUE À LA CITÉ FRONTALIÈRE DE KIPUSHI ("Welcome to the border town of Kipushi"), the road was completely clogged with eighteen-wheelers sitting at idle. Every one of the trucks was jammed to the brim with cargo, strapped to the beds with thick ropes and half-covered in blue and pink tarpaulins.

"We call this *heavy-charge road,*" Philippe said. "Each truck is weighed at the border, and because most of them are overweight, they are charged for excess cargo."

Because there were so many trucks clogging "heavy-charge road," we were forced to drive down the wrong side of the road for several kilometers to bypass the jam, swerving sharply to dodge oncoming vehicles.

"The trucks can wait three or four days to cross the border," Philippe explained. "They are filled with ore from across Katanga—copper, cobalt, nickel, and zinc from Lualaba and Haut-Katanga, and also gold, coltan, cassiterite, and wolframite from Tanganyika."

Tanganyika Province is part of the old Katanga region, located immediately north of Haut-Katanga Province. It is a very dangerous area overrun by numerous Mai-Mai militias. Aside from a few groups like Mai-Mai Bakata Katanga, the Mai-Mai militias are not as active in the Copper Belt part of Katanga, as it is more heavily secured by the army. The name Mai-Mai means "water-water," based on the belief that they have magical powers that can turn enemy bullets into water. The militias originally took up arms to support Joseph Mobutu against Laurent Kabila's invasion in 1997. Soon after, the Mai-Mai degenerated into roving bands of hoodlums fighting for territory, and they turned to mining to fund their efforts. Tanganyika Province happens to contain substantial coltan reserves, along with significant deposits of tin, tungsten, and gold. Each of these metals is required in the manufacture of microprocessors. The Mai-Mai were sitting on a treasure chest, and since the turn of the millennium, they have resorted to violence to compel the local population to extract the riches for their benefit. Most of the minerals are smuggled out of the country into formal supply chains via Rwanda and Uganda, or across the Kipushi border point with Zambia.[9]

Not long after passing the sign that welcomed us to the border region of Kipushi, we arrived at a junction and turned off "heavy-charge road" onto a single-lane route called Kipushi Road, which passed through a remote area of dense forest. There were no other vehicles on this road—no trucks, no horns, no sounds at all—just the hot, dry breeze.

Philippe pointed out the window. "There are many artisanal sites in this forest. *Creuseurs* from the villages walk here in the morning to dig." I asked if there were children digging in the forest. "Yes, of course," Philippe replied. "What else will they do? There are no schools in the villages. Each member of the family must earn for the collective to survive." Philippe and I subsequently spent a day exploring these sites, each of which consisted of small patches of hacked-up terrain being excavated by a few dozen artisanal miners, including children. They were mini versions of what I was about to see in Kipushi.

About ten minutes after turning off "heavy-charge road," we arrived at a security checkpoint that was manned by five FARDC soldiers. Philippe motioned for me to remain quiet and to keep my mobile phone out of sight. The soldiers scrutinized my documents, asked a series of questions about our intentions, and eventually allowed us through. A few minutes later, we were in the heart of Kipushi, a typical border town with a heavy military presence. In addition to the usual churches, hair salons, mobile phone top-up kiosks, and local groceries, there were numerous bars and dance clubs, presumably to cater to military personnel. We were still a few hundred meters away from the KICO mine when I heard a loud droning that drowned out all other noise in the area.

"That is the main ventilation fan at KICO that blows air down the primary shaft so workers can breathe," Philippe explained.

I asked how deep the shaft was.

"More than one kilometer."

The KICO compound was fenced off and heavily guarded. We parked at a distance from the main entrance and walked along the perimeter of the concession. Just to the west, there was a giant, defunct open-pit mine several hundred meters in diameter.

"This is where Gécamines originally exploited the mine," Philippe said.

Looking into the pit, I could barely make out a few dozen people scraping at the bottom of the crater in various trenches. Philippe explained that Gécamines had already excavated most of the copper, cobalt, and zinc from the open pit years ago, but artisanal miners still scavenged the site for whatever scraps they could find, like birds picking at bones after the big cats have finished gorging. Beyond the abandoned pit, I could discern an immense craterous landscape with a few thousand bodies moving over it.

"That is the primary artisanal mining area," Philippe said. "It goes all the way into Zambia."

I was ready to march over to explore the mining area, but Philippe explained that we first had to secure permission from Ivanhoe officials. While the artisanal miners were technically digging outside of the KICO concession, Philippe assured me that the KICO security guards would not let us anywhere near the artisanal mining site without permission.

"They do not want journalists taking photos and writing stories about the conditions next to their concession," Philippe said.

We walked over to the main gate of the KICO compound and were greeted by armed guards. We were required to pass a Breathalyzer test prior to entering the site. Once inside, the compound impressed in scale and sophistication. KICO had a dedicated power supply and included comfortable residential facilities for Ivanhoe employees from abroad, as well as a gym and a recreation area. There were numerous cargo trucks, SUVs, forklifts, and excavators parked at the site. The Congolese employees wore beige uniforms with neon yellow stripes around the waist and arms, as well as yellow hard hats and industrial gloves. Aside from a few green trees planted outside the main office structure, the entire compound consisted of concrete, metal, and dirt.

We were led by guards into a conference room with a large square table. The walls of the room were covered in detailed schematics of mineral deposits and mine shafts. When the KICO staff arrived, I presented my request to survey the artisanal mining area. After answering questions about why, for how long, to what end, and so forth, we were granted permission to survey the artisanal mining area next to the KICO mine, but only with one of the KICO security guards as an escort. I was concerned that the guard's presence would prevent us from conducting interviews and receiving candid answers, but fortunately, he became bored after following us for a short time and returned to the compound, allowing Philippe and me to speak freely with the artisanal miners.

The Kipushi artisanal mining area was located in an open swath of earth just south of the abandoned Gécamines pit. It was a vast lunar wasteland spanning several square kilometers—a bizarre juxtaposition to the advanced KICO mining compound sitting right next to it. KICO had first-world mining equipment, excavation techniques, and safety measures. The artisanal site seemed to be time-warped from centuries before, populated by peasants using rudimentary tools to hack at the earth. More than three thousand women, children, and men shoveled, scraped, and scrounged across the artisanal mining zone under a ferocious sun and a haze of dust. With each hack at the earth, a puff of dirt floated up like a specter into the lungs of the diggers.

As we walked along the periphery of the site, Philippe reached down and handed me a stone about twice the size of my fist. "*Mbazi,*" he said.

Heterogenite. I studied the stone closely. It was dense with a rugged texture, adorned with an alluring mix of teal and azure, speckles of silver, and patches of orange and red—cobalt, nickel, copper. This was it. The beating heart of the rechargeable economy. Heterogenite can come in the form of a large stone, such as the one Philippe handed to me, or as smaller pebbles, or weathered down into sand. Cobalt is toxic to touch and breathe, but that is not the biggest worry that the artisanal miners have. The ore often contains traces of radioactive uranium.

I dropped the stone and followed Philippe deeper into the mining area. Most of the artisanal miners cast suspicious glances as I walked by. A teenage mother stopped digging and leaned against her shovel under the murky daylight. She gazed at me as if I were an invader. Dust swallowed the meager infant strapped to her back, head cocked at a right angle to its fragile body. Philippe asked if she would be open to speaking with us. "Who will fill this sack while I talk to you?" she responded angrily. We walked farther through the mine and found a group of six males caked in dirt and mud, ages eight to thirty-five.

"*Jambo,*" Philippe greeted the group, the Swahili word for "hello."

"*Jambo,*" they replied.

The group was digging inside a five-meter-deep pit about six or seven meters wide at the surface and three meters wide at the bottom, similar to the pits described by Frederick Stanley Arnot in 1886. The younger boys dug with small shovels closer to the surface, while the men dug deeper into the claylike sediment. The bottom of the pit was submerged in about a foot of copper-colored water. The oldest member of the group was Faustin. He was lean and hardened, with a face compressed toward the center. He wore plastic slippers, olive trousers, a light tan T-shirt, and a baseball cap.

"Most people digging here come from Kipushi," Faustin said. "Some people also come from villages on the Zambia side."

He pointed into the vague distance. There was no formal border crossing in this part of Kipushi, just an invisible line somewhere beyond the artisanal mining area that the local population crossed each day.

Faustin explained that he, his brother, brother-in-law, wife, cousin, and three children worked in a group. "We work with the people we trust," he said. Each day, they filled large raffia sacks with mud, dirt, and heterogenite stones that they dug out of the pit. They broke down larger stones into pebbles using a metal mallet so that they could fit more into each sack. Once the sacks were full, they carried them to nearby pools of water to sift the contents through a *kaningio* (metal sieve). The sieved heterogenite stones were then loaded back into the sacks. It took several such cycles each day to obtain enough heterogenite pebbles to fill one large raffia sack.

"By the end of one day, we can produce three sacks of heterogenite," Faustin explained.

I asked him what they did with the sacks.

"We take them over there near KICO. The *négociants* come to that place. We sell the cobalt to them."

"What do the *négociants* do with the heterogenite?" I asked.

"They transport the sacks to the *comptoirs* and sell it to them."

"Why don't you take the cobalt to the depots yourself?"

"I don't have a motorbike. Some other *creuseurs* can do the transportation to the *comptoirs* themselves, but this is a risk, because you must have a permit to transport ore in Congo. If the police find us when we are transporting the ore without the permits, we will be arrested," Faustin explained.

I asked what kind of permit was required. Faustin was not sure of the details, only that it was too expensive for most artisanal miners. Philippe filled in the details. "There are three different permits required for transporting ore. The price depends on how much ore is being transported and the distance it is transported. *Négociants* must pay something like eighty or one hundred dollars per year to transport one ton of ore no more than ten kilometers. A *comptoir* will have to transport many tons of ore, and maybe the distances could be up to fifty kilometers. The mining companies must transport thousands of tons, and it could be more than three hundred kilometers if they are traveling from Kolwezi to Kipushi, so the fee in this case can be thousands of dollars each year."

The ore transportation fees seemed to be little more than a money grab by the government. Why else charge people for driving rocks from one place to another? The fees also made it impossible for most artisanal miners to access markets directly due to their inability to pay the tax. Being cut off from the marketplace forced them to accept submarket prices from *négociants* for their hard labor, further reinforcing the state of poverty that pushed them into artisanal mining to begin with.

I asked Faustin and the members in his group about their health. They complained of persistent coughs and headaches. They also suffered minor injuries such as cuts and sprains, as well as back and neck pain. None of them wanted to come to the artisanal mining area to dig each day, but they felt they had no choice.

"What I can tell you is there is no other work for most people who live here," Faustin said. "Yet anyone can dig cobalt and earn money."

I worked through the arithmetic of just how much the members of Faustin's group were able to earn. The eight individuals in the group produced on average three sacks of washed heterogenite ore per day, and each sack weighed an average of forty kilograms. The *négociants* that came to the site paid 5,000 Congolese francs per sack, or about $2.80. This payment implied an income of roughly $1.05 per team member per day. The children did not actually receive any money; they simply worked to help the family. The heterogenite in Kipushi had a cobalt grade of 1 percent or less, which was much lower than the heterogenite closer to Kolwezi, where cobalt grades could exceed 10 percent. The low grade of cobalt in Kipushi had a direct bearing on the meager incomes earned by the artisanal miners who worked in the area.

After I finished speaking with Faustin's group, two of the boys, André and Kisangi, eight and ten years old, offered to demonstrate the sieving process. I followed them from the pit as they dragged a raffia sack bursting with dirt and stones. It probably weighed more than they did. After thirty meters, we arrived at a washing pool that was used by several groups of artisanal miners to sieve stones from dirt. The pool was about six meters in diameter and half a meter deep. There was a rusted metal bucket and a shovel at one end, and a copper-colored metal sieve about one meter by one meter lying in the water near the bucket. The pool of water was a putrid, bubbly, copper-colored swamp. Boys like André and Kisangi who sieved and washed stones were called *laveurs*, and women and girls were called *laveuses*.

The boys tipped the sack over and emptied the contents by hand into a large pile next to the washing pool. André stepped bare-skinned into the noxious water and picked up the sieve by two handles at one end. He lodged the other end of the sieve into the dirt at the edge of the pool. Kisangi used the small shovel to scoop the contents of the sack onto the sieve. André then vigorously yanked the sieve up and down through the surface of the water, separating dirt from stone. His tiny shoulders looked as if they would pop out of their sockets with each jolt. After a few minutes, only pebbles remained in the sieve. André appeared exhausted and barely managed to hold the sieve above water while Kisangi scooped the pebbles out by hand and placed them in a pile. The children would repeat this arduous process another ten or fifteen times to sieve all the stones from the sack, and they had to sieve several sacks each day.

"Our mother and sister pick up the stones and put them in that bucket," Kisangi explained. "They use the bucket to fill another sack with these stones."

From pit, to pool, to sack of stones—the family had subdivided the steps involved in getting cobalt out of the ground and packed for transport by *négociants*. The *négociants* then sold the cobalt into the formal supply chain via nondescript depots along the highway. Laundering minerals from child to battery was just that simple.

Philippe and I left the rinsing pool and walked farther into the artisanal mining area over rolling craters and shifting shades of brown. An oppressive haze hung in the air. There were no trees to be found and no birds in the sky. The earth had been stripped bare as far as the eye could see. It seemed as if half the teenage girls at the site had infants strapped to their backs. Boys as young as six took wide stances and summoned all the strength in their bony arms to hack at the earth with rusted spades. Other children teetered under the weight of stuffed raffia sacks they dragged from pits to pools. I spoke with more family groups, all of whom operated in a similar fashion to Faustin's family. I passed by more putrid washing pools and scores of pits filled with men and boys hacking and shoveling. Every so often, a group of exhausted children could be found sitting in the dirt under the harsh afternoon sun, eating dirty bread.

Somewhere close to the border with Zambia, or perhaps just on the other side, I came across several young women dressed in sarongs and T-shirts, standing in shallow pits with about six inches of coppery water at the bottom. They were not kin to each other but worked in a group to keep safe. Sexual assault by male artisanal miners, *négociants,* and soldiers was common in mining areas. The women said they all knew someone who had been shoved into a pit and attacked, the likely cause of at least some of the babies strapped to teenage backs. Sexual assault was a scourge in almost every artisanal mining area I visited. The women and girls who suffered these attacks represented the invisible, brutalized backbone of the global cobalt supply chain. No one at the top of the chain even bothered making press statements about zero-tolerance policies on sexual assault against the women and girls who scrounged for their cobalt.

A young woman named Priscille stood in one of the pits with a plastic bowl in her right hand. She rapidly scooped dirt and water with the bowl and flung it onto a sieve a few feet in front of her. Her motions were precise and symmetrical, as if she were a piece of machinery designed only for this purpose. After the sieve was filled with gray-colored mud and sand, Priscille yanked the sieve up and down until only the sand remained. That sand contained traces of cobalt, which she scooped with her plastic bowl into a pink raffia sack. I asked Priscille how long it took her to fill one sack with the sand.

"If I work very hard for twelve hours, I can fill one sack each day," she replied.

At the end of the day, the women helped each other to haul their fifty-kilogram sacks about a kilometer to the front of the site where *négociants* purchased each from them for around $0.80. Priscille said that she had no family and lived in a small hut on her own. Her husband used to work at this site with her, but he died a year ago from a respiratory illness. They tried to have children, but she miscarried twice.

"I thank God for taking my babies," she said. "Here it is better not to be born."

By evening, I finished the last interview and made my way back to the front of the artisanal mining area near the edge of the KICO compound. Scores of artisanal miners had dragged sacks of heterogenite to the front of the mine to sell to the *négociants*. I was expecting to see a team of formal mineral traders, perhaps with government uniforms or badges, but instead, the *négociants* were young men dressed in jeans and casual shirts. Unlike the dirt-crusted artisanal miners, their clothes were clean and bright. Most of the *négociants* arrived on motorbikes along with a few pickup trucks, which they used to transport the sacks to the depots. There were hundreds of white, blue, orange, and pink raffia sacks stacked next to the artisanal miners. The *négociants* took a cursory look inside the sacks and offered a fixed price that the artisanal miners had to accept. Philippe told me that women were always paid less than men for the same sack of cobalt.

"For this reason, the only women you will see selling the cobalt are the ones who work on their own," he explained.

I asked Philippe what would happen if an artisanal miner were to fill the bottom half of a sack with dirt and the top half with heterogenite.

"The *négociants* will find out at the depot. They will bring a gang to attack the *creuseurs*. No one would ever buy cobalt from that person again."

I watched a few *négociants* load sacks onto their motorbikes. They tied the sacks where a second passenger might sit, compressing the machine to its limits. One *négociant*, Eli, said that prior to being a *négociant*, he used to sell mobile phone top-up minutes for Africell in Lubumbashi, but his cousin convinced him to obtain authorization to be a *négociant*. The fee was $150, and it had to be paid annually.

"Now I make two or three times in a day what I used to make," Eli said.

I asked if I could see what the authorization document looked like.

"It expired two years ago!" Eli replied.

"What happens if a police officer asks to see your permit when you are transporting minerals?"

"We pay a fine. Maybe ten dollars, but this does not happen often."

After speaking to a few more *négociants,* I wandered back into the mining area to take a final look before darkness fell. The devastated landscape resembled a battlefield after an aerial bombardment. The survivors of the day's assault clambered out of the craters and trudged back to their huts to catch what little rest they could before returning to endure the ordeal all over again the following day.

A lone girl stood atop a dome of dirt, hands on her hips, eyes cast long across the barren land where giant trees once ruled. Her gold-and-indigo sarong fluttered wildly in the wind as she surveyed the ruin of people and earth. Beyond the horizon, beyond all reason and morality, people from another world awoke and checked their smartphones. None of the artisanal miners I met in Kipushi had ever even seen one.

After my visit to Kipushi, I went to investigate the depots to which the *négociants* sold the cobalt excavated by the artisanal miners. The depots were the unremarkable yet vital junctions between the informal and formal cobalt supply chains. Most of the depots for cobalt from Kipushi, as well as the smaller artisanal sites in nearby forests, were located on "heavy-charge road." They consisted of wooden shacks with large pink tarpaulins draped across the front. The names of the depots were painted in black letters atop the tarps—$Depot, Depot Jaafar, and Cu-Co, the symbols in the periodic table for copper and cobalt. The prices per kilogram that the depots offered for heterogenite were posted at the front, written in black marker on flattened raffia sacks based on cobalt concentrations from 0.5 percent to 2 percent in increments of one-tenth of a percent. I visited nine depots in a six-kilometer stretch northeast of Kipushi, and all but two were operated by Chinese agents. None of the Chinese agents were willing to speak with me. The other two depots were run by Indians—Hardeep and Amit—both from the state of Punjab.

Hardeep and Amit said they came to the DRC on work visas for jobs in the hospitality sector. They were both university graduates and spoke fairly good English, but they said jobs were very hard to come by back in India. The owner of the hotel at which they worked in Lubumbashi (they did not want to tell me the name of the hotel or the owner) also happened to moonlight as a mineral trader. He placed Hardeep and Amit in two depots—Depot Tiger and Depot 233. Hardeep and Amit reported to the depots every day at ten in the morning and remained until sunset. They kept money from their transactions inside a padlocked metal box, which it seemed anyone could probably steal if they set their minds to it.

"We use the Metorex to determine the purity of the cobalt," Hardeep explained. He showed me a small laser handgun that when pointed at a sample of heterogenite returned a reading of the grade of cobalt.

"The samples from Kipushi are usually one percent," Amit said.

At the end of each day, Hardeep and Amit drove the heterogenite sacks back to Lubumbashi. They said that their boss sold the heterogenite to a processor in Lubumbashi, but they did not know which one or the price paid by the processor. According to Philippe, there were two main mining companies that bought the heterogenite from Kipushi—Congo DongFang Mining and CHEMAF. Both companies had cobalt processing facilities in Lubumbashi, and both happened to operate the only two "model sites" for artisanal cobalt mining in the DRC. We will pay them a visit.

The prices paid at Depot Tiger and Depot 233 for a kilogram of heterogenite with 1 percent grade was 200 Congolese francs (about $0.11). A forty-kilogram sack, therefore, sold for about $4.40. The *négociants* at Kipushi paid Faustin about $2.80 per sack. Authorization to transport ore and a means of conveyance meant that the *négociants* operating in Kipushi were able to retain almost 40 percent of the value of each sack of heterogenite. It seemed a needless layer in the supply chain that shifted value away from the people who worked the hardest. For that matter, the depots equally seemed to be a needless layer in the supply chain, siphoning yet more value out of the system by providing an informal and untraceable entry point for artisanal cobalt into the formal supply chain. There was nothing to stop mining companies from going to the artisanal sites themselves and directly paying the women, men, and children who dug their cobalt—aside from the negative optics associated with having direct links to hazardous, penny-wage artisanal mining areas teeming with children.

There was a toxic feeling in Kipushi that I was unable to shake for several days after my visit. The earth, air, and water at the site seemed to be utterly contaminated, which suggested that every moment the artisanal miners spent digging in the mine exposed them to harmful substances that could have serious consequences to their health. To understand these consequences better, I met with a researcher at the University of Lubumbashi named Germain, who had been gathering data on the public health and environmental impacts of mining in the Copper Belt. Germain was a methodical researcher with an activist's spirit. He told me he had to be very cautious about his work, as some of his findings had not been well received by mining companies or the Congolese government. Here is some of what he described:

> In the studies we conducted, the artisanal miners have more than forty times the amount of cobalt in their urine as the control groups. They also have five times the level of lead and four times the level of uranium. Even the inhabitants living close to the mining areas who do not work as artisanal miners have very high concentrations of trace metals in their systems, including cobalt, copper, zinc, lead, cadmium, germanium, nickel, vanadium, chromium, and uranium.

Germain pointed out that indirect exposure to heavy metals by people who did not even work as artisanal miners still had negative health consequences on them, especially for children—"Even if children do not work in the mines, indirect exposure to heavy metals from their parents is worse for them than direct exposure for the adults. This is because a child's body cannot remove heavy metals as well as adults can." Germain added that humans weren't the only ones suffering toxic contamination—wildlife such as fish and chickens that he tested also showed very high levels of heavy metals.

Contamination by heavy metals of the local population and the food supply was causing a range of negative health consequences across the Copper Belt. For instance, Germain had recently documented a high rate of birth defects in mining communities, such as holoprosencephaly, agnathia otocephaly, stillbirth, miscarriages, and low birth weight.[10] Germain said that in most cases, the child's father had been working as an artisanal miner at the time of conception and that samples of cord blood taken at birth revealed high levels of cobalt, arsenic, and uranium. Respiratory ailments were also common—"Inhalation of cobalt dust causes 'hard metal lung disease' which can be fatal," Germain said. "Also, prolonged contact with cobalt by the artisanal miners can cause them to suffer acute dermatitis."

Cancers were also on the rise in artisanal mining communities, especially of the breast, kidney, and lung. "Exposure to nickel and uranium are the biggest causes of cancer," Germain said. Cases of lead poisoning were also widespread. Samples of dust taken inside homes throughout the Copper Belt had an average of 170 micrograms of lead per square foot. Germain explained that the lead dust probably came from the clothes of mine workers, as well as metal processing at some of the large mines. By way of comparison, the Environmental Protection Agency in the United States recommends a maximum safe limit of 40 micrograms of lead per square foot inside homes. Levels as high as 170 micrograms per square foot can cause neurological damage, muscle and joint pain, headaches, gastrointestinal ailments, and reduced fertility in adults. In children, lead poisoning can cause irreversible developmental damage as well as weight loss, vomiting, and seizures.

Germain lamented that the public health system in the Congo was not equipped to handle the scale and severity of negative health outcomes being suffered by the people who lived in mining communities. "There is no training of doctors to diagnose and treat health ailments arising from contamination by heavy metals," he said. Many villages and artisanal mining communities did not have basic medical clinics available to them to treat simple ailments, let alone seizures or cancers. Germain felt there were many parties responsible for the public health problems being faced by mining communities, but he had particularly strong words for foreign mining companies:

> The mining companies do not control the runoff of effluents from their processing operations. They do not clean up when they have chemical spills. Toxic dust and gases from mining plants and diesel equipment spreads for many kilometers and are inhaled by the local population. The mining companies have polluted the entire region. All the crops, animals, and fish stocks are contaminated.

Germain noted that the country's Mining Code contained provisions that were meant to prevent toxic dumping by mining companies, but none of these provisions or any other laws on environmental protection were adequately enforced. "Before getting a concession, the mining companies must submit a plan on waste management to the government. Of course, they do not adhere to their plans. But the government is not sending people to monitor their activities either."

I asked Germain why he thought the Congolese government had not engaged him to assist with a more extensive testing program and system of enforcement of waste management at the big mines. He sighed and explained that government officials predictably wanted to maximize mining royalties, which meant maximizing the extraction of ore, which meant letting mining companies do as they pleased so long as the royalties were paid. The research Germain was doing was a hindrance, not a benefit, to this agenda. He had in fact received pressure to cease doing the kind of testing he described to me. "It is not just because of the foreign mining companies," he explained. "Congolese companies are just as guilty of dumping waste matter into the environment. They don't like the work I do either."

Germain understandably felt that there was little chance the public health consequences of mining across the Copper Belt would improve until companies were compelled to adhere to minimum standards of sustainability and environmental protection. "Just like in America," he said.

"What would it take to get there?" I asked.

Germain reached for a thoughtful answer, but remained silent and only offered a weary shrug.

A pattern emerged early in my trips to the Congo—word would spread about my forays into artisanal mining areas, and not long after, a call was made to one of my guides or a message was left at my guesthouse asking for a meeting. No sooner had I met with Germain than did Philippe inform me that he had been asked to arrange a meeting with an organization called Investissements Durables au Katanga ("Sustainable Investment in Katanga"), or IDAK. IDAK is actively involved in the DRC's artisanal mining sector, and three members of the organization's leadership—Alex, Fortunat, and Mbuya—asked me to meet with them in a church in Lubumbashi. We sat on plastic chairs in what appeared to be a storage room. There were no lights, just a table lamp and two open windows, which allowed the noise from the traffic outside to flood the room. The IDAK leaders seemed keen to impress upon me the organization's importance in assisting artisanal miners.

"We founded IDAK in 2011 to provide a forum for representatives of local government, national government, civil society, and mining companies to discuss challenges facing the mining sector and to find solutions in a collaborative manner," Alex explained. "IDAK is trying to improve cooperation between stakeholders and build the capacities and skills of civil society to support the artisanal miners."

Alex added that IDAK had international support for its efforts and received most of its funding from Deutsche Gesellschaft für Internationale Zusammenarbeit ("German Society for International Cooperation"), a consulting firm that advised the German government and corporations on sustainability and international development.

"The funding was initiated by German car companies to help clean their cobalt supply chains," Alex said.

The IDAK team shared a copy of a comprehensive guide they published in 2014 that outlined their recommendations on corporate social responsibility in the Congolese mining sector.

"This guide includes a plan for the removal of children from artisanal mining," Mbuya explained.

In addition to focusing on child labor, IDAK's CSR plan described programs for strengthening local communities, building and staffing schools, promoting alternate livelihoods, and improving public health capacity and infrastructure. It all sounded very promising, but I could not help but wonder why so little of it seemed to be happening. I described what I had seen in Kipushi—hundreds of children digging in the dirt for meager income, thousands of people suffering toxic exposure, and no monitoring of any kind regarding labor abuses.

"Yes, we have these problems, but without IDAK, the situation would be worse," Fortunat said.

The IDAK team must have read the poorly hidden skepticism on my face, because they spent another hour describing all of the organization's efforts to improve conditions for artisanal miners. They also stressed the importance of their role in mediating conflicts between artisanal miners and foreign mining companies.

"If there is a land dispute, we try to resolve the matter constructively. If there is an accident at the mine, we advocate for the rights of the injured miners," Mbuya said.

I knew from meeting just a few people like Makaza at Mukwemba that conflict resolution on land disputes was an important initiative, although I never heard of a single case in which the dispute had been resolved in a manner that was favorable for the displaced people.

I asked the IDAK team what they felt was the biggest obstacle to their efforts at removing children from artisanal mines. Unsurprisingly, they said, "Poverty."

"Parents are pressured to bring their children into the mines to work. If parents earned a good wage, children could be in school instead of working at a mine," Mbuya said.

It seemed obvious enough, so why were "good wages" so elusive?

Would something as simple as a reasonable wage solve some of the challenges being faced by artisanal miners or at least attenuate the levels of child labor? Let's say for a moment that paying a decent wage to adult artisanal miners would help keep children in school instead of working in mines and that it would also help families afford medical care when they were ill or injured, save money to help withstand income shocks or other misfortunes, and alleviate strain and violence in the community. Let's say a decent wage for adults might accomplish all of this and more—who should pay it? Foreign mining companies would argue that they do not employ artisanal miners, so the responsibility is not theirs, even though the cobalt from artisanal digging ends up in their supply chains, and even though in some cases they allow artisanal miners to work on their concessions to boost production. The government of the DRC would argue that they do not have the money to support good wages or other income schemes, even though mining concessions are sold for billions of dollars and royalties and taxes in the billions are collected each year based in no small part on the value of the minerals excavated by artisanal miners. Cobalt refiners, battery manufacturers, and tech and EV companies would argue that the responsibility should be borne downstream, even though the scramble for cobalt only exists because of their demand for it. Therein lies the great tragedy of the Congo's mining provinces—no one up the chain considers themselves responsible for the artisanal miners, even though they all profit from them.

My meeting with IDAK revealed that there were tangible efforts at the local level to address abuses in the artisanal mining sector, even if those efforts did not seem to be translating into meaningful progress on the ground. Philippe offered a theory, "IDAK has the correct goals, but there is no chance to realize their goals so long as the government is corrupt and the Chinese rule Katanga. The Chinese pay billions to the government, and the politicians close their eyes. Organizations like IDAK and other civil society organizations are allowed to exist only to show they exist." The more time I spent with Philippe, the more I appreciated the depth of his concerns about the plight of artisanal miners in the Congo. When enough trust had developed between us, he told me that he had himself been an artisanal miner. He spent four years digging for cobalt around Likasi. During that time, he suffered numerous lacerations, rashes, respiratory ailments, and a broken leg in a pit wall collapse. After the collapse, he stopped working for two months to recover. When the time came to return to the mines, he made the difficult decision not to do so. "I could have been killed that day. What would happen to my wife and children?" Philippe moved his family into his brother's home in Lubumbashi while he took time to get on his feet. He worked odd jobs to get by, but his heart remained with those who toiled in the mines. According to Philippe, the problems in the mining sector went back generations:

> If you really want to understand what is happening in the Congo's mining sector, you must first understand our history. After independence, the mines were managed by the Belgians. They took all the money, and there was no benefit for the people. After the Belgians, we had "Africanization" with Mobutu. He nationalized the mines, but again, they only benefited the government, not the people. With [Joseph] Kabila, we created the Mining Code in 2002, and this brought foreign investment into the mining sector. They said the Mining Code would improve the lives of the Congolese people, but today, their lives are much worse. Now you can see—never have the people of Congo benefited from the mines of Congo. We only become poorer.

Philippe formed a group to support artisanal mining communities. His team focused on trying to help children stay in school. Completing their educations, he felt, was the only way to help break the cycle of poverty. He agreed with IDAK that poverty was the primary factor that led to the exploitation of artisanal miners, but he also pointed to another, equally insidious force: "There is an agenda to promote a false picture of the conditions here. The mining companies claim there are not any problems here. They say they maintain international standards. Everyone believes them, so nothing changes." Philippe's words got me thinking about the press statements from corporations espousing their compliance with international human rights standards and zero-tolerance policies on child labor. The Global Battery Alliance and Responsible Minerals Initiative were supposed to be assisting with adherence to these norms via on-ground assessments of cobalt supply chains and monitoring of artisanal mining sites for child labor. I asked Philippe if he had ever seen or heard of these initiatives. Here is what he said:

> They tell the international community about their programs in Congo and how the cobalt is clean, and this allows their constituents to say everything is okay. Actually, this makes the situation worse because the companies will say—"GBA assures us the situation is good. RMI says the cobalt is clean." Because of this, no one tries to improve the conditions.

Philippe was describing a smoke screen set up by powerful stakeholders that served to obscure the harsh realities under which cobalt was mined. The more time I spent in the Congo, the more his words rang true. To this day, I never met anyone associated with the GBA or the RMI in the Congo, nor did I ever hear about any inspections of artisanal mining areas from any colleagues in the DRC being conducted under their banners. My efforts to speak with these coalitions about my findings met without response until the summer of 2020 when the then director of the Global Battery Alliance, Mathy Stanislaus, agreed to a call. We had a congenial conversation about artisanal mining in the Congo and a recapitulation of the GBA's various initiatives. When I pressed Mr. Stanislaus on what I had seen on the ground, he acknowledged that there were some problems, at least as relates to child labor.

"According to the OECD [Organisation for Economic Co-operation and Development], up to seventy percent of the cobalt from the DR Congo has some touch with child labor. There are large gaps of information on the supply chain, so we have to fix the information flow in a trusted way," he said.

Let's start with the second sentence. What exactly does it mean to "fix the information flow?" Fixing it for the artisanal miners would suggest a genuinely independent and objective assessment of the realities on the ground. Fixing it for everyone else would suggest the opposite. And trusted by whom? Same problem. Consumer tech and EV giants, mining companies, and the Congolese government would be unlikely to trust the same flow of information that the artisanal miners would trust. This is the precise tension that Philippe identified as being a barrier to meaningful progress for artisanal miners. The prevailing information flow depicted a false reality that conditions were not so bad and that they were being monitored to root out problems. A more accurate information flow would depict the opposite—conditions on the ground for the artisanal miners were hazardous and subhuman, and there were tens of thousands of children who mined for cobalt under these conditions every day.

Consider the first sentence, because this is the important one. If the OECD and its constituents concede that 70 percent of 72 percent of the world's supply of cobalt "has some touch" with child labor, that would imply that half of the cobalt in the world was touched by child labor in the Congo. This fact alone indicted a preponderance of the global supply chain of cobalt, yet child labor was far from the only problem in the Congo's artisanal mining sector. How much of the Congo's cobalt was "touched" by the hundreds of thousands of Congolese people suffering the consequences of toxic exposure to cobalt, uranium, lead, nickel, mercury, and other heavy metals? How much was touched by the infants who inhaled hazardous mining dust every day at artisanal mines? What about the noxious gas clouds and toxic dumping that contaminated the air, land, crops, animals, and fish stocks of the Copper Belt, and what about the millions of trees chopped down to make way for enormous open-pit mines? Let us not forget the unknown number of people who were injured or worse in mining accidents. By the time one tallied such a list, how much cobalt would be left in the world that was untouched by catastrophe in the Congo?

The full magnitude of these catastrophes had yet to be revealed to me. Any notion that Kipushi had offered even a glimpse of the severity of insult being suffered by the Congo's artisanal miners would be harshly dispelled, one mile at a time, on the road to Kolwezi.

3

The Hills
Have Secrets

Likasi and Kambove

> The white man is very clever. He came quietly and peaceably with his religion. We were amused at his foolishness and allowed him to stay . . . He has put a knife on the things that held us together and we have fallen apart.
>
> —Chinua Achebe, *Things Fall Apart*

NOTHING LOOKS THE SAME after a trip to the Congo. The world back home no longer makes sense. It is difficult to reconcile how it even inhabits the same planet. Neatly arranged mountains of vegetables at grocery stores seem vulgar. Bright lights and flushing toilets seem like sorcery. Clean air and water feel like a crime. The markers of wealth and consumption appear violent. Most of it was built, after all, on violence, neatly tucked away in history books that tend to sanitize the truth.

We are rarely asked, if ever, to confront the untold suffering that has been endured by Africa. Imagine for a moment what it was like for an African person to be ripped from her home; separated from husband and children; chained, branded, beaten, raped, and incarcerated—all before being forced into the putrid cargo hold of a slave ship, crammed next to hundreds of agonized men, women, children, and babies. Or what it was like to spend six weeks in this cargo hold without room to sit upright, locked down by flesh-ripping shackles day and night. Or to have to use a bucket for a toilet in front of hundreds of people as the ship crashed through waves. Or to try to comfort an inconsolable child who was frightened, feverish, and seasick. Or to be one of the gravely ill, but still living, who was thrown into the ocean like so much refuse. Or to survive this hell only to arrive in the Americas and be sold into slavery, where the real torture began.

Imagine for a moment the toll taken on a person, a family, a people, a continent across centuries of the slave trade, followed by a century of colonization. Empires were built and generations of wealth were amassed across the Western world in this manner. Perhaps that is the most enduring contrast of all between our world and theirs—our generally safe and satisfied nations can scarcely function without forcing great violence upon the people of Africa. The catastrophe in the mining provinces of the Congo is the latest chapter in this unholy tale.

According to a mid-level manager at Congo DongFang Mining (CDM) who goes by the name of Hu, the people of the Congo, and Africa more generally, suffer exploitation because they are lazy.

"If the Africans worked harder, they would not be so poor. Chinese people have discipline. African people do not. They drink and gamble. They allow their leaders to exploit them. This is why they are poor."

I met Hu at the Royal Casino, one of the private Chinese clubs in Lubumbashi. We sat poolside in the open air. Chinese men drank and smoked as heavy-beat club music thumped through the speakers. Congolese people were not allowed inside the club, except when the strippers arrived around 9:00 p.m.

As he drank his beers, Hu from Chengdu let his opinions fly. "The Africans will always be poor because they do not want to learn. In China, we have the best education in the world. Chinese people study very hard, and look how quickly our country has become a world power."

Hu lit a cigarette and waved his hands in scattershot motions as he continued. "Also, the Africans lack management ability. They do not take interest in details. This is why they can only be laborers. Even as laborers, they do not perform well. They only want to have fun."

Hu continued by offering his thoughts on poverty in Africa. "I think they like being poor because they receive foreign aid and do not have to work. If they did not like being poor, why do they spend all day on Sunday in church instead of working?"

Hu went on like this for a while, and I forced myself to listen. After numerous failed attempts to speak with CDM management or to gain access to the company's mineral-processing facility in Lubumbashi, Hu was the first CDM employee who agreed to meet with me. Given the company's position as one of the chief buyers and exporters of artisanal cobalt from the DRC, I wanted to learn as much as I could about CDM's operations and perhaps gain access to contracts or production data, but Hu took the occasion instead to vent his opinions about Africans. It was a frustrating meeting, to say the least.

I can only assume that Hu felt comfortable sharing his perspectives on Africans because he assumed that like so many of the Indians in Africa, I too was a bigot. Indians have a long history on the continent dating back to the 1840s, when the British began shipping them to Africa to work as debt bondage slaves on railroads and plantations. The debts were manufactured through the imposition of exorbitant land taxes. If a peasant could not afford the taxes, he was told he could work it off by laying railroad in East Africa. Illiterate peasants were made to sign contracts they could not read, agreeing to discharge their debts as indentured workers. They often toiled for lifetimes, receiving little pay. In Africa, a hierarchy was soon established—Africans at the bottom, Indians and Arabs above them, and Europeans at the top. Skin tone dictated the hierarchy back then, and it still does today—simply swap out the Europeans with the Chinese.

LIKASI

The stretch of road from Lubumbashi to Likasi passes through a broad expanse of open terrain and rolling hills. A dreary pall obscures the horizon. All is shaded in copper and rust. Villages cling to the roadside like fingertips at a cliff's edge. Redbrick huts reach deep into the bush. Women cook cassava by open fires. Toddlers make friends of dirt. Teenage girls line up at the nearest well with yellow plastic containers to fill their supply of water for the day. Spires of silver smoke rise from deep within the forest where men burn trees to make charcoal, their only source of heat and light. This land that is home to the world's largest reserves of an element crucial to the manufacture of the most dominant form of rechargeable energy in the world still awaits the arrival of electricity.

Although the two-lane highway paved by SICOMINES has greatly assisted with movement through the Copper Belt, the road remains narrow and treacherous. Cars, SUVs, and minivans loaded with passengers and stacked with goods up to three meters high on the roofs strike out from behind slow-moving cargo trucks crammed with minerals in a mad dash to overtake them. The roadside is littered with hundreds of skeletal remains of vehicles whose drivers miscalculated the distance and speed required to overtake in time. I once saw a minivan stuffed with sacks of cobalt and mattresses tied to the roof swerve into the opposite lane to overtake a cargo truck, then swerve right back to avoid an oncoming passenger bus, only to career out of control right in front of my jeep and wipe out across the highway. We slammed the brakes and narrowly avoided the same fate. It took an hour for local villagers to clear the wreckage from the road. In time, everything of value would be picked clean from the vehicle—engine parts, seats, and tires—until only metal and rust remained.

Traffic slows to a crawl at each of the *péage* checkpoints on the highway. Gaunt children swarm vehicles to sell vegetables, charcoal, and bushmeat. Dull soldiers with AK-47s question passengers who clearly do not belong. Officials from the Direction Générale de Migration (DGM) insist on scrutinizing travel documents. One time, a fellow in a lime-green jumpsuit who called himself "Captain Mike" approached me at the checkpoint just before Likasi and announced that he was a member of the Congolese secret service and needed to inspect my luggage. Such charades are common, making the process at checkpoints at times lengthy and frustrating. Eventually, it all runs its course and vehicles are allowed through.

Copper first lured the Belgians to the hills near Likasi in the early 1900s. The behemoth deposits fired their imagination, and they founded a mining town called Jadotville in 1917, after Jean Jadot, the first president of UMHK. Copper is not the only thing the Belgians found near Likasi. They also discovered uranium on April 11, 1915. The deposits had an average concentration of 65 percent U_3O_8 (triuranium octoxide), making it the highest-grade source of uranium in the world at the time. UMHK promptly built a uranium mine called Shinkolobwe southwest of Likasi. The global market for uranium in the 1920s was limited to use in pigments for ceramics, not unlike cobalt, so the mine was not nearly as profitable as the nearby copper mines and was ultimately closed in 1937. Soon after, the Manhattan Project identified Shinkolobwe as the ideal source for the high-grade uranium required to build an atomic bomb. On September 18, 1942, at an office in Midtown Manhattan, the owners of UMHK agreed to sell uranium from Shinkolobwe to the U.S. Army for around one dollar per pound. Shinkolobwe provided roughly 75 percent of the uranium that was used for the bombs dropped from the *Enola Gay* on Hiroshima and Nagasaki in August 1945.[1] Although Shinkolobwe has been nonoperational for decades, rumors persist that rogue army officials and organized criminals excavate uranium and sell it on the black market to the likes of Iran, North Korea, and Pakistan. One such operative named Arran also happens to exploit child laborers at a cobalt-mining death trap called Tilwezembe, just a bit farther down the road to Kolwezi.

A stroll through the streets of Likasi reveals a curious collection of crumbling buildings, old art deco structures from the colonial period, and the original tree-lined avenues where the Belgians once lived. The small city center is built around a khaki-colored two-story building with aqua trim, Le Mairie de Likasi ("the Town Hall of Likasi"). Storefronts display vegetables, dried fish from the nearby Lufira River, and chai (tea), a word that entered Swahili from the descendants of the Indian debt bondage slaves trafficked by the British to Africa. Of the three major cities in the mining provinces, the streets in Likasi are unquestionably the worst. They are perpetually being dug up, repaved, and rerouted. Heavy haulers clog the upturned roads. Children in bright uniforms climb over rock piles and ditches to get to school. A single accident on the primary road through town can lock down vehicular movement for hours.

Likasi is home to a few copper-cobalt mines and processing facilities, a demolition factory, and a chemical manufacturing plant that produces sulfuric acid, which is used to process copper-cobalt ores at many industrial mining sites. Numerous artisanal mining areas are scattered across a chain of hills and forest that stretch from Likasi to the nearby town of Kambove, whose immense copper deposits were hailed by the geologists Jules Cornet in 1892 and John R. Farrell in 1902. Many of the artisanal sites are guarded by informal militia units, some of which are paid by mining companies. The units typically consist of a "general," who leads a force of ten to twenty young men armed with Kalashnikovs, handguns, and machetes. The militias are particularly active in some of the villages and artisanal mining sites near Kambove.

"Kambove is the most lawless area of mining in the Copper Belt," a local guide, Arthur, explained. "It is more like the coltan mines in Tanganyika."

As I explored the mining areas in and around Likasi and Kambove, the conditions proved to be much worse than I expected.

Early mornings are cool in the Copper Belt even during the peak heat of the dry season. Temperatures drop once the sun goes down due to the altitude and lack of humidity. Moisture builds during the night, and at sunrise, silver mists weave through the hills like lost spirits. There are numerous villages scattered in the remote areas around Likasi and Kambove.

I managed to explore a few of them, including one that had particularly bleak conditions. My guide, Arthur, asked me not to disclose the village's name due to the risks of negative repercussions, but he did say that I could mention the name of a similar village that used to be in the area called Kamatanda.

"You can tell people that the village I am going to show you is just like Kamatanda used to be," he said.

Kamatanda was once situated adjacent to an old Gécamines copper-cobalt mine north of Likasi. Most of the residents of the village, including almost all the children, dug and washed heterogenite from roughly 2014 to 2018, at which point a Chinese mining company purchased the concession and took over the land in the surrounding hills, including Kamatanda. Arthur said that the army was sent to force more than one thousand inhabitants to leave Kamatanda, not unlike what happened to Makaza near the Étoile mine. The inhabitants of other villages in the area lived under the constant threat of also having to leave their homes one day. Their only prayer was that there should be nothing valuable in the dirt under the next village.

To reach the artisanal mining village Arthur wanted to show me, we drove from Likasi on a dirt road far into a remote area, parked in what seemed to be the middle of nowhere, and proceeded on foot along a path of rock and dirt that was too jagged for the vehicle. The morning mists had already evaporated as we trudged through thin straggles of dry brush. Before long, the crunch beneath our feet gave way to a sea of voices. The village appeared suddenly—a crumbling collection of huts, hacked-up earth, and a small stream just two or three meters wide that snaked through the terrain. There was no electricity or sanitation in the village. Scores of children stood in the water, bent double as they sieved dirt from heterogenite pebbles. A cacophony rose from the hills—sloshing water, hacking shovels, and frenetic shouting. It was like a beehive, impossible to focus on any one person at a time. The villagers looked poorer than the people I'd met in Kipushi. Their clothes were more tattered, and most everyone was filthy and emaciated. Piles of stone, white raffia sacks, and refuse were strewn around the stream. Plantain trees near the dilapidated huts provided the primary form of sustenance. Manioc and onions grew in a small agricultural field. The stream had a rank stench of sewage. A handful of armed men patrolled the scene. They wore no uniforms—just jeans and shirts, baseball caps and sneakers.

Arthur led us toward the militia, sometimes also referred to as *commandos*. He said that we needed their permission to speak to the inhabitants. The commandos were familiar with Arthur, as he and his colleagues provided medicine, cooking oil, sacks of flour, and other supplies to a few villages in the area. Arthur approached the head of the militia, Bukasa, a thin, long-faced man with yellow teeth and bloodshot eyes. Bukasa wore jeans, sneakers, and an Adidas T-shirt. Arthur explained in Swahili that I was a professor from America who had come to assist with fundraising. Bukasa granted our request to survey the village and speak to some of the inhabitants, but he instructed us not to venture beyond the primary village area.

We walked along the stream that transected the village and observed the artisanal mining operation in action. Boys between eight and thirteen years of age whacked large mud-caked heterogenite chunks against each other with their bare hands to reduce the size of the stones. They did not have mallets or hammers as did most of the artisanal miners in Kipushi. Once the boys had reduced the size of the stones, they passed them to another group of children, which included girls, to wash in the stream. Although a few of the children had *kaningios,* most of them rinsed the stones by using one layer of a torn raffia sack. Two children held the ends of the sack like they were going to fold a bedsheet. Another child loaded the middle of the sack with mud and stones. The children holding the sack then lowered it beneath the surface of the stream. The boys worked in unison as they rapidly lifted their right arms, dropped them, lifted their left arms, dropped them. They went back and forth, right to left, agitating the mud and dirt to pass through the sack. Eventually, the sack held only heterogenite pebbles. The children loaded the pebbles into other raffia sacks and carried them to Bukasa's team, who loaded them into a Hilux pickup truck. The commandos transported the sacks to Likasi in the truck. I asked Arthur if he knew to which depots in Likasi the ore from the village was sold. He said there were many, but the primary ones were Depot Jin, Depot Diop, and Depot Hao. According to Arthur, all three depots sold their ore to Chinese mining companies. He also suggested that Bukasa and his team were on the payroll of one of the Chinese mining companies. "They call it 'private security,'" he said.

A subsequent visit to Depots Hao, Jin, and Diop revealed just a few transactions taking place, albeit during limited surveillance on a single afternoon. The transactions I observed were between the Chinese agents, who operated the depots, and Congolese *négociants,* who arrived with stuffed raffia sacks on motorbikes. I counted twenty-six raffia sacks in total stacked at the depots, and Arthur assured me that all the heterogenite from the three depots went to processing facilities run by Chinese mining companies in Likasi and Lubumbashi. He made his case plainly: "The mining companies can say they do not buy cobalt from these villages. But where do they think the cobalt goes? If no one is buying it, why are they digging it?"

Although most of the families in the village were familiar with Arthur, few were willing to sit for extended conversations. Some were no doubt anxious about speaking to an outsider in the presence of the commandos, and others simply did not want me getting in the way of their work. Two brothers who did speak with me were Denis and Awilo, ages ten and eleven. The boys were washing stones when Arthur spotted them. He guided them to a quieter area for us to speak. They wore brown shorts, plastic flip-flops, and tattered T-shirts, one green and the other azure. Denis hid from the sun under an oversize baseball cap with a Chinese dragon emblem on the front. The boys did not know who their father was. Their mother worked at a guesthouse in Likasi. She visited them once or twice a month.

"We live with our grandmother," Denis said. "We have two older brothers, but they went to Zambia."

The boys expelled metallic coughs as they spoke. They complained of itching and burning skin on their legs, as well as chronic pain in their backs and necks. They had been breaking and washing stones in the village for as long as they could remember and had never attended a day of school. They said they awoke each morning anxious to return to the stream.

Denis and Awilo took me to meet their grandmother Solange, who was sitting in the dirt, peeling manioc with a small knife. She wore a clean but faded brown-and-yellow blouse and skirt. Her eyes were deep-set. Her fingers seemed disjointed and arthritic. Her skin was dry liked cracked earth. Solange explained that the boys' father left to be with another woman when they were babies. The same thing happened to her when she was twenty-eight, and she was left on her own to raise four children. She was unable to stay in Likasi after that, so she moved to a nearby village, where her brother was living. She said that when she first left Likasi in the mid-1980s, there was no artisanal mining taking place. The original Belgian copper mines were run by Gécamines, and most of the men who lived in Likasi and Kambove worked at them. After Gécamines closed the mines, people started digging for themselves.

"At that time, what they earned from the copper was enough," Solange said. "We did not have to send our children to dig."

Solange said that everything changed in 2012. "[Joseph] Kabila sold the mines to the Chinese. They made it seem like a blessing. They said we should dig cobalt and get rich. Everyone started to dig, but no one became rich. We do not earn enough to meet our needs."

Solange finished peeling the manioc and poured water from a yellow plastic container into a metal pot. She placed the manioc in the pot, then used a match to light kindling. She coaxed the fire to life and placed the pot on top. As the manioc cooked, she grew pensive. "Look at my grandchildren. This is what cobalt has done to Congolese children. They have no more future."

For most of the day, my presence had been tolerated by the commandos, but Bukasa began to stare with consternation as I spoke to several more children, including a boy named Kiyonge. He was nine, small for his age, and wore frayed black shorts and a muddied shirt with a smiley-face emoji on the front. He pressed his fingers against his left eye constantly. I asked him what was wrong, and it turned out he had a sty in his eyelid that appeared to be causing him quite a bit of pain. The closest medical clinic was back in Likasi, so if a villager became unwell, injured, or had a painful sty in his eye, his only choice was to suffer through it. Kiyonge also had a patch of missing hair about the size of a silver dollar behind his right temple. His skin was covered in rashes, and he spoke in the grainy voice of an old man.

"We used to live in Milele. Two years ago, my mother brought me and my brothers here. She left after a few months to bring my two sisters, but she did not return," he said.

Kiyonge lived in the village with his three older brothers. He said that they dug for cobalt, but he was too small to dig, so he washed stones in the creek.

Kiyonge showed us the hut in which he and his three brothers lived. It was a thatched structure with a plastic sheet tied on top as a makeshift roof. Shorts and shirts were hanging to dry on a string. Inside, the hut was roughly three meters by three meters with a hard dirt floor. One white plastic bowl sat in a corner, and there was one large metal pot surrounded by large stones for cooking and heating. There were also some knives, spoons, plastic containers, and a hodgepodge of clothes. The boys boiled manioc and onions that grew in a field next to the village to make rudimentary fufu, a staple dish of the poor in the DRC. They slept on mats on the ground. During the rainy season, they draped the hut in as many spare pieces of plastic tarp and ripped up raffia sacks as they could find. Water from the storms inevitably seeped through and muddied the ground on which they slept.

"If you want to learn more about children who dig cobalt, you must go to Milele," Kiyonge said. "There are thousands of children there. Many of the children from that place are brought by sponsors to villages like this one."

Arthur explained that by "sponsor," Kiyonge meant commandos or *négociants*. They were known to traffic children from other villages and even neighboring provinces into artisanal digging sites such as Kiyonge's village to boost production. Milele was located far to the north of Likasi. I was not able to find a guide willing to take me there, as the area was controlled by particularly violent militias.

After a few hours, I had spoken with several children and a few mothers and grandmothers in the village. I had also observed the process of washing and sorting the ore in the stream. There was only one question that remained: Where was the ore coming from? Kiyonge said his older brothers were in another area digging for heterogenite. It was the same area outside the village that Bukasa prohibited me from seeing. Kiyonge said there was a back way through the brush to get to the area without detection and offered directions. Arthur and I walked past the dilapidated huts into an area of brush and eventually arrived in a range of dirt about the size of a soccer field. Most of the trees and bushes had been cleared away, and the ground seemed as if it had been plowed. I saw several young men and teenage boys in the field, along with dozens of raffia sacks arranged in stacks of three or four, each filled to various degrees with stones and dirt. There were also at least fifteen tunnel openings distributed across the field, each of which was roughly a meter in diameter. I asked Arthur how many people might be underground. He said he was not sure but estimated it would be at least one hundred.

This was the first time I saw tunnel digging for cobalt in the Congo. There were so many questions I wanted to ask: How deep did the tunnels go? How many people were down there? How did they descend and return? How did they get ore to the surface? Did the tunnels have any supports? How did the diggers breathe underground?

Unfortunately, I was unable to explore the tunnel digging area any further. There were a few commandos patrolling the field, and Arthur did not want us to linger a moment longer and risk being seen. Based on my observations that day, it seemed that deep within an otherwise unremarkable hill, far removed from any signs of civilization, there was something akin to an ant colony of humans who tunneled, excavated, washed, packed, and fed valuable cobalt up the chain to the companies that produced the world's rechargeable devices and cars. I never in all my trips to the Congo saw or heard of any of these companies or their downstream suppliers monitoring this part of the supply chain, or any of the countless places like it.

The more villages I visited in the Congo, the more I appreciated how challenging it was for a child to go to school. Most of us take education for granted and often compete mightily to obtain the best one possible, but children like Denis, Awilo, and Kiyonge had no chance at completing even a few years of elementary school. A few of the larger villages around Likasi had schools, but most of them did not, especially in remoter areas. I met with a teacher named Josephine in Likasi who used to work in one of the village schools near the town. She lived with her husband and three children in a small home in the Quartier Mission part of the city. She was in her thirties, energetic, and liked writing poetry. Josephine was passionate about child education and often worked for months without pay.

"The government is supposed to pay the salaries for the teachers, but they do not provide funding, so the schools must charge fees," she said.

"How much are the fees?" I asked.

"Five dollars each month."

Josephine said that most families in poor villages around Likasi were not able to pay the school fees on a consistent basis and that as a consequence, parents often sent their children to work instead. Digging for cobalt was the surest way to walk home each day with at least some money. It seemed unimaginable that the difference between receiving an education and having to engage in hazardous child labor was a handful of dollars. I asked whether foreign aid from governments or grants from charitable foundations might help bridge the gap, or perhaps cash payments to families on condition that children remained enrolled in schools. Such initiatives had proven to be effective in other poor countries at increasing school completion rates among vulnerable children.

Josephine said that she was aware of a few schools that had received support from UNICEF in the past, but when the financial support ended, many children had to go back to work. She also felt that cash payments to

families were not the solution. To start, the closest school might be several
kilometers away, which made it impossible for a child to attend consistently, especially during the rainy months. In addition, "many children
themselves do not wish to be in the school. There is too much pressure for
them to work, even if they can afford the fees. In the last year, I started
with thirty-six children. After two months, I had only seventeen. Even
those children worked every morning before they came to school. They
were always tired and hungry. How can they learn in this condition?"
Josephine explained that the beleaguered state of many children and a
lack of motivation among teachers who often went unpaid for extended
periods resulted in the fact that even when village children managed to
attend schools, many ended up reaching the age of thirteen or fourteen
with only rudimentary literacy skills. According to Josephine, the educational system in rural Congo was completely broken.

Josephine's observations left me frustrated. It seemed that on any
given day, a poor family in the Congo almost always needed income first
and education second or not at all. Food, medicine, repairs to a hut, or
any other expense required that every member of a family earned whatever they could, including the children. The dividends of an education
were too theoretical and too far into the future for those who survived
day-to-day, especially when the schools lacked the support they needed
to provide an adequate education. It was no wonder that impoverished
families across the Congo's mining provinces relied on child labor to
survive. At times, it felt like cobalt stakeholders up the chain counted on
it. Why help build schools or fund proper education for Congolese children living in mining communities, when the children could just dig up
cobalt for pennies instead?

KAMBOVE

The next stop on our journey is the mining town of Kambove, located
about twenty-five kilometers northwest of Likasi. To fully appreciate
Kambove, we take a slight detour to Paris, circa July 10, 1873. On this

day, Edmund Dene Morel was born to an English schoolteacher and a French civil servant. Morel's father died when he was only four years old, so his mother moved back to England to raise him. In 1890, around the same time that Joseph Conrad began his journey up the Congo River, Morel secured a job as a clerk at a Liverpool shipping line known as Elder Dempster. The company handled all the cargo for King Leopold's Congo Free State. Because Morel knew French, Dempster instructed him to review shipping transactions with the Belgians. Morel became fascinated with Africa and read everything he could about the continent. He soon encountered testimonies from missionaries in the Congo Free State that described widespread atrocities. These testimonies were rejected as falsehood by Leopold's propaganda machine. Like most people of the time, Morel was inclined to believe a king.

Sometime in 1900 and quite by accident, Morel was comparing the official figures of Elder Dempster's shipping returns with the sale of rubber by the Congo Free State on the Antwerp market when he noticed something peculiar. The flow of rubber out of the Congo into Belgium seemed to be increasing by leaps and bounds, yet the entire value of the rubber, aside from transport costs, was represented in the ledgers as a credit. This discrepancy suggested to Morel that labor costs must be nil. Morel wondered whether the natives were being paid in goods instead of currency, but the ledgers indicated that most of the imports into the Congo Free State consisted of weapons such as ball cartridges, rifles, cap guns, and manacles. Morel reasoned that "the statistics afforded, therefore, conclusive proof in themselves that the natives of the Congo were being systematically robbed . . . By what processes, then, were the natives of the Congo being induced to labour since commerce apparently played no part in the affair?" Morel recalled the reports of atrocities submitted by missionaries and concluded that the Congo Free State was operating by virtue of "the reduction of millions of men to a condition of absolute slavery, by a system of legalized robbery enforced by violence."[2]

By analyzing data, Morel uncovered one of the greatest human rights catastrophes in history. He investigated the data further and calculated that during the years 1895–1900 there was a discrepancy of 23.5 million

Belgian francs in the stated value of exports of rubber and ivory from the Congo and the value stated on arrival in Antwerp.[3] Someone was skimming tens of millions of francs in profit from this system of "absolute slavery," and it could only be one person—King Leopold II.

Morel published a book, *Affairs of West Africa,* in 1902, which included a blistering indictment of the Congo Free State. He assigned responsibility for the exploitative system to Leopold, who had "invented a form of slavery more degrading and more atrocious than any slavery which has existed previously."[4] Morel's book led the UK House of Commons to debate the issue on May 20, 1903. Roger Casement, British consul to the Congo Free State, was ordered to conduct a formal inquiry. Casement published *The Casement Report* in early 1904 based on his investigations in the Congo rain forest and the testimonies of the natives he met, all of which confirmed everything the missionaries had been saying and that Morel had deduced from import-export data.

Morel and Casement met in England and formed the Congo Reform Association (CRA) in March 1904 to bring down Leopold's colonial regime. The CRA became the first international human rights organization of the twentieth century, driven by the power of data (Morel) and survivor testimonies (Casement). Joseph Conrad, Arthur Conan Doyle, Mark Twain, and Booker T. Washington were among the many supporters of the CRA. By 1908, Leopold was forced to sell the Congo Free State to the Belgian government, bringing an end to one of the most brazen systems of slavery in the history of Africa. Or so it seemed.

Leopold showed the world that the Congo was teeming with riches. The minerals in Katanga had only recently been prospected when the Belgian government took over. The scramble was on.

More than a century after Morel and Casement's extraordinary campaign to end slavery in the Congo, a new system of "legalized robbery enforced by violence" thrives in the mining provinces. The artisanal mining sites near Kambove are cases in point. UMHK set up the first mines in Kambove to exploit the copper in the 1910s, and Gécamines built the city in

1968 to establish a full-time workforce for mining exploitation. The financial collapse of Gécamines in the 1990s created substantial hardship in Kambove. The entire town was supported by the company, and overnight, thousands of people were forced to fend for themselves without jobs or an alternate source of income. The collapse of Gécamines also unleashed waves of shady deals and graft that have plagued the Congolese mining sector for decades. Almost every industrial copper-cobalt mine I visited was resuscitated through crooked dealings that siphoned value away from the local population into the hands of kleptocrats and foreign stakeholders. Leopold's model remained intact.

Here is an example. In January 2001, Laurent Kabila sold rights to all the old Gécamines mining sites around Kambove to a mining company called Kababankola Mining Company (KMC). KMC was owned 20 percent by Gécamines and 80 percent by a company called Tremalt Limited. Tremalt was controlled by a power broker from Zimbabwe, John Bredenkamp, who had helped ensure the deployment of Zimbabwean military forces to support Laurent Kabila against a Rwandan-Ugandan invasion of the DRC in 1998. These were incidentally the same forces that had helped Kabila take control of the Congo from Mobutu just one year earlier. Without Bredenkamp's support, Kabila would have been toppled by his former allies within weeks. Kabila owed Bredenkamp, and KMC was one of the ways he repaid the debt. Tremalt paid the paltry sum of $400,000 for the rights to the six mining concessions around Kambove. The deal raised red flags, and the United Nations ordered an inquiry. In October 2002, the UN published a report in which it determined that the concessions sold to KMC for $400,000 had a fair market value of over $1 billion, an even more egregious delta between purchase price and market value than what Morel uncovered with the Congo Free State a century earlier.

In the aftermath of the UN's investigation, Bredenkamp pulled out of the scheme and sold Tremalt for $60 million to an Israeli American businessman named Dan Gertler, who already owned diamond and copper mines in the DRC. Gertler was a childhood acquaintance of Laurent Kabila's son Joseph, who helped him purchase his first diamond concession in the Congo in 1997. Gertler also paid Laurent Kabila $20 million for a monopoly on all diamond trading in the DRC beginning in September 2000. Like Bredenkamp, Gertler's ventures drew international scrutiny. The IMF and the World Bank conducted investigations into the security of some of the collateral (diamonds) against which their loans to the DRC had been provided, similar to their concerns over the SICOMINES deal in 2009. These investigations uncovered that Gertler's name appeared more than two hundred times in the Panama Papers and that many of his deals for mining assets in the DRC were executed through the notorious Mossack Fonseca shell companies. In December 2017, the United States Department of the Treasury sanctioned Gertler for human rights abuses and corruption. But the dodgy dealings with the Kambove mines don't end there.

Since 2016, a new company controls the mines in Kambove—China-based Huayou Cobalt. Huayou purchased the mines through a 72–28 joint venture with Gécamines called MIKAS. The prevailing sentiment is that Joseph Kabila arranged the Huayou deal in Kambove and that he accepted financial payments to do so. The largest-ever leak of financial information from Africa confirmed these suspicions. The leak occurred in the summer of 2021 and revealed that a shell company called the Congo Construction Company (CCC), whose accounts were held at the Kinshasa branch of BGFIBank, acted as a financial intermediary between Chinese mining companies and Kabila's family. One of Kabila's sisters owned a 40 percent stake in the bank branch, for which she never paid a dollar, and the branch was operated by one of Kabila's brothers. An investigation conducted by Bloomberg revealed that "in total, about $65 million flowed through CCC's accounts between January 2013 and July 2018, of which $41 million was withdrawn in cash, making it impossible to track the beneficiaries of all the funds. Still, bank records show that at least $30 million was routed, via transfers or in cash, to people and entities directly linked to the Kabilas or companies owned by the presidential family."[5] It appears that the Kabila family used CCC to accept payments from Chinese mining companies to close mining deals across the Copper Belt. The Kabilas also used the bank to channel at least $138 million in public funds to themselves.[6] It may never be known just how much money Joseph Kabila extracted from Chinese mining contracts and construction deals. His apparent ransacking of mining assets and public funds would put even Leopold to shame.

The MIKAS-operated mines of Kambove are located a few kilometers north of the town. According to locals, the mines are exploited in a mixed industrial-artisanal system, and there is no tracking or clarity as to what proportion of the production derives from machines versus hands. At the time of my visit, the MIKAS mines were heavily secured by a mix of Republican Guard and private security. When I attempted to access the concessions, I was stopped by soldiers at a roadblock not far into the hills. I settled instead for interviews in Kambove with artisanal miners who said they worked at the mines.

I met four men and four teenage boys who said they worked as artisanal miners in three of the MIKAS mines north of Kambove. They reported that they left their homes early in the morning to walk to a gathering point where they were picked up by MIKAS cargo trucks and transported to the mines. They said that some people who lived in the hills closer to the mines walked to the sites. Based on the testimonies of the workers I interviewed, there were somewhere between two and three thousand artisanal miners who worked at the MIKAS mines. Mpoyo, a twenty-two-year-old resident of Kambove who worked at one of the MIKAS mines, described the system: "It is mostly artisanal mining at Kamoya South. Sometimes MIKAS uses the excavators, but as I said, it is mostly artisanal mining. Most people dig in the main pit, and some people dig around the pit. We do not have to dig deep, because already the pit is so deep."

According to Mpoyo and the other interviewees, there was no system of washing and sorting stones at the MIKAS mines. The artisanal miners excavated the ore, hammered it down to size, and loaded it into raffia sacks. I asked what happened to the sacks after they were loaded, and the workers told me that agents from the MIKAS mines purchased the sacks from them, just like the system Makaza described at Étoile. In fact, the MIKAS artisanal miners were paid the same amount per forty-kilogram sack, roughly $1.10. The artisanal miners loaded the sacks onto MIKAS cargo trucks, and the trucks transported the ore to the MIKAS concentrator in Kambove for processing. From the concentrator, the semi-processed copper and cobalt were likely exported to the parent company, Huayou Cobalt.

Mpoyo and the other artisanal miners said that they worked in groups at the mines and that they earned an average of about $2.20 per day based on their typical production of two sacks each. They stated that almost all the production at the four sites was artisanal. They also asserted that SAEMAPE officials were present at the MIKAS mines and that they tallied the weight of each day's production, which determined MIKAS's royalty payment to the Congolese government. If true, it would mean that the government agency tasked with monitoring artisanal miners and protecting their interests was part of the system of illegally utilizing artisanal miners on industrial sites. I would encounter similar reports at other industrial sites farther along the road to Kolwezi.

The artisanal miners working at the MIKAS mines stated that working conditions were harsh. They clocked ten- to twelve-hour days hacking and hammering for cobalt with no personal protective equipment or other safety gear. They did say, however, that there was a medical clinic at each site that was available to patch up minor injuries. They reported chronic back and neck pains and injuries such as lacerations and sprains. They also said there had been one major pit wall collapse at one of the MIKAS mines, Kamoya Central, in May 2018. Several artisanal miners suffered serious injuries in the collapse, such as broken legs, and a few were killed, although no one could say exactly how many.

Assuming there were somewhere between two and three thousand artisanal miners working in the MIKAS mining sites above Kambove, and that each miner produced two forty-kilogram sacks of ore per day, their aggregate production would be somewhere between 160 and 240 tons of copper-cobalt ore per day. It was a massive sum of artisanal production taking place on an industrial site, and it was not the only one. Most of the major mining concessions located between Likasi and Kolwezi would prove to have artisanal miners working on them. In some cases, artisanal miners were responsible for all the production taking place.

Although I was unable to gain access to the MIKAS copper-cobalt mines north of Kambove, I was able to enter another large artisanal mining site in the Kambove area called Tocotens. It was an abandoned Gécamines copper-cobalt mine located a few kilometers southeast of the town. Artisanal miners from Kambove walked into the mine to dig each day. I did not see any security or armed militia at the time of my visit. Inside the site, there were several hundred teenage boys and young men digging in and around a large pit to extract ore. Younger boys and girls washed stones in rinsing pools that appeared every bit as putrid as the ones in Kipushi. The mine was topped by a repellent blanket of haze formed by a combination of the dirt kicked up by all the hacking at the site with the grit spewed out by cargo trucks grinding their way through Likasi's poorly maintained roads. The artisanal miners at Tocotens sold their production to informal depots located next to the site.

"We sell the cobalt to the *comptoirs*," an earnest artisanal miner named Patoke explained, pointing to several rudimentary depots advertised by pink and white tarps situated next to Tocotens.

Just like Depots Hao, Jin, and Diop in Likasi, the Tocotens depots were all operated by Chinese agents. None of them were willing to exchange more than a few words with me.

Although Tocotens was a former Gécamines mine, the diggers I met working at the site were too young to remember the impact that the collapse of Gécamines had on Kambove. Patoke's father, Mbese, remembered those days well:

I worked at Tocotens for Gécamines. The company gave us a good wage. They provided a home to each family. They provided school for our children. When we had another child, they gave us one more sack of flour each month.

After Gécamines left, we had no wage. We tried to dig in the mines. I had to go to Lubumbashi to sell the ore, but I could only earn ten percent of what I earned before.

Like Solange, Mbese seemed nostalgic for the days prior to the crash of Gécamines. Were things really that much better? During Mbese's time, Gécamines provided jobs with fixed wages to tens of thousands of citizens in the mining provinces. The company built schools and hospitals, provided insurance schemes, and cultivated pride in its employees. It also trained hundreds of mining engineers who had prestigious jobs with competitive salaries. Some even went on to work for major mining companies abroad. Unfortunately, the entire system was erected on a shaky foundation. The company fell into ruin in large part due to the apparent theft of funds by executive management, mining officials, and elite government figures, chief among them Joseph Mobutu. In the waning days of his reign, Mobutu is said to have pilfered massive sums of money from the company's coffers. Financial collapse was inevitable, and the consequences on the people in the mining provinces linger to this day, passed on from father to son, like Mbese and Patoke and thousands of others.

Beyond Tocotens, there were a few other artisanal mining areas that I visited near Kambove. Most of them were informal digging sites located in the forests south of the main highway. The largest of these sites had a name—Shamitumba. It was located about ten kilometers south of Kambove, down the same dirt road that led to Shinkolobwe. A year after my visit, the site was shut down by the Tshisekedi government when high levels of uranium were discovered in the dirt. Most of the informal artisanal sites in the forests south of Kambove were formed when local villagers started digging somewhere and found heterogenite. Some of the sites had single digging zones roughly fifty meters across; others had several digging areas that were up to a few hundred meters in size.

Like Kipushi, the diggers in these remoter artisanal areas tended to work in family groups, with men and older boys excavating trenches five to six meters deep. I did not see any tunnels at any of these sites. The dirt was more copper-hued than in Kipushi, with varying shades of rust, light brown, and gray. As the digging areas expanded into the surrounding forest, trees were chopped down and brush was cleared. The wood was burned to make charcoal that the artisanal miners used for heating and cooking in their villages. Most of the diggers lived in villages in the nearby forest, although some walked or cycled from Kambove each day. There were easily several thousand people digging and washing heterogenite at these sites, including hundreds of children. Similar to the village Arthur showed me, none of these sites were in any way being monitored or audited by stakeholders up the chain. A barrel-chested artisanal miner from Kambove named Kabenga described how he worked in a group that included his brother, cousin, two sons, wife, and daughter.

"We come here because the ore is good and we do not have to dig too deep," Kabenga said. He added that the ground was softer in the forest than in other artisanal mines around Kambove. He also preferred the fact that there were no soldiers or militia at the sites. Kabenga said that by the end of the day, he could load three sacks of washed heterogenite onto his bicycle. It would take him and his sons more than an hour to push the load back to town.

I saw *négociants* on motorbikes at a few of the artisanal sites in the forest. They transported the heterogenite to depots in Kambove for those artisanal miners who did not have bicycles or the enormous strength and stamina required to wheel three or four forty-kilogram sacks of stones uphill on a dirt road for several kilometers. Although I could not confirm, it seemed most likely that the *négociants* sold their hauls to depots in Kambove. It is possible that they took the sacks to Likasi, but that was an additional distance of twenty-five kilometers, which meant greater fuel costs. There were no other depots in the area outside of these towns. As to the question of where the cobalt went from the depots, I can only say that of the thirty-plus depots I saw in or around Likasi and Kambove, almost all of them were operated by Chinese buyers.

Although the hills just north of Kambove near the MIKAS mines proved impossible to access due to the presence of security forces, I wondered whether there might be artisanal mining areas deeper in the hills to the north or northwest and, if so, whether they might be accessible. I asked a few colleagues, and Arthur reported that there were at least a few artisanal mining spots deeper in the hills beyond Kambove that were exploited by local villagers. He said that he had only been to one of these areas about two months earlier, and at the time, there were not any militias or other security forces operating in the vicinity. The coast seemed clear, so we planned a visit.

We drove a few kilometers west of Kambove, then turned north into the hills up a narrow path of dirt and rubble. It was a slow, bumpy grind. The engine began to smell of burning oil as we plowed in low gear up the unforgiving terrain. We continued for almost an hour, parked near a clearing, and continued by foot about fifteen minutes deeper into the mountains. The hill face was jagged and rocky, with scant foliage other than dry brush and shrubs. I saw only one large tree, standing atop an adjacent hill, its pale plumage shaped like a feeble dome around a narrow trunk. We arrived at the artisanal mining area, and I saw at least two hundred children and several hundred adults digging in a shallow-water trench that snaked eastward through the hills. Two girls clambered out of the trench not far from where I was standing, fifteen-year-old Nikki and fourteen-year-old Chance. Nikki wore a peach shirt and chocolate-brown skirt, and her hair was tied back in a ponytail. Chance wore a pink frock cut at the knees with white polka dots. Nikki's daughter appeared to be around one year old, and Chance's son seemed no more than a few months. The girls were caked in mud from the knees down, and their babies seemed feeble and sickly.

Nikki and Chance were the youngest mothers with whom I spoke during all my time in the Congo. I never ascertained where their parents were or whether they were even alive. During our brief exchange, I learned that the girls lived in a village about a thirty-minute hike away from the artisanal mining area. They woke around dawn each day to trek through the hills to scavenge for cobalt.

"We dig together. We wash our stones in this water. At the end of the day, we can fill one sack," Nikki said.

I asked Nikki and Chance what they did with the sack once it was full, given how remote their location was.

"Some men sell it for us," Nikki replied.

"What men?" I asked.

Nikki's daughter began to cry loudly. Nikki did her best to console the infant by instinctively rocking and patting her, but the baby only cried more. Nikki seemed to be getting frustrated, so I turned to Chance and tried to ask a few more questions of her, but she said she had to return to digging. She gently placed her sleeping son into a cardboard box next to the trench and climbed down in labored movements into the muck. Nikki was having no success at consoling her daughter. She tried to feed her, but the infant did not respond. Her cries turned to shrieks. Was she colicky? Had she soiled herself? How did one care for a baby in circumstances such as these, especially when the mother herself was a child? Arthur motioned that we should continue down the trench. As we moved on, I peeked inside the cardboard box at Chance's son. His diminutive chest pumped up and down rapidly as he slept under the scalding sun, inhaling unknown hazards into his tiny lungs.

We walked deeper into the hills along the trench in which the artisanal miners were working. We watched as people shoveled and washed stones in groups of four or five. Not many of the artisanal miners were interested in being observed, fewer in speaking. We arrived at length at a group of boys, ages twelve to seventeen. The eldest, Peter, wore blue jeans, plastic slippers, and a red shirt with the letters *AIG* stitched on the front. Imagine that on a remote hill deep in the Congo's mining provinces, a child can be found digging for cobalt, wearing a muddy shirt with the logo of the behemoth American financial services company that had to be bailed out for $180 billion during the 2008 financial crisis. Imagine what even 1 percent of that money could do in a place like this, if it were spent on the people who needed it, not stolen by those who exploited them.

Peter was surprisingly energetic and open to talking with us. He explained that the boys in his group were brothers and cousins originally from a village near the town of Manono, which was a few hundred kilometers to the north in the heart of coltan territory. Lithium deposits had also recently been discovered in Manono, which several foreign mining companies were moving to exploit given the increasing demand for the metal in the manufacture of lithium-ion rechargeable batteries. Manono had a grim reputation as being the northern corner of Le Triangle de la Mort. The other two towns that form the "Triangle of Death" are Mitwaba and Pweto, so called because the Mai-Mai militias operating in the region were known to utilize particularly harsh methods to force the local population to dig for coltan and gold. Reports from the area describe torture, murder, and chopping off hands and feet—techniques passed down the generations from Leopold's terror squads.

"Two years ago, the Mai-Mai took us from our home and brought us to a cobalt mine near Milele," Peter explained.

Milele was the same place that Kiyonge, the child with the sty in his eyelid, had mentioned as being home to thousands of children who dug for cobalt.

"The Mai-Mai sold us to a Lebanese man named Ahmad. He made us dig, and he took all the money. He said we had to repay him for bringing us to Milele. We ran from that place and came to Kambove," Peter said.

Hearing about child trafficking in Milele a second time from children around Likasi and Kambove seemed more than coincidence. I was eager to learn as much as I could this time about the operation and prepared a list of questions in my mind: How many Mai-Mai militias were involved in the child trafficking system? How many people like Ahmad bought children from the militias? How many children had been taken from Peter's village near the town of Manono? How many children in total were digging for cobalt in Milele when Peter lived there?

Before I could ask the first question, a ruckus boomed across the hills, followed by shouting and gunshots. Peter jumped into the trench. I spun around and saw seven men armed with Kalashnikovs and handguns sprinting toward us. The men shot at the sky and quickly encircled Arthur and me. They trained their weapons at us and shouted like berserkers, red-eyed and stinking of liquor. They asked if we had taken any pictures and demanded to see our phones. They ripped my backpack off my shoulders, shoved me around, and started rummaging through my belongings. One of them found my notebook and started leafing through it. Fortunately, he could not read English.

The situation was getting out of hand. I looked anxiously toward Arthur. The blood drained from his face, but in a calm and steady voice, he asked me to show the men my *engagement de prise en charge* with Mr. Lukalaba's stamp and signature. By this time, the contents of my backpack were scattered in the dirt, so I searched for the folder in which I kept the document and found it under one of the commandos' boots. I retrieved the papers and presented them to the man wearing a black beret, assuming he was the head of the militia. Arthur pointed to Mr. Lukalaba's signature and explained that we were under the protection of the governor's office. The man in the beret barked back, but Arthur persisted calmly. The signature seemed to settle their aggressiveness, and they ordered us to leave immediately, but not before demanding again to inspect my phone for photos. I steered them to an album that had no recent images, which seemed to satisfy them. The militia hounded us out of the mining area, firing a few more shots in the air as we left.

As we exited the artisanal mining area, I caught a glimpse of Nikki one last time. Her daughter had finally calmed down and was sleeping on her back as she dug in the trench. Nikki stared at me blankly, coldly . . . then with the slightest tremble in her eyes, her expression changed to that of a terrified child. Our eyes locked in recognition. I think we both understood that she was doomed.

WILDERNESS

The experience in the hills northwest of Kambove left me shaken, but there was still one more place to explore in the Likasi-Kambove area—the remotest wilderness close to the Zambian border. I was told there were a few large mines for copper, cobalt, and gold starting around thirty kilometers south of the highway, as well as numerous artisanal mining sites scattered in the mountains. Few researchers, if any, had ever ventured into this area. Not even the locals knew where most of the artisanal mines were located. The region was secured by the army, and access required formal authorization. I was told that my best chance to obtain permission was to approach the SAEMAPE office in Likasi.

I visited the SAEMAPE field office in Likasi and met two affable young men, Jean and Pathé. They were still wearing their official gray-and-orange SAESSCAM uniforms more than sixteen months after SAESSCAM had been renamed SAEMAPE, because none of the staff in the mining provinces had yet been provided new uniforms. These types of bureaucratic delays were endemic to the DRC. To this day, the official national identification cards used by every citizen in the DRC to prove their citizenship have not been updated since 1997, when the country was called Zaire. As a result, most people use their voter registration cards as a substitute form of identification. Why are the Congolese people still using their Zaire national ID cards from 1997? Because new national ID cards require that the government conduct a new national census, and the last one was conducted in 1984.

I explained to Jean and Pathé that I had come to the Congo to understand the nature of artisanal mining as part of a research project and that I was curious to explore some of the remoter mining sites in the mountain wilderness. They were surprisingly supportive of my request, perhaps out of a sense of boredom, because it seemed that they did little other than sit in their offices all day. They told me they would need to make some phone calls, so I left them to it. I was later informed that they had received permission to take me to one industrial gold mine deep in the mountains, called Kimpese, and also to one artisanal mining site located on the way to Kimpese. Permission, however, had only been granted for the three of us. The trip to Kimpese was the only one I took to a mining area without a guide I trusted. It did not go as planned.

Jean and Pathé picked me up the following morning in a midsize SUV. Jean was lean with deep-set eyes and had the habit of biting off the end of each word as he spoke. Pathé was shorter, more deliberative, with a strong chin and narrow cheeks. They were both Lubumbashi natives and graduates of the University of Lubumbashi. They explained that Kimpese was located just over thirty kilometers south of the highway. The plan was to go first to Kimpese and then tour the artisanal mine on the return journey.

"There is a small village on the road about halfway to Kimpese. From that village, we can walk approximately one kilometer to reach the artisanal zone," Jean explained.

A few kilometers west of Kambove we peeled onto a dirt road heading south. To call it a "dirt road" would be akin to calling the Congo a democratic republic. It was even harder to navigate than the path Arthur and I took to get to the artisanal mining area where we were run off by commandos. It was more like a track of jagged rocks, deep holes, and mounds of dirt unfit for vehicular passage. Our pace slowed to a grind as we plowed through the terrain. A few patches of flat earth offered momentary reprieve to our battered spines.

"It is not possible to take heavy machinery to Kimpese," Jean explained. "You will see only small equipment for excavation."

I asked how many people worked at the site. Jean said there were three thousand people at Kimpese and that they dug "through artisanal techniques."

I took the risk of asking whether there were any children working at Kimpese. Without hesitation, Pathé replied, "Yes, there are children."

"How many?"

They did not know.

I was surprised that a SAEMAPE official admitted to the existence of child labor at a formal mining site, especially since most government employees that I met took great pains to deny or diminish the existence of child labor in artisanal mining. One senior parliamentarian in Kinshasa once told me that the international community was mistaken about the issue of child labor at artisanal mines in the Congo. According to him, they were actually Pygmies.

As we drove deeper into the mountains, the sense of remoteness and isolation intensified. There was absolutely nothing to be seen except rock, dirt, and trees. I asked where such a large population of people working at Kimpese might live.

"There are villages in the mountains," Pathé responded. "Some people also live at the mine itself."

"Who pays them for the work they do?"

"The army pays them."

I asked what the army did with the production from the mine. On cue, a cargo truck with Chinese markings packed with sacks of ore barreled down the dirt road in the opposite direction. We had to swerve into the brush to avoid a collision. As the truck rolled by, Pathé pointed to it and said, "The Chinese companies have arrangements to buy most of the ore from the army."

After more than an hour of bumps and jolts, the SUV started to make a loud grinding sound. We stopped, and Jean climbed under the vehicle to inspect the problem. He discovered a large stone jammed into the axle. We tried for about thirty minutes to dislodge it, but it would not budge. I asked how much farther it was to Kimpese, and Pathé estimated fifteen or sixteen kilometers—too far to hike. The village near the artisanal mining area that we had been authorized to visit was another kilometer or two down the road, so we decided to head there. Pathé pulled out a satellite phone and made a call asking for another vehicle to meet us in a few hours.

As we walked down the dirt road through the mountains, all was silent save for the wisps of white-hot air blowing through the trees. The breeze was completely absent of moisture. No sooner did I blink than did the film on my eyes evaporate like mist on hot coals. We arrived at last in a small village that consisted of thirty open-air wooden huts with thatched roofs along the western side of the road. Immediately behind the huts, the terrain dropped sharply into a valley. On the other side of the road, thick forest sloped up a steep hill face. The village had no electricity, and the only source of water was a well at the far end of the settlement, tucked between two jacaranda trees. A lone child, maybe three years old, wearing a pale brown frock, shuffled languidly across the dirt staring at her feet. Behind her, two soldiers sat on plastic chairs. They wore the distinctive uniform of the Republican Guard—military fatigues, black boots, and red berets. There were several piles of stuffed raffia sacks next to them. They manned a makeshift *péage* crossing that consisted of a long wooden pole propped across the road by two vertical branches at either end. At ten dollars, it was the most expensive toll crossing I encountered in the mining provinces.

There were only a handful of women and children in the village when we arrived. Most of the inhabitants were out digging at the artisanal mining area. At closer inspection, the huts appeared to be more like dorms that housed two or three families each, which suggested that a few hundred people lived in this isolated settlement. I asked Jean and Pathé if it would be possible to speak with some of the villagers before we hiked to the artisanal mining site. They seemed reluctant but settled on a single interview. After speaking with a few of the women in the village, they selected a young mother named Marline. We met inside her hut and sat on the dirt. The belongings of the families that shared Marline's hut consisted of three plastic containers of water, one large plastic bowl, a stack of manioc, metal pots for cooking, knives and cutlery, and clothes piled in two corners. There was a small, faded poster of Jesus on one of the walls, along with numerous spiderwebs in the corners of the hut. A short, brown lizard clung to one of the walls and stared at the motley collection of visitors.

Marline was twenty years old and held a baby in her lap. She wore a faded red skirt and a green blouse. Her hair was cut short, and she spoke in a soft, mossy voice. Although she was sitting only two feet in front of me, I knew there were several impenetrable barriers between us. First, she had been selected by Jean and Pathé. Although they had admittedly been forthcoming about the fact that there were children at Kimpese, they might still have selected someone they knew would say what they preferred to be said. Jean and Pathé were also present in the hut and would translate from Swahili as they saw fit. Marline would also bear in mind the presence of the Republican Guard when determining what she should and should not say. Finally, I was well aware that I had to spend the remainder of the day with Jean and Pathé and that we were down to just one site visit since Kimpese was out of the question, so I too had to be judicious about the questions I asked lest they determine it would be better to return to Likasi and alert others that I was not to be trusted.

I began by asking Marline where she was from. She said that the people living in the settlement were all from a village not far from Kambove. She explained that the villagers "came with the army" to the settlement to work in nearby mining areas. She normally went to the mining site each day, but her daughter had been sick recently, so she was staying in the village to tend to her. I asked how the artisanal system worked at the village. Marline said that the villagers usually worked all day at the mine and carried back sacks of cobalt before it was dark. Each Saturday, a truck came to the village to load the sacks. They were given a weekly wage by the buyers of 15,000 Congolese francs (about $8.30) for men and 10,000 (about $5.50) for women. Items they paid for the previous week from town, such as flour, cooking oil, vegetables, and beer, were also brought at that time by the buyers. I asked who the buyers were. Marline said it was usually the army.

A crowd of women and children from the village, as well as the two Republican Guard soldiers, had started to congregate around Marline's hut while we were speaking. Jean and Pathé did not seem keen to continue talking with an audience, so they suggested that we should start hiking to the mining site. As I stood up, I looked over at Marline and her baby and wished I could find a safe place to ask her the questions I really wanted to ask: Did the villagers have a choice when they came here with the army? How many other settlements like this were there in the mountains? Did the soldiers use violence to make them dig? Were they free to return to their home villages if they wished to? What happened if they were injured at the site? With each passing day in the Congo, my list of unanswered questions only seemed to grow.

We embarked on our march up the incline through the trees toward the artisanal site. The forest was dry and sharp, but our passage was eased by a narrow path that the villagers had trodden going to and from the mining area. We had proceeded no more than ten minutes when we heard the first gunshot. Two more shots followed in quick succession. Brisk footsteps came crunching through the brush. The Republican Guard soldiers from the village were racing toward us. They spoke in firm and escalating tones to Jean and Pathé, then continued swiftly up the hill.

"There has been an accident," Jean said.

"What happened?"

"A boy fell. His head hit a stone."

"Is he okay?"

"He is dead."

The army was closing off the area. We were ordered to leave.

Jean and Pathé took me straight to the hobbled SUV without stopping in the village on our way back. When their colleagues arrived with the second vehicle, I returned with Jean to Likasi while the others worked to repair the SUV. I inquired the next day if it might be possible to try again to see Kimpese or perhaps some other artisanal site in the mountains, but permission was not forthcoming. I never managed to return to the remote wilderness near the Zambian border, nor in any depth to the hills around Likasi and Kambove, but I saw enough to conclude that there was a secret world of artisanal mining hidden in these hills that operated in an even more oppressive manner than the more visible sites like Kipushi and Tocotens. Thousands of tons of cobalt were being fed from this shadow economy into the formal supply chain by a ragged population in conditions that at times were next of kin to slavery.

That evening, I recounted the day's events to Arthur. He had been anxious about the trip and was relieved when I returned safely. The entire region of wilderness stretching to the border with Zambia was a black hole even to locals. Arthur was not sure how many mining sites were hidden in the area. "It could be fifty, one hundred, two hundred. Some sites are exploited for a few months until the ore is exhausted. Bigger sites like Kimpese have been there for years."

I asked Arthur if he thought the army had forcibly relocated the villagers to the settlement to dig for cobalt.

"No one wants to live out there! But there is cobalt and gold, so the army takes the poorest people and makes them dig."

I asked Arthur whether he heard anything in town about the accident, but there had been no reports. He surmised that the child would probably be buried in the hills, like so many others who dug and died without a trace.

Arthur took a long sip of his beer and stared morosely. "What did that child die for?" he asked. "For one sack of cobalt? Is that what Congolese children are worth?"

4

Colony to the World

The great historical tragedy of Africa has been not so much that it was too late in making contact with the rest of the world, as the manner in which that contact was brought about; that Europe began to "propagate" at a time when it had fallen into the hands of the most unscrupulous financiers and captains of industry; that it was our misfortune to encounter that particular Europe on our path, and that Europe is responsible before the human community for the highest heap of corpses in history.

—Aimé Césaire, *Discourse on Colonialism*

OF ALL THE HAZARDS one encounters in the Congo, perhaps the most dangerous one is history. It is a force as unrelenting as the great river that bends the land to its will, and like the river, it clouds everything in its path. My friend Philippe told me on my first trip to the Congo that I could not truly understand what was happening in the mining provinces without first understanding the nation's history. But where does one begin? There is no single starting point, least of all in a land with such an epic and tragic past as the Congo, but if we were to try to identify a place and time that we might call the beginning of this journey, we might settle on the mouth of the Congo River in the year 1482. Everything that is happening in Katanga in the twenty-first century is the result of an unrelenting sequence of events that began at that place and time. The trajectory, however, was not irreversible. There was a fleeting moment of hope at the dawn of independence in 1960 when the fate of the Congo could have been so different . . . but hope was destroyed before it ever had a chance. History made sure of it. More than any king, slave trader, warlord, or kleptocrat, history reigns supreme in the Congo, darkening the land like a gathering storm, the moment before the first bolt rips the sky.[1]

INVASION AND THE SLAVE TRADE: 1482–1884

The saga began on the Iberian Peninsula in the early fifteenth century with the age of discovery, which from the perspective of those who were "discovered" would be more accurately called the age of invasion. Prince Henry the Navigator of Portugal dispatched ships in search of African gold. The inhospitable waters along West Africa proved impenetrable to European ships until the Portuguese developed the caravel in the 1440s— an agile vessel with lateen-rigged sails that allowed it to tack into the wind. The caravel carried Europeans beyond the Canary Islands for the first time: in 1445, they passed the mouth of the Senegal River; in 1462, they reached Sierra Leone; and in 1473, they sailed beyond the Gulf of Guinea and discovered that the shore of Africa turned southward again. Following this discovery, an explorer named Diego Cão sailed farther south than any European yet and set anchor in Loango Bay near the mouth of the Congo River in 1482. The age of invasion completed its tragic reconnaissance of the global south when Christopher Columbus reached the Americas in 1492, and Vasco da Gama sailed around Africa to India in 1498.

When Diego Cão arrived at the mouth of the Congo River, he became the first European to meet the people of the Kongo Kingdom. At one point, he asked the name of the mighty river that turned the ocean brown with sediment more than a hundred kilometers from the coast. The Kongo people replied with *nzere* ("the river that swallows all others,"), but Cão's cartographer misheard and recorded the river's name as "Zaire." Cão returned to Portugal to report his findings. Within a few years, the Portuguese had built a slave-trading mission at Loango Bay. From the early 1500s until the end of the slave trade in 1866, one-fourth of the 12.5 million slaves stolen from Africa and shipped across the Atlantic would depart from Loango Bay.

Throughout the entire period of the Atlantic slave trade, Europeans remained largely restricted to the coasts of Africa and had virtually no knowledge of the interior. The one person most responsible for opening pathways into the interior of Africa was David Livingstone. Born in Scotland in 1813, Livingstone traveled to Cape Town in 1841 to preach Christianity to the natives. Hungry for adventure, he endeavored to cross the Kalahari Desert in 1849. In 1851, he became the first European to see the Zambezi River, at which point a new dream was born—was there a navigable river from the coast of Africa into the heart of the continent? The existence of such a river could facilitate Livingstone's dream of bringing "commerce and Christianity" to Africa, which he felt would assist in the final extirpation of slavery.

Livingstone continued his explorations and discovered by 1856 that the Zambezi was not a waterway from coast to interior. During his journeys, Livingstone survived twenty-seven bouts of malaria thanks to his discovery of the ameliorative properties of quinine. For centuries, malaria had prevented European exploration of the African interior. Although quinine was not a cure for malaria, it helped prevent a death sentence. Quinine proved to be the first of two crucial developments that facilitated European colonization of Africa. The second development involved boiling water. Beginning in the 1850s, the steam engine revolutionized transport. Steamboats carried goods quickly and less expensively across rough seas. They could also forge upstream to allow exploration of rivers into the African continent. Although the Zambezi proved not to be navigable from coast to interior, Europeans were hopeful that with the assistance of steam power, the Nile might be.

From 1859 to 1871, Livingstone explored the Great Lakes region along the eastern Congo in search of the source of the Nile. In March 1871, he arrived at the banks of the Lualaba River at a village called Nyangwe, located at the edge of the Congolese rain forest. Arab slave dealers refused him passage beyond Nyangwe, and a dejected Livingstone returned to Ujiji in western Tanzania. By this time, it had been several years since anyone had heard from Livingstone, and there was great interest in determining whether he was still alive. Efforts to discover Livingstone's fate by a Welsh orphan turned American journalist, Henry Morton Stanley, sealed the Congo's fate.

Stanley was born as the illegitimate child of a teenage mother in Wales. He grew up in an orphanage, made his way to America, fought on both sides of the Civil War, and eventually found work as a journalist for *The New York Herald*. When Livingstone disappeared somewhere in East Africa, Stanley saw an opportunity to become famous. He pitched *The Herald* on the nineteenth-century equivalent of a reality-TV search for Livingstone. He would send dispatches from the field and either find Livingstone or evidence of his death. Stanley eventually found Livingstone sick and weary at Ujiji in November 1871. According to his apocryphal account, he uttered the famous words, "Dr. Livingstone, I presume?" Stanley spent four months with Livingstone and came to see him as the father he never had.

Stanley felt inspired to finish Livingstone's work by discovering the source of the Nile. On October 17, 1876, he saw the Lualaba River for the first time, at the opposite end of the Congo River system that Diego Cão discovered almost four centuries earlier. In all that time, no one had managed to trace the Congo from its source to the Atlantic coast. Stanley ventured down river on a steamboat and reached Nyangwe, where Arab slave traders had prevented Livingstone from pressing forward in 1871.[2] Stanley's solution was to pay one of the largest Arab slave dealers in Africa, Tippu Tip, to travel with him. Tip would use the occasion to expand his slave-trading empire into the upper Congo.

Stanley pressed into the upper Congo and passed seven cataracts on February 7, 1877, at a place he named Stanley Falls (Boyoma Falls). It was here that Stanley heard a local tribe call the river *ikuta yacongo*. He realized the Lualaba River was not the source of the Nile. It was the Congo River. Stanley forged through withering conditions, and in March 1877, he arrived at the beginning of a 320-kilometer section of cataracts at a place he named Stanley Pool (Malebo Pool) in the spot that would become modern-day Kinshasa. Stanley and his surviving crew eventually reached the mouth of the Congo River at Boma on August 10, 1877. In so doing, Stanley demonstrated that the Congo River was navigable in three sections from the coast deep into the African interior. Livingstone's dream was achieved, but it became a nightmare for the people of the Congo.

By 1877, most of the African continent had already been staked by Britain, France, Germany, Portugal, Spain, and Italy. The vast midsection of the continent remained the only unclaimed territory. Stanley's journey opened the Congo to the eyes of Europe, and King Leopold II of Belgium made his move. Leopold formed a holding company called the Association Internationale du Congo (AIC) with himself as the sole shareholder. The stated purpose of the AIC was to fulfill Livingstone's dream of bringing Christianity and commerce to the heart of Africa. Leopold offered Stanley a job—return to the Congo and secure treaties from local tribes on behalf of the AIC.

Stanley's escapades negotiating treaties for the AIC involved the first time that batteries played a role in the exploitation of the Congolese people. George Washington Williams, an African American minister traveling in the Congo, uncovered Stanley's ruse as a way of intimidating tribal leaders into signing his treaties. He wrote about it in *An Open Letter to His Serene Majesty Leopold II*:

> A number of electric batteries had been purchased in London, and when attached to the arm under the coat, communicated with a band of ribbon which passed over the palm of the white brother's hand, and when he gave the black brother a cordial grasp of the hand the black brother was greatly surprised to find his white brother so strong, that he nearly knocked him off his feet in giving him the hand of fellowship. When the native inquired about the disparity of strength between himself and his white brother, he was told that the white man could pull up trees and perform the most prodigious feats of strength.

By early 1884, Stanley had secured more than four hundred treaties from native tribes, amassing a massive stretch of land across the Congo. None of the tribal leaders fully understood that they were ceding authority of their lands to the AIC, and they certainly could not read the language in which the agreement was written. Nevertheless, Leopold had what he needed to make the case that the Congo was his at an imperialist extravaganza called the Berlin Conference.

On November 15, 1884, the major colonial powers of Europe convened in Berlin to discuss how they might carve up Africa. Leopold's emissaries presented the territories of the AIC as a free-trade zone and stipulated that the Congo River would remain open for shipping without tariffs. The conference ended with the General Act of Berlin, which set out the terms of the European dissection of Africa. Leopold dissolved the AIC, and on May 29, 1885, he declared himself to be the personal owner and king sovereign of the *Congo-Vrijstaat*—the Congo Free State. His new patch of personal property in Africa was seventy-six times the size of Belgium.

COLONIZATION: 1885–1960

Leopold unleashed a harsh colonial machine designed to extract maximum value from the Congo's resources and maximum labor output from the Congolese people. He enlisted an army of mercenaries, the Force Publique, to compel the local population into servitude. The first target on Leopold's list was ivory, but mass poaching of elephants across Africa soon caused ivory prices to plummet. Leopold's entire experiment was close to failure when a new invention saved him just in time—the rubber tire.

In 1885, a German named Karl Benz designed a vehicle with an internal combustion engine and ironclad wooden wheels suitable for slow speeds. To support higher speeds, Scottish inventor John Boyd Dunlop devised an air-filled rubber tire, or pneumatic tire, in 1888. As the nascent automobile industry grew, demand for rubber grew with it. Just as the DRC is blessed with the world's largest cobalt reserves needed to meet demand for today's electric vehicle revolution, so too was Leopold's Congo blessed with millions of square kilometers of rubber trees needed to meet demand for the first automobile revolution.

Leopold's Force Publique coerced the native population to extract rubber sap from the vines of rubber trees deep in the Congolese rain forest. They whipped natives into submission using the *chicotte,* a flesh-shredding whip fashioned from twisted hippopotamus hide. They kidnapped the wives and children of village men and ordered them to meet a quota of three to four kilos of rubber sap per fortnight. If they returned from the forest without meeting their quotas, the hands, noses, or ears of their loved ones were chopped off. Rubber exports from the Congo Free State increased ninety-six-fold from 1890 to 1904, making it the most profitable colony in Africa.

Joseph Conrad witnessed the atrocities of Leopold's regime when he journeyed on the Congo River, beginning on June 13, 1890. He kept a diary in two black penny notebooks filled with impressions that would one day yield his excoriating meditation on the colonial desecration of Africa, *Heart of Darkness.* "The Belgians are worse than the seven plagues of Egypt," Conrad wrote in a letter to Roger Casement, whom he befriended in Matadi before venturing upriver. The truth of the Congo Free State remained shrouded from the world until E. D. Morel's data dive in 1900, which motivated the British to order Roger Casement to conduct the first human rights investigation of the twentieth century.

Casement departed upriver on June 5, 1903. He spent one hundred days investigating conditions and documenting survivor testimonies of murder, slavery, and mutilation by Leopold's Force Publique. Casement issued *The Casement Report* on January 8, 1904, and he joined forces with Morel to create the Congo Reform Association to bring an end to Leopold's regime.[3] Leopold was forced to sell the Congo Free State to the Belgian government on November 15, 1908, netting him a tidy sum of several hundred million dollars on top of what he had already profited. The Belgians took control of the "Belgian Congo" and regretfully continued the system of forced labor for rubber extraction that Leopold began. Rubber prices began to collapse on the world market, and the Belgians were wringing their fingers over how to keep the colony profitable. In the nick of time, they discovered Katanga's mineral deposits.

Beginning in 1911, Union Minière du Haut-Katanga (UMHK) used forced labor to compel the local population to mine copper and other minerals from Katanga. Copper production grew from 100,000 tons in 1940 to 280,000 tons in 1960, equal to 10 percent of global production. Farther north, the Belgians sold a seventy-five-thousand-square-kilometer concession of rain forest filled with palm oil trees to the Lever brothers, whose new soap recipe required palm oil. Following Leopold's model, the Lever brothers used forced labor in the extraction of palm oil under a quota system. The riches they generated helped build the multinational powerhouse Unilever.

The bloodbath of World War II showed Africans that their European owners were not as enlightened as they portrayed themselves to be, leading to a wave of anti-colonial sentiment across the continent. Protests for independence escalated in the Belgian Congo during the late 1950s, led by a meteoric nationalist leader, Patrice Lumumba.

HOPE BORN AND DESTROYED: 1958–JANUARY 1961

After suffering centuries of slavery and colonization, the Congo had a narrow opportunity at independence to be reborn as a land of freedom and self-determination. Four figures rose to the forefront of the Congolese fight for independence. The first was Patrice Lumumba, a charismatic leader of humble origins. He was joined by a close friend and ally, Joseph Mobutu. The third figure, Joseph Kasa-Vubu, was a popular Congolese freedom fighter, and the fourth, Moise Tshombe, was the head of a political party that favored autonomy for Katanga.

The country's first elections were held just prior to independence— Lumumba was elected prime minister, and Kasa-Vubu was elected president. A ceremony was held on the day of independence in Léopoldville to mark the handover. King Baudouin of Belgium boasted, "The independence of the Congo constitutes the culmination of the work conceived by the genius of King Léopold II, undertaken by him with tenacious courage and continued with perseverance with Belgium." An agitated Lumumba delivered an unscheduled response that pulsed with the anger of millions of Africans who were enslaved by the "genius" of their colonial overlords. He decried the "humiliating slavery" forced on the Congolese by the Belgians and lauded the Congolese struggle for freedom "amid tears, fire, and blood." He warned that the people of the Congo would never forget the "grueling labor, demanded from us in return for wages that did not allow us to satisfy our hunger . . . or to raise our children as creatures very dear to us" and that the Congolese people had "seen our raw materials stolen" under the guise of laws that were "cruel and inhuman." Lumumba ended his incendiary speech with a declaration to the Belgian king: "*Nous ne sommes plus vos singes*"—"We are no longer your monkeys."[4]

Eleven days after independence, the Belgians executed a brazen plan to keep control of what mattered most in the Congo—the minerals of Katanga. They backed Moise Tshombe in announcing that Katanga Province had seceded from the Congo. UMHK provided crucial financial support to Tshombe's administration, and Belgian troops expelled the Congolese army from Katanga. With surgical precision, the Belgians had severed Katanga Province like a hand from the body of the nation, and with it, 70 percent of the government's income. The country was crippled before it ever had a chance.

Lumumba wrote to the United Nations asking for assistance in expelling the Belgians and reunifying the country. The UN responded with the largest ground operation since its creation to help stabilize the nation, but the forces were not authorized to expel Belgian troops. Lumumba turned instead to the Soviet Union for help. The possibility that the Congo, and especially Katanga, might come under Soviet influence put the United States, the United Nations, and Belgium into overdrive to dispatch Lumumba. On August 18, 1960, President Dwight Eisenhower met with his national security council to discuss the situation in the Congo and proclaimed that the U.S. had to "get rid of this guy."[5] The CIA hatched a plot to assassinate Lumumba using toothpaste poisoned with cobra venom; they settled instead on a plan to recruit Lumumba's friend and the head of the army, Joseph Mobutu, to overthrow him.

On September 14, 1960, Joseph Mobutu announced that he had seized control of the government. Mobutu had the army behind him, as well as the logistical and financial backing of the United States, United Nations, and Belgium. Mobutu expelled all Soviet troops and placed Lumumba under house arrest. On November 27, 1960, Lumumba managed to escape. The U.S., UN, and Belgium provided their intelligence services to assist with his recapture. Around midnight on December 1, 1960, Lumumba was caught and imprisoned by Mobutu's forces. His supporters organized a counteroffensive and soon occupied half of the country. The incoming Kennedy administration was worried that Lumumba might return to power and persuaded Belgium to send Lumumba to their stronghold in Élisabethville to be executed.

Patrice Lumumba was flown to Élisabethville on January 16, 1961, driven to an isolated mansion, and tortured by six Belgians and six Katangans, including Moise Tshombe and his second in command, Godefroid Munongo. In an ironic twist of history, Munongo was the grandson of King Msiri. In 1891, Belgian mercenaries dispatched by Leopold had assassinated Msiri to take control of Katanga, and exactly seventy years later, Msiri's grandson joined with the Belgians to assassinate Lumumba and hand Katanga back to the Belgians. After torturing Lumumba for hours, Tshombe and the Belgians shot him dead. They chopped up the body and threw the parts into barrels of sulfuric acid. Lumumba's skull, bones, and teeth were ground to dust and scattered on the drive back, save just one tooth, taken as a souvenir by the Belgian commissioner of the Katangan police.

HELL ON EARTH: FEBRUARY 1961–2022

With the nationalist threat neutralized, the United Nations sent troops to force Katanga to reunify with the Republic of Congo, which is all Lumumba ever wanted. Kasa-Vubu, Tshombe, and other Congolese leaders met in March 1961 to hash out the future of the nation. They agreed to create a confederation of sovereign states to replace the Republic of Congo. The UN and U.S. demanded a unified Congo and the secretary-general

of the UN, Dag Hammarskjöld, subsequently brokered a separate deal
with Kasa-Vubu to reject the agreement in exchange for financial assistance. Tshombe felt betrayed and attacked UN forces in Katanga. All-
out war erupted in the streets of Élisabethville. Hammarskjöld flew to
Élisabethville to broker a peace deal with Tshombe, but his plane was
shot down during its descent to the airport on September 18, 1961.
Rumors persist that Tshombe ordered the attack.

UMHK continued to support an independent Katanga by paying mining taxes directly to Tshombe's government. Tshombe's forces fought the
UN in Katanga for another two years, until President Kennedy sent U.S.
fighter jets to support a decisive UN offensive. Tshombe conceded defeat
on January 14, 1963. The Congo was finally reunified after three and
a half years of fractious violence, and new elections were held in May
1965 with Kasa-Vubu emerging as president. Kasa-Vubu's presidency
was short-lived—on November 24, 1965, Joseph Mobutu executed his
second coup and took complete control of the government.

Mobutu ran the Congo for thirty-two years, just as Leopold did—a
personal wealth machine. He nationalized UMHK under Gécamines
on December 31, 1966, and he took direct ownership of several mining
concessions. He siphoned billions of dollars from the country's mineral
exports into personal bank accounts, becoming one of the ten richest
people in the world during the 1980s. On October 27, 1971, Mobutu
renamed the country the Republic of Zaire, based on what he thought
was the original name of the Congo River during the time of the Kongo
Kingdom, when it was actually a Portuguese cartographer's incorrect
rendering of the word *nzere*.

Mobutu remained in power for decades, despite overt corruption, by
embracing the U.S. cause against communism, which brought him the
unwavering support of Presidents Nixon, Bush, Reagan, and Clinton.
Katanga's minerals flowed to the West, and the proceeds flowed into
Mobutu's bank accounts. However, that which Katanga gives, it can also
take away. Copper prices peaked at $1.33 per pound in April 1974 and
plunged to $0.59 per pound in June 1982 as low-cost producing nations
increased output. Copper production by Gécamines peaked in 1988 at

nearly 480,000 tons, and five years later, it plummeted to 30,000 tons. When the Soviet Union collapsed in 1991, Mobutu's value to the West collapsed with it. A genocide in neighboring Rwanda proved to be the catalyst for his final downfall.

On April 6, 1994, a plane carrying President Juvénal Habyarimana (a Hutu) of Rwanda was shot down on approach to Kigali International Airport. Hutus blamed Tutsis, and a massacre erupted. After one hundred days, Hutu Interahamwe had slaughtered at least eight hundred thousand Tutsis. More than two million refugees fled across Zaire's borders into the Kivus. The Interahamwe set up a ministate in the Kivus headquartered near Goma and continued to stage attacks against Tutsis. The degeneration of Zaire under Mobutu made it possible for its comparatively diminutive neighbors to contemplate an invasion. The head of the Rwandan army and current president of Rwanda, Paul Kagame, seized the opportunity. Kagame orchestrated an attack on the Kivus in conjunction with Uganda, using a Katangan front man and longtime opponent of Mobutu—Laurent-Désiré Kabila.

Kabila merged several rebel groups into an army called the AFDL and promptly led a battalion of forces to take control of Katanga. He took up residence in the Karavia Hotel in Lubumbashi and arranged meetings with Western investment banks, De Beers, and mining companies from America and Europe to divvy up the spoils of war. The remaining AFDL forces led by Kagame's loyal aide-de-camp, James Kabarebe, marched west toward Kinshasa. A decrepit Mobutu fled to Morocco, where he eventually died in exile. Kabila was sworn in as president of the Democratic Republic of the Congo on May 29, 1997. He portrayed himself as the rightful successor to Patrice Lumumba and promised to bring freedom and prosperity to the Congolese people.

Like Mobutu and Leopold before him, Laurent Kabila ran the Congo as a kleptocratic system of personal enrichment. Kabila executed deals with foreign mining companies and funneled the money into personal accounts. Kabila made a fatal error, however, when he turned against those who helped put him in power. On July 26, 1998, Kabila ordered all Rwandan and Ugandan troops to withdraw from the country. Rwanda and Uganda promptly backed new rebel armies led by James Kabarebe with the mission of overthrowing Kabila. One week later, Kabarebe invaded the Congo for the second time.

What followed on August 2, 1998, and for years thereafter became known as "Africa's Great War," an internecine explosion of violence involving nine African nations and thirty militias that laid waste to the DRC and resulted in the death of at least five million Congolese civilians. Kabarebe highjacked a Boeing 727 from the airport at Goma and flew his troops to the doorstep of Kinshasa to stage an attack on the capital. Kabila managed an eleventh-hour agreement to secure military assistance from Zimbabwe in exchange for mining assets, including the infamous Tremalt deal for the mines near Kambove. Troops from Zimbabwe were joined by forces from Namibia, Angola, Sudan, and Chad, each in exchange for stakes in Katanga's mineral resources. Armies from Rwanda, Uganda, and Burundi took control of the eastern Congo and marched across the country toward Kinshasa. War raged for two years before the UN sent peacekeepers to stabilize the situation.

Laurent Kabila was assassinated by one of his bodyguards on January 16, 2001. Kabila's son, Joseph, succeeded him and inherited a country in ruins. In a bid to jump-start the nation's economy, Joseph Kabila resuscitated the country's mining sector under a new Mining Code in 2002 that was designed to attract foreign investment. Kabila also initiated a peace process to end conflict with Rwanda and Uganda. A final agreement signed on December 17, 2002, required Rwanda and Uganda to withdraw all troops from the DRC. The countries subsequently created spheres of control in the Congo to continue exploiting its minerals. Rwandan forces took control of the coltan trade in the Kivus, and Ugandan forces took control of the gold trade and fought bitterly with the Rwandans for control of the Congo's lucrative diamond mines.

With the eastern Congo mired in conflict, Kabila turned his attention to making money by closing mining deals in Katanga. He secured the SICOMINES deal in 2009, which opened the doors for a Chinese takeover of Katanga. Kabila brokered several other deals with Chinese mining companies in exchange for kickbacks funneled through his accounts at BGFIBank. Kabila's second term as president ended in December 2016, although he clung to power for two more years before elections were finally held on December 30, 2018. Kabila's handpicked successor, Félix Tshisekedi, was declared the winner. Despite questions about the credibility of the results, Tshisekedi's inauguration on January 25, 2019, marked the first peaceful transfer of power in the Congo since the country's independence in 1960.

Although many in the Congo were worried that Tshisekedi would promote Joseph Kabila's interests, within a few months of taking office, Tshisekedi initiated an anti-corruption campaign targeting the mining sector. He spoke critically about some of the harms being caused by Chinese mining companies, and he pursued stronger ties with the United States. According to U.S. ambassador Mike Hammer, human rights was an important part of the agenda: "When President Tshisekedi came to power in January 2019, one of my first conversations with him referred to our concerns on human trafficking and child labor issues. He assured me that he was committed to human rights." On the same topic, a Western diplomat added off the record, "President Tshisekedi does not want to continue the practice of complete Chinese exploitation of his country, whereas Kabila and his cronies depend on the Chinese because it filled their pockets."

Tshisekedi continues to apply pressure to Chinese mining companies to improve transparency, labor standards, and sustainability practices. Displeased with Tshisekedi's actions, Kabila is said to be scheming with Chinese backers to run again in the 2023 elections to retake control of the country, or to ensure the victory of someone else who will support their agenda.

The stage is set for the next contest to control Katanga's riches. Will the Western-leaning Tshisekedi consolidate power, or will Kabila reclaim the nation and push it further toward China? The flow of cobalt is at stake, and with it, control of our rechargeable future. Who is to say that, either way, anything would improve in the lives of the Congolese people? From the moment Diego Cão introduced Europeans to the Kongo in 1482, the heart of Africa was made colony to the world. Patrice Lumumba offered a fleeting chance at a different fate, but the neocolonial machinery of the West chopped him down and replaced him with someone who would keep their riches flowing.

Cobalt is but the latest treasure they have come to loot.

5

"If We Do Not Dig, We Do Not Eat"

Tenke Fungurume, Mutanda, and Tilwezembe

This realization of a great human tragedy will be vivid and historically enduring in the measure in which we are able to fashion for ourselves a mental vision, which shall also be an accurate one, of its victims.
— E. D. Morel, *History of the Congo Reform Movement*

TRAVELING WEST FROM LIKASI can be a grind. The road is often choked with traffic and clogged at *péage* checkpoints. Cargo trucks rumble down the narrow highway, packed to the brim with minerals. "You can determine the state of the global economy just by sitting along the road halfway between Likasi and Kolwezi and watching how many trucks filled with copper cathode and cobalt concentrate go by," said Asad Khan, CEO of a Congolese construction company called Big Boss Congo. "When the economy is booming, the road is jammed with trucks coming out of the mines." By this metric, the global economy was doing very well during my visits to the DRC. The road was perpetually congested with big-wheel haulers, dented pickup trucks, rusted cars, sputtering motorbikes, and warped-wheel bicycles laden with sack upon sack of copper and cobalt. Fuel supplies were often unable to keep up with demand, which led to a hunt for "Gaddafis," the term for hustlers that stockpile gasoline in plastic containers when supplies are plentiful, then resell it at a hefty premium when they dwindle. I found myself on the hunt for a Gaddafi more than once during my field research in the Congo.

The heavy traffic and perpetual mining activity west of Likasi has resulted in dangerous amounts of air pollution. A thick cloud of fumes, grit, and ash suffocates the land. Sky and earth meet vaguely above the hills at some obscure and unattainable frontier. Villages along the road are coated with airborne debris. Children scamper between huts like balls of dust. There are no flowers to be found. No birds in the sky. No placid streams. No pleasant breezes. The ornaments of nature are gone. All color seems pale and unformed. Only the fragments of life remain.

This is Lualaba Province, where cobalt is king.

The stretch of road between Likasi and Kolwezi passes by two of the largest industrial mines in Africa—Tenke Fungurume and Mutanda. The third big mine before Kolwezi is Tilwezembe. It is perhaps the largest industrial site that functions almost entirely as an artisanal mining area. The model of mixed industrial-artisanal production at Étoile near Lubumbashi and the MIKAS mines north of Kambove skews increasingly artisanal at many of the industrial mines in Lualaba Province. Corporations atop the cobalt chain stake their reputations on the impervious wall that is supposed to exist between industrial and artisanal production. Such assertions are as meaningless as trying to claim that one can discriminate the water from different tributaries while standing at the mouth of the Congo River.

TENKE FUNGURUME

Seventy-five kilometers northwest of Likasi sits the largest mining concession in the Congo: Tenke Fungurume (TFM). The mine is named after the two towns that border the western (Tenke) and southern (Fungurume) ends of the concession. TFM spans more than 1,500 square kilometers, covering an area slightly larger than greater London. Thousands of people once lived in villages across the concession, but they were evicted when the rights were sold in 2006 to a joint venture between the U.S. mining company Phelps Dodge (57.75 percent), Tenke Mining Company (24.75 percent), and Gécamines (17.5 percent). In 2007, Phelps Dodge merged with Phoenix-based mining giant Freeport-McMoRan (56 percent), and Tenke Mining Corp was acquired by Lundin Mining (24 percent), leaving 20 percent for Gécamines.

In 2016, Freeport sold its stake in TFM to China Molybdenum (CMOC) for $2.65 billion. The sale ended the presence of any U.S.-based mining companies in the DRC and cleared the way for the Chinese takeover of the Congo's copper-cobalt mines. The sale of such a valuable mining asset by Freeport at the dawn of the cobalt revolution was a puzzling move. Preferring not to be identified, one of the senior executives who managed the TFM concession for Freeport provided an explanation: "The reason we sold TFM was purely financial. Freeport was on the wrong end of an oil and gas investment that put significant burden on the company's financial position. There were commitments to the market to halve the debt within a year, and the only way to do that was by selling assets."

CMOC consolidated ownership of TFM in 2019 and currently controls 80 percent of the mine. CMOC subsequently invested $550 million to acquire a 95 percent stake in an undeveloped copper-cobalt deposit near TFM called Kisanfu, positioning the company to be one of the world's top cobalt producers for years to come. In 2021, the largest lithium-ion battery maker in the world, China-based CATL, paid $137.5 million to acquire a 25 percent stake in Kisanfu, advancing Chinese dominance across the rechargeable battery supply chain.

TFM produced an impressive 15,700 tons of cobalt in 2021,[1] although the Congolese government formally charged CMOC in February 2022 with understating production in order to minimize its tax and royalty payments.[2]

The bustling roadside town of Fungurume is the main entry point to TFM. Residents crowd the highway, adding to the congestion in the area. The road is further obstructed by an array of vendors selling charcoal, bushmeat, and mobile phone top-ups. Wandering around Fungurume, one gets the sense of a village that developed too quickly. The population of Fungurume ballooned from 50,000 in 2007 to more than a quarter million in 2021, which has created considerable strain on infrastructure, housing, and employment. Small businesses are crammed next to each other along the town's dirt paths, including bakeries, auto repair shops, barbershops, restaurants, and a large bazaar where one can buy clothes, pots and pans, plastic containers, dried fish, and vegetables. There are a few schools in Fungurume, the largest of which is a two-story pink building protected by a black metal fence. Most of the homes are one- or two-room brick structures with metal roofs. Piles of chopped wood are scattered in random spots around town. Patches of pale green grass offer a timid contrast to the dominant reds and browns of brick and dirt. Locals gather around the homes that are lucky enough to have a satellite dish to watch soccer matches. Music thumps from speakers sitting in the dirt outside businesses, creating an incomprehensible cacophony of sound. Women are adorned in colors that were once vibrant but have slowly faded with sun and grit. Men smoke, drink, and gamble. Other than the very young, no one smiles.

The main entrance to the TFM concession is located just west of Fungurume. There are two heavily guarded checkpoints prior to entering the mine. The first checkpoint has a metal gate surrounded by barbed wire fencing. There is a small stream of foul, sludgy water that passes beneath a bridge next to the fence. At each visit, I saw women washing clothes in the stream while children swam nearby. About 250 meters north of the first checkpoint, there is a second and more heavily guarded security entrance. A sign greets visitors with the words WELCOME TO TENKE FUNGURUME MINING written in English, French, and Mandarin. Security jeeps with triangular pink flags atop metal poles pass back and forth through the second gate. Although CMOC maintains that it adheres to Congolese law and does not permit artisanal mining to take place on the TFM concession, I saw dozens of artisanal miners at each visit digging into the pit walls of the mine, including just behind the second checkpoint.

There is in fact so much artisanal mining that takes place on the TFM concession that an entire village of artisanal miners has spawned a few kilometers west of Fungurume, called Fungurume 2. One afternoon, I sat at this village and watched dozens of motorbikes laden with sacks of ore race down dirt paths from deep within the TFM concession. I was told they were *négociants* who had purchased artisanally mined cobalt from diggers on the TFM concession and were en route to sell their loads at depots in the area. According to locals, much of the ore is sold from the depots right back to CMOC.

After the second security checkpoint, the road continues north into the immense TFM concession. The walls of the pit mines loom high above the landscape. There are a few industrial areas off the main road, followed by a residential complex farther north for foreign workers. The residential complex has at least two hundred individual homes situated along tree-lined streets, as well as tennis courts, a gymnasium, and pool. There is an office complex north of the residential area, and north of the office complex, there is a private landing strip for corporate jets. Beyond this point, most of the concession is wilderness. A second road leads west from the main residential complex toward the town of Tenke, which is about half the size of Fungurume. TFM's massive copper-cobalt processing facility is situated near Tenke. It uses a two-stage process called solvent extraction and electrowinning (SX-EW) to produce copper cathode and cobalt hydroxide. Toxic solvents and acids used in the processing are supposed to be disposed of responsibly. My visit to Tenke proved otherwise.

The truth of what is happening in and around the TFM mine is best uncovered by speaking with the residents of Fungurume. To call the relationship between Fungurume and TFM acrimonious would be putting it mildly.

"They kicked us from our homes!" an elderly man with patchy skin, Samy, exclaimed. "We lived on that land for three generations before the mining companies came. We grew vegetables and caught fish. They threw us out, and now we cannot find enough food to feed our families . . . We have no jobs in this area. How do they expect us to live?"

Many Fungurume residents repeated Samy's anger about being kicked off the concession in 2006. They said that they were given little warning and no compensation or relocation assistance. One of my translators, Olivier, described the situation best:

> Imagine if a mining company came to the place where you live and they kick you out. They destroy all your belongings except whatever you can carry in your own hands. Then they build a mine because there are minerals in the ground, and they keep you out with soldiers. What can you do if there is no one to help you? Maybe you would feel it is your right to go back to that place where you lived and dig some of the minerals for yourself. That is how the people in Fungurume feel.

Digging for scraps of cobalt on the TFM concession became the only way many people in Fungurume could survive. The Freeport executive who explained the rationale behind the sale of the concession acknowledged as much: "There were always illegal miners, mainly on hills that were not active mining zones. We would have waves that would come into active mining zones. We had an uneasy truce. If you don't interfere with the industrial mining equipment, if you are not bothering anyone, we will leave you to it. We had a security force, but you have to pick and choose your battles. You can't be everywhere on the concession." The "uneasy truce" between Freeport and Fungurume became more of a simmering battlefront after CMOC took over. Large numbers of artisanal miners continued to venture onto the concession, and every so often, CMOC ordered its security forces to prevent access when the numbers became too great. When the CMOC security forces could not cope, the army was brought in to help. That is when the battlefront erupted.

One such eruption took place in August 2021, when the residents of Fungurume began to riot over blockaded access to the mine. A mob swarmed the highway to prevent the passage of cargo trucks into TFM. As the fever escalated, the mob started to attack other vehicles that were driving by. Asad Khan was driving back from Kolwezi to Lubumbashi and got caught up in the violence. He said that ten or twelve people grabbed onto his SUV and were using bricks and metal objects to smash his windows. "That's when I thought I was going to die," Asad said. "I panicked and put my car in reverse sixty to seventy kilometers per hour, driving zigzag, and when I made a sharp turn at high speed, the men fell off my car."

An even worse eruption took place in June 2019. Artisanal miners were digging on the TFM concession in large numbers, including inside some of the main pits. CMOC's security forces could not handle the situation. A Fungurume resident named Promesse explained what happened next:

> The army sent soldiers to remove the *creuseurs* from the concession. They shot their guns in the air. They beat the men to make them leave. Many people became angry. They shouted, "This is Congo, not China!"
>
> The next day, two trucks that were full with ores drove out from the mine. The same men from Fungurume blocked the road. They beat the drivers and set the trucks on fire.

Promesse said that after the trucks were set on fire, a battalion of fully armed FARDC soldiers swarmed the area and suppressed the mob with gunfire. Several people were killed, and numerous homes and businesses were burned.

The tensions between the residents of Fungurume and CMOC go beyond periodic blockades of access to the concession and include a palpable discontent about the lack of support that was promised to the community.

"They said they would build schools and make jobs, but we are still waiting," a Fungurume resident named Eric said. "They care only about the cobalt. The people of Fungurume are like pests to them."

"When they bought the concession, they think they also bought the people of Fungurume. They think they can control us like prisoners," another resident added.

Another man, Kafufu, whose right arm was missing, offered the following lament about the TFM mine:

Do you know there are hundreds of workers who live on that concession? Until CMOC came, their dormitories were close to Fungurume, so they would come here to buy supplies and eat at restaurants. This helped support our livelihood. Then they moved all the workers to "Bravo Camp." It is much farther inside the concession, so the workers do not come to Fungurume or Tenke anymore.

Kafufu lived in Tenke and was visiting his brother in Fungurume when he saw me speaking to a group of locals. He said he wanted to take me to Tenke straightaway because there was something urgent he needed to show me. I asked if it could wait until the next day, but he was insistent that I accompany him that day. After rounding up my interviews, I drove with Kafufu to Tenke. The town was situated immediately west of several immense open-air pit mines on the TFM concession. Kafufu led us north of Tenke into a more sparsely populated area of small huts. We stopped the jeep and continued by foot. He walked toward a few dilapidated huts, some of which were made of wood with thatched roofs. "That is my home," he said, pointing to one of the thatched huts. I had not noticed it when we were farther south, but up close, I could see that everything in this part of Tenke—the ground, the trees, the huts, the bicycles, the people—was covered in a thin layer of mustard-colored dust. I focused on two children sitting outside a hut, no more than five years old, filling empty plastic bottles with dirt. Their skin, clothes, and faces were draped in the mustard-colored powder.

"What is it?" I asked.

"It is dried sulfuric acid," Kafufu replied. "They use it in the mine to process the ores."

"How do you know?"

"I used to work there," Kafufu said, pointing to the TFM concession with his only hand. He was a graduate from the University of Lubumbashi and said that CMOC had provided him with extensive training for work at the processing facility.

"My arm was crushed in an accident. They gave me wages for one week, and they paid for the surgery," Kafufu said.

I asked Kafufu when the accident occurred.

"That was two years ago," he replied. He had not been able to work since that time.

Given his knowledge of the processing facility, Kafufu was able to explain how the system worked: "First, they take the ores to the crushing plant for milling. They have metal rollers as big as a car that can crush the ores like sand. After this, they leach the sand using sulfuric acid to separate the copper and the cobalt. This makes some gas that is filled with hydrofluoric acid, sulfur dioxide, and sulfuric acid."

The problem, according to Kafufu, was that CMOC did not contain the gas. "They let it blow over our homes. It falls on our food and our water. It falls on everyone who lives here," he said.

I looked at the two boys playing in the dirt, wrapped in a blanket of poison. I tried to imagine how their parents must feel, watching their children being contaminated each day and feeling powerless to protect them. Although violence was never an acceptable response, I could understand why the people of Fungurume might feel desperate enough to set fire to a few trucks.

The women of Fungurume typically begin their days with the Sisyphean task of wiping away the grit that has settled on their homes overnight. Most of the men in town, such as Franck and his fourteen-year-old son, Gloire, try to sleep in. They are often awake much of the night digging on the TFM concession. I met Franck and Gloire in their small home near the northwestern edge of Fungurume. A thin, pale green sheet was draped over the entrance of the home in place of a front door. Inside, the dwelling consisted of two rooms, one in which Gloire, his mother, father, and two younger brothers slept on mats on the dirt; the other in which they cooked, ate, and listened to the radio. Although some of the homes in Fungurume had spotty electricity, theirs did not. They bought batteries to power their flashlight and radio. The price of the batteries was more expensive than I would have imagined—two dollars (roughly one day's income) for a pack of four AA batteries. The price seemed particularly exorbitant since they were living right next to one of the largest battery-component metal-making mines in the world.

When I met Gloire, he was sitting with his back against the wall with his legs outstretched in front of him. His jaw was clenched tightly, and he was covered in sweat. There was a small wooden table in the corner near him on which some of the family's clothes were stacked; the rest were hanging on a string outside. One small opening in the brick wall across the room from Gloire served as a window but offered little ventilation. The mud-brick home and metal roof heated like an oven beneath the morning sun. Ghostly clouds of dust floated through the cracks between metal and stone. Gloire wore a pair of dark brown trousers and a dark green T-shirt with white trim. He shifted and fidgeted constantly, ever in search of a comfortable position.

Gloire explained that he went to school in Fungurume until the third year, at which point his family could no longer afford the fees of six dollars per month. At age eleven, Gloire said he started digging with his father on the TFM site.

"We go to the concession at night. We pay the guards, and they let us dig in the pits. It is more certain to find cobalt there. If we cannot pay the money, we sneak inside the concession and dig. Sometimes we are chased by dogs, but mostly, we are not disturbed," Franck said.

"We know the land, so we know where to go to find good ore in the ground," Gloire added. He said that there was a large amount of malachite and heterogenite on the concession, which were sources of copper and cobalt. "We fill the sacks with these stones. They are very heavy, so we place them on a bicycle to carry them out."

I asked Gloire what they did with the ore once they got the sacks out of the concession.

"We sell it to the depots in Fungurume."

"What do they do with it?"

"They take it to TFM."

On the morning of August 19, 2018, Franck and Gloire woke up a little earlier than usual. Gloire remembered switching on the radio and listening to reports of refugees fleeing clashes between rival ethnic groups in Ituri Province along the border with Uganda. There had been clashes before, but this one was reported to be particularly violent and was causing a mass exodus of displaced people. Later that day, Gloire spent some time running errands for the family—he bought manioc at the market and repaired the front wheel on the family's bicycle. That night, Gloire and his father ventured into the TFM concession. They hiked by moonlight for more than an hour to a large pit. Numerous artisanal miners had been excavating it for weeks. While they were digging, one of the walls of the pit collapsed. Gloire and five others were buried in an avalanche of stones and dirt. Franck and the other artisanal miners dug out the people who had been buried. Everyone survived, although some suffered serious injuries.

Gloire gingerly pulled up his right trouser leg to show me his injury. It looked as if someone had ripped off the bottom half of his calf muscle and placed a tight, thin piece of pink skin over the gash. The bone on the outside of Gloire's ankle was missing, and that area was also sealed by a tight piece of pink skin. Franck pointed to Gloire's shin to show me where it was shattered. There was a sharp indentation at the spot. The leg was a mangled mess.

The night of the accident, Franck carried his half-conscious son on his back all the way home. He and Gloire's mother tended to the agonized child all night, and the next morning, they rushed him to a medical clinic in Fungurume. Gloire was in excruciating pain, but the clinic did not have any painkillers other than acetaminophen, which was incapable of dulling his discomfort. The clinic also did not have antibiotics to treat a potential infection, nor an x-ray machine with which to determine the extent of the bone damage. A nurse cleaned and bandaged Gloire's leg and sent him home.

Ever since the pit wall collapse, Gloire had been suffering extreme pain and sharp fevers. He was unable to walk, change his clothes, or go to the toilet on his own. His mother and father were powerless to alleviate his pain or seek treatment for his injury. As best as I could determine, Gloire required surgery, a cast, and extensive rehabilitation, which he could only secure at a proper hospital in Kolwezi or Lubumbashi. Following Gloire's

injury, the family came under financial hardship and had to find a way
to replace the lost income.

"I take another son to dig with me now," Franck said.

"Are you worried you or he might get injured like Gloire?" I asked.

"Yes, of course, but if we do not dig, we do not eat."

Franck took me to see the depot where he said he sold the ore he dug
from the TFM concession. It was in an abandoned brick shack that appeared to have been repurposed for cobalt trading near the eastern end
of Fungurume just off the highway. It did not have a name, only a price
list posted at the front, written in black marker on a raffia sack. There
were two other depots immediately adjacent, also without names. All
three depots were operated by Chinese men dressed in casual clothes,
none of whom were open to conversing with me. I returned to observe
the depots toward the end of the following day, and I saw Congolese men
load sacks from all three depots into a gray cargo truck. I followed the
truck down the highway and watched it drive into the TFM concession.
Although Franck said that most of the artisanal miners he knew sold ore
to these depots and a few other ones in the area, he also said that many
people sold their cobalt to *négociants*. I asked what the *négociants* did
with the cobalt. According to Franck, they transported it to a village about
ten kilometers southwest of Fungurume, and they did so only at night.

Night markets for cobalt trading was something new. I never heard
of anything like it in Haut-Katanga Province, but in Lualaba Province,
I encountered rumors of three such markets in villages in the forest. I
only managed to track down one of them, and that was the one Franck
mentioned. I traveled one night down a bumpy dirt path deep into a remote area, passing by numerous motorbikes heading in both directions.
The motorbikes heading southwest were loaded with sacks of cobalt; the
ones heading northeast were either empty or carrying passengers where
the sacks used to be. Aside from the motorbike headlights, all was black.

I arrived in the village to an obscure aura of pit fires and flashlights
glowing within a spectral haze of dust. The huts, mostly made of bricks,
were laid out in a broad clearing in the forest. Clothes hung on lines
draped from one hut to another. Plastic bottles, cigarette butts, and stray

trash were strewn about. There were numerous Congolese *négociants* bartering with Chinese agents at the front of several huts. In addition to *négociants,* there were also artisanal miners selling cobalt to the Chinese buyers. I surmised that the artisanals probably lived in nearby villages and had come to the marketplace to sell the cobalt they excavated from nearby digging sites akin to the ones I saw in the forests south of Kambove.

I learned from a few *négociants* at the village that they typically made three or four runs each night from Fungurume, for which they earned around ten to fifteen dollars per run. It was a substantial income for one night of work that might take an artisanal miner weeks to earn. I also confirmed that the Chinese buyers paid some of the villagers to use their huts as depots. Based on the volume of transactions I witnessed, it seemed plausible that hundreds of tons of copper-cobalt ore were being purchased through this marketplace each year. The informal and all but untraceable nature of the marketplace made it impossible to discriminate the source of cobalt once it was thrown into the same batch of acids for processing industrially mined ore. What else could the purpose of this kind of remote night marketplace be, other than to launder artisanally mined cobalt into the formal supply chain completely out of view, and certainly beyond the scope of any tracing or auditing of cobalt supply chains that were purportedly taking place? Can any company at the top of the chain legitimately suggest that the cobalt in their devices or cars did not pass through a village marketplace like this?

The deeper I ventured into the mining provinces, the murkier the bottom of the cobalt supply chain proved to be, and the more resistant to claims that the flow of cobalt was adequately monitored for child labor or other abuses.

The strained relationship between the residents of Fungurume and the TFM mine was illustrative of a broader crisis unfolding across the mineral provinces of the Congo—foreign mining companies expropriated large swaths of land, displaced villagers, contaminated the environment, offered little to no support to the local population, and left them to eke out a meager existence in dangerous conditions as artisanal miners on the land they once lived on. Perhaps no one I met in Fungurume illustrated the consequences of this crisis more than a sixteen-year-old boy named Makano. I found Makano in his brick house near the southwestern edge of town. When I entered the home, I was met by the stench of decay. A noisome odor hung in the air like an apparition. Makano sat insensate on the dirt, scrawny limbs extending from a wasted trunk. I could feel the heat radiating from his burning frame. He spoke in a voice devoid of tone, emerging from his throat like a grainy whisper:

> My father died three years ago. I am the oldest son, so it was my responsibility to earn money for my family. I started digging in the fields in the south of Fungurume with a group of boys who were my friends. We dug in small pits. Some days, we found ore; some days, we did not. We were not earning much this way, so we felt we must go to the [Tenke Fungurume] concession.

Makano did not have a bicycle, so he said he had to carry one sack of stones off the concession each night. I asked what he did with the sack, and he said he sold it to the depots in Fungurume.

"We know the purity of cobalt is good, but they never pay more than two dollars for one sack," Makano said.

On the night of May 5, 2018, Makano went to dig on the TFM concession with his friends. They dug for several hours and were preparing for the long walk home before dawn. Makano was climbing out of a six-meter pit with a heavy sack of cobalt on his shoulders when he lost his footing and crashed to the bottom. The next thing he remembered, he was in the Gécamines hospital in Kolwezi.

"My left leg and my hip were broken. I had cuts all over my body. My head was swollen," Makano said.

It took all the family's money to pay for the treatment and initial surgery to save Makano's life. He stayed in the hospital for a week, after which time his mother, Rosine, had to bring him home, even though his injuries were not healed.

Rosine helped Makano pull down his trousers to show me his injury.

There was a festering gash in his right hip and a long scar down his right leg where the doctors had placed a metal rod to support the shattered bones. The wounds appeared to be infected. Makano was burning with fever and clearly needed antibiotics and medical care immediately, or else he seemed likely to go into septic shock.

"I know my son is dying," Rosine said tearfully. "He needs to go to the hospital, but I do not have any money."

She looked at me, desperate and despondent.

"Please help us."

Rosine was neither the first nor the last mother in the Congo who would ask me to help her child. It was impossible to assist them all, so whom does one help? In what manner and for how long? Much of my research in the DRC was self-funded, so I lacked the capacity to assist in any meaningful way in even the severest cases. Even if one were to assume that it was feasible for me to help everyone I met, how could I possibly assess the array of unforeseeable negative consequences that could befall a family even with the most well-intentioned assistance? What might happen if word leaked that I had left money with Rosine to help her son? Might another equally desperate mother not do whatever it took to get that money from Rosine to save her child? This was but one of many potential risks to ill-conceived assistance. Nevertheless, Makano was sitting right there in front of me in the dirt, slowly dying. How could I take this child's story and turn my back on him?

I did what I could to assist Makano as discreetly as possible. Although it would probably not buy the child as much time and medical care as he needed, at this stage, every day was precious. I left Makano and Rosine knowing that I had at best provided a short stay on his bleak prognosis. Guilt took hold as my thoughts turned to Gloire, Marline, Nikki, Chance, Kiyonge, Kisangi, Priscille, and so many others. Their situations may not have been as extreme as Makano's when I encountered them, but that was only because I met them at different points on the same journey to the same dismal terminus.

I wandered through Fungurume back across the highway, through the dusty maze of huts and shops. I knew the metallic taste of the town by now and spat out the bitter paste every few minutes. As the ruckus from the highway faded, I caught the sound of a chorus. The uplifting voices drew me to the Église Alliance Chrétienne Internationale (International Christian Alliance Church). Inside, I found a large room packed with congregants. They sang passionately, led by a vibrant pastor atop a small wooden platform. A child looked at me, his wide eyes alight and comforting. I understood at last how the people of the Congo survived their daily torment—they loved God with full and fiery hearts and drew comfort from the promise of salvation.

Although their love was powerful, the evidence was mounting that it was all but unrequited.

MUTANDA

Seventy kilometers west of Fungurume sits the crown jewel of Glencore's mining operations in Africa—Mutanda. Rich red earth stretches from the highway up to the foothills of the concession, where the massive mountains of the pit walls rise high above the horizon. Prior to suspending operations in January 2020, Mutanda was the largest cobalt-producing mine in the world. The complex is a contained rectangular zone of roughly 185 square kilometers, consisting of several titanic open-air mining pits more than 100 meters deep. Hundreds of thousands of trees would have been clear-cut to make way for these craters in the earth. From the reports of locals, it does not appear that many, if any, trees were planted to replace them. Glencore historically maintained a 70 to 80 percent holding in the mine in conjunction with various other parties, including Gécamines and Dan Gertler. As of February 2017, Glencore acquired 100 percent of the mine through its Congolese subsidiary, Mutanda Mining Sarl (MUMI), making it the only major copper-cobalt mine in the DRC that is not a joint venture with Gécamines. Like TFM, Mutanda has its own mineral-processing facility that uses the same SX-EW process requiring large amounts of sulfuric acid. The concession has a residential area for foreign mining staff, a recreational area, and a small golf course.

At its peak in 2018, Mutanda produced 27,300 tons of cobalt,[3] which accounted for almost 30 percent of global production and positioned Glencore as the largest cobalt mining company in the world.

On August 8, 2019, Glencore announced that it was suspending operations at Mutanda for two years beginning in January 2020. The company cited insufficient sulfuric acid supplies for its processing facility as well as "adverse conditions" in the cobalt market, even though TFM and other industrial mines appeared to have more than enough sulfuric acid to continue operations uninterrupted. It is true, however, that cobalt prices dropped 40 percent from 2018 to mid-2019, hence many industry analysts believe that the move was an effort by Glencore to reduce the global cobalt supply and boost prices.

A senior official at Gécamines offered a different theory: "Glencore shut Mutanda to pressure the Congolese government to provide better terms on taxes." The official explained that despite heavy opposition from Glencore, including an in-person meeting in Kinshasa between then CEO Ivan Glasenberg and Joseph Kabila on March 7, 2018, the DRC government declared cobalt to be a "strategic" substance on November 24, 2018. Doing so initiated an increase in the royalty rate from 3.5 percent to 10 percent that mining companies had to pay for extracted cobalt. The new policy also established a 50 percent tax on superprofits. The tax on superprofits was to be triggered when a commodity's price increased by more than 25 percent above levels that were cited in the mining company's initial bankable feasibility study to assess the geologic reserves in the concession prior to commencing operations. If the price of cobalt rose enough, mining companies would be on the hook for the superprofit tax. Cobalt prices on the London Metal Exchange in fact increased by more than 100 percent from their lows in the summer of 2019 to the summer of 2021. A lot of money was at stake for Glencore, which had paid the Congolese government $626.9 million in taxes and royalties in 2018 from the Mutanda site alone and $1.08 billion in total taxes and royalties from all its mining operations in the DRC. The $1.08 billion represented an impressive 18.3 percent of the entire Congolese national budget that year. Glencore appeared to have financial leverage with which to pressure the Congolese government, but the plan did not work, nor did rumors of graft and shady dealings. For years, the company has been under investigation by the U.S. Department of Justice, the UK's Serious Fraud Office, and the Office of the Attorney General of Switzerland for alleged money laundering, bribery, and corruption relating to its mining operations in the DRC.[4]

Although I made efforts to gain access to the Mutanda complex during visits in 2018, 2019, and 2021, I was not granted permission. The story of Mutanda, however, does not end there.

Like most industrial mines in the Congo, Mutanda has grown across the years. In 2015, Glencore purchased a massive tract of undeveloped land north of the highway across from the main MUMI concession. Like the TFM concession, there were thousands of villagers who had been living on the land for generations. In this case, however, they refused to move. In fact, Glencore's purchase of the land signaled to the villagers that there must be something valuable in the dirt. They started digging in the hills, and soon, one of the largest artisanal mining cooperatives in Lualaba Province, Coopérative Minière et Artisanale du Katanga (COMAKAT) organized the operation at a site named Shabara. Mining cooperatives were originally established under the 2002 Mining Code as a means of managing artisanal miners in authorized Zones d'Exploitation Artisanale (ZEAs). The cooperatives were charged with registering workers, paying their wages, ensuring safe working conditions, and preventing child labor at the ZEAs. Even though Shabara is not an authorized ZEA, a full-fledged artisanal mining operation under COMAKAT has been thriving there for years.

Unlike the main Mutanda complex, I managed to gain entry to the Shabara mine. To reach the site, I exited the highway near Mutanda and drove north on a dirt road past a village called Kawama. The once-quiet village had grown rapidly in recent years following an influx of artisanal miners. The deluge of people transformed Kawama into a hodgepodge of dwellings scattered around massive termite mounds. Some of the homes were older brick huts that had been in the village for many years, and others were more like plastic tents that looked like they had been thrown up the previous week. There were Gaddafis selling gasoline in yellow containers, women selling charcoal, and two mobile phone top-up kiosks.

The dirt road to Shabara transected the village and veered up a steady incline for more than a kilometer. As the altitude increased, I was able to see a broad expanse of lightly forested savannah and rolling hills. I arrived at the entrance of the mine, which was secured by armed guards. They waved me through as a guest of COMAKAT and led me to a small, mustard-colored concrete structure with the words BUREAU ADMINISTRATIF COMAKAT painted above the main door. One of the senior COMAKAT managers as well as a SAEMAPE official greeted me and took me on a guided tour of the mine on foot. The presence of a SAEMAPE official suggested that the Congolese government was collecting royalties from the production at Shabara, even though it was technically an illicit artisanal mining operation on an industrial concession.

The Shabara mine was massive. It stretched for dozens of square kilometers over rolling hills and pits up to a cliff's edge that overlooked a wide swath of countryside. There was at least one large depot filled with more than a thousand pink raffia sacks stuffed with ore. Cargo trucks ferried dirt around the site. Excavators scraped and gouged at the earth. The COMAKAT official led me deeper into the mine past several large digging areas toward the primary excavation zone. I was expecting to see something similar to Kipushi or perhaps Tocotens. I thought perhaps there would be two or three thousand artisanal miners at most, digging in trenches and stuffing sacks. As we rounded a broad ridge and the main pit revealed itself, the scene hit like a thunderclap. In all my time in the Congo, I never saw anything like it.

An explosion of human beings was crammed inside the enormous digging pit, which was at least 150 meters deep and 400 meters across. More than fifteen thousand men and teenage boys were hammering, shoveling, and shouting inside the crater, with scarcely room to move or breathe. None of the workers wore an inch of protective gear—just shorts, trousers, flip-flops, and maybe some shirts. It was a storm of colors—red, blue, green, yellow, and orange melded inside the pink-stone pit. At least five thousand raffia sacks filled with ore were stacked at the edge of the excavation area, a growing tally from that morning's production alone. The pit was not dirt and stone—it was a solid mountain of rock and heterogenite being chiseled and hammered into pebbles by raw human force.

The COMAKAT official led me into the pit along a narrow path of jagged rock. Men and boys walking up the other way with stuffed raffia sacks draped over their shoulders like a human cargo train were instructed to clear the way for our descent. The soles of my sneakers tore off by the end of my time at Shabara, but many of the artisanal miners were barefoot. As we descended into the pit, I was able to make out that the diggers were organized in groups of five to ten people each. Some groups jammed thick stretches of rebar into a crack in the mountain and hammered it with large metal mallets to break off a boulder-size chunk of rock. Other groups used smaller bits of rebar and mallets to break down the boulders into stones and pebbles. Other groups of mostly younger boys loaded the pebbles into the sacks. In dozens of areas around the pit, artisanal miners descended and emerged from tunnels. Some of them teetered high above the pit, like an ibex perched on a mountain face.

I was unable to ask questions of the COMAKAT official inside the pit amid the thunderous clanking of metal on stone. I could only observe as this sea of humanity matched brute force against the unforgiving rock. Dust and grit rose from the earth like smoke from a wildfire. It was impossible to fathom how a spectacle such as this could exist in the twenty-first century. One might imagine such a scene millennia ago, perhaps as tens of thousands of oppressed laborers in Egypt excavated thousands of tons of stone to build the great pyramids . . . but at the bottom of trillion-dollar supply chains during the modern era? This could not be what adherence to international human rights norms or 100 percent participation in third-party audits with cobalt suppliers was supposed to look like.

A fight broke out nearby to where I was standing. The COMAKAT official blew a whistle tied around his neck and charged toward the fracas. Tempers were sure to flare inside the suffocating pit as the artisanal miners pushed themselves to the limits under the searing sun. While the COMAKAT official dealt with the brawl, I locked eyes with some of the nearby workers. Some gazed back curiously, others defensively, and some looked right through me as if I were just another chunk of stone in the dirt. The COMAKAT official eventually returned and led me out of the pit. As we ascended, the detonation of sound receded, and I felt as if I could finally breathe again.

I continued on the walking tour through the Shabara mine with the COMAKAT official. My mind was buzzing with questions, but I did not know how much more time I would have, so I tried to determine which were the most important ones to ask. The first was about wages.

"We pay the artisanals between four and five dollars a day depending on what tasks they do," the COMAKAT official responded. This was the highest average daily income of any artisanal miners that I documented anywhere in the Copper Belt, aside from the tunnel diggers in the Kasulo neighborhood of Kolwezi.

"How much ore does this mine produce?" I asked.

"We produce between fifteen thousand and seventeen thousand tons of ore each month," the official said.

It was a staggering sum. I asked who bought all the production.

"We have contracts with the Chinese," the official replied.

According to the COMAKAT official, Glencore did not buy any of the production from Shabara because they were at loggerheads over the presence of artisanal miners on the concession. Instead, I was told that many of the major Chinese mining companies operating in the Copper Belt bought the production. Who else could absorb fifteen thousand tons of heterogenite per month? The official explained that their agreements with the Chinese buyers stipulated that COMAKAT kept 20 percent of the sale price, which they used to cover operating expenses. There was bound to be quite a bit of profit left over for the owners of the cooperative.

After a two-hour tour, we returned to the COMAKAT office near the entrance of the mine, at which point the official who gave me the tour made it clear why I had been allowed to visit the site.

"The foreign mining companies leave no place for Congolese people to work. We have lived on this land for so long. We will not leave," he declared.

The official said he was aware that I was a researcher from America, and he wanted me to help raise awareness of the plight being faced by the artisanal miners who worked at Shabara and across the Copper Belt. He echoed the sentiments of Makaza near Étoile, Samy in Fungurume, and so many others I met—the Congolese people were being pushed over the cliff's edge by foreign mining companies that kept appropriating more of their land each year. The COMAKAT official drew a line in the dirt with his declaration, "We will not leave," but the issue was not as simple as pitting artisanal miners against foreign mining companies. The Congolese government directly contributed to the crisis by auctioning off massive parcels of land for billions of dollars and passively sitting back to collect concession fees, royalties, and taxes. Very little of these funds were being redistributed for the benefit of the Congolese people. So long as the political elite were content to continue the tradition of government-as-theft established by their colonial antecedents, the people of the Congo would continue to suffer.

Based on what I saw at Shabara, COMAKAT was managing an astounding artisanal mining operation on part of Glencore's Mutanda concession that was producing roughly 180,000 tons of copper-cobalt ore per year. Considering that it was just one of the many industrial mining sites in which artisanal mining was the dominant mode of production, two facts seemed indisputable: 1) the artisanal contribution of total cobalt production in the Congo could easily exceed even the highest estimates of 30 percent, and 2) the massive amount of artisanal production from the Congo had to flow into the formal supply chains of big tech and EV companies. Where else could 180,000 tons per year of cobalt ore possibly go?

Shabara was just the beginning. There were several more industrial mines in Lualaba Province where artisanal production was the norm. Although Shabara was the only one I managed to investigate directly, I took testimonies from dozens of people who worked at the others. Perhaps none was more dreadful than Tilwezembe.

TILWEZEMBE

West of Shabara, the road pushes deeper into the fringes of a grim waste-land. Villages recede from the roadside into a vaguely discernable land-scape choked by haze. The smog that was once heavy and obscuring near Lubumbashi has become stifling and oppressive. All seems darker here. The path forward is no longer clear. Whatever semblance of life existed up to this point vanishes entirely when we reach Tilwezembe.

Tilwezembe is a smaller mining site than many of the industrial copper-cobalt concessions in Lualaba Province, but it plays an outsize role in the violent and degrading nature of mining in the Congo. Based on ev-erything I have seen and heard, Tilwezembe is the largest industrial site at which almost nothing but artisanal production takes place. The con-cession is located a few kilometers west of Mutanda and just under two kilometers south of the highway down a dirt road near the village of Mupanja. Mupanja is located near the end of the Lualaba River, which flows more than three thousand kilometers in a bold arc across the heart of the African continent before emptying in the Atlantic. Henry Morton Stanley started his epic journey down the Congo River about one thou-sand kilometers due north of Mupanja. The Belgians built a hydroelec-tric dam next to Mupanja in 1953 to provide power to UMHK's copper mines in the area. The dam formed a lake, which the Belgians named Lac Delcommune after Alexandre Delcommune, who led the first Bel-gian campaign in 1891 into Katanga to try to sign a treaty with Msiri on behalf of King Leopold. He was also the first person to greet a battered Stanley when he finally reached Boma in 1877 after tracing the Congo River. After independence, the Congolese renamed Lac Delcommune to Lac Nzilo ("Young Lake").

In addition to providing hydroelectric power to the mines, the river is also a source of fish and fresh water for local communities. *Fresh,* how-ever, is not the correct word—the water is heavily polluted, a condition that local residents attribute to toxic runoff from nearby mines. The

environmental researcher at the University of Lubumbashi whom I met after my visit to Kipushi, Germain, took samples from the river water near
Mupanja and found particularly high levels of lead, chromium, cobalt,
and industrial acids. When I inspected the water, it had an unnaturally
dark color and was topped with slicks and sludge. There were a few areas
of bubbly foam collected along the riverbank, in addition to scatterings
of dead fish. I recalled the words of Reine, the student in Lubumbashi,
who said that my heart would cry when I saw what the mining companies had done to the forests and rivers. I felt both sadness and outrage as
I watched children splashing innocently in the toxic waters. Men fished
for dinner from the bridge above the river, and women washed clothes
along the riverbank as white-breasted cormorants floated by. The people
of Mupanja were being contaminated in every possible way.

Mupanja is a bustling roadside village. It has numerous shops selling
clothes and shoes, pots and pans, charcoal, bushmeat, and the morning's catch. FARDC soldiers patrol the area and leer at young women.
Despite being located right next to a hydroelectric dam, the village does
not have reliable electricity. Most of the homes are redbrick with metal
roofs. Bedsheets are used as front doors, except at one home where I saw
an American flag being used. Village girls walk to and fro with plastic
containers of water balanced on their heads, while others smash large
wooden pestles into mortars to crush cassava leaves that will be boiled
for dinner. Children catch insects inside empty liquor bottles. Plastic bottles, cardboard boxes, and other trash are strewn across the dirt paths
between the homes. When the piles get too big, they are burned, releas-
ing a foul stench into the air.

A local fisherman named Modeste, who had lived in Mupanja for many
years, spoke about the changes he had seen since cobalt took over. "Ten
years ago it was a peaceful village. Now people come from all places to
dig cobalt . . . There is too much alcohol and prostitution in the village . . .
There are always soldiers here . . . People kill each other for cobalt."

Violence had become an increasingly serious problem in Mupanja in recent years. No one I approached felt comfortable offering details about specific incidents, but many people nodded when I asked whether the FARDC soldiers were responsible. Alcohol was the village's second major problem. Men drank heavily before and after work at Tilwezembe, which inevitably led to more violence. The third major challenge faced by the residents of Mupanja was flooding. During the stormy season, water from the river pushed inland and often swamped parts of the village. Repairing or rebuilding homes was an annual ordeal for the residents. Many simply abandoned their huts after the roofs were ripped off in a storm, leaving the exposed brick walls behind for the next family that deigned to live here.

Tilwezembe is owned by Glencore via its 100 percent ownership of Canada-based Katanga Mining, which in turn owns a 75 percent stake in Tilwezembe (Gécamines owns the other 25 percent). The mine is roughly eleven square kilometers in size and has deposits of several hundred thousand tons of copper and cobalt. Perhaps the most important thing to know about Tilwezembe is that industrial operations were formally ceased at the mine in 2008. Not long after, artisanal mining took over.

Tilwezembe has one of the most well-developed artisanal mining operations of any industrial mining site in the DRC, even though there is not supposed to be any artisanal mining taking place at the site. Tales of child labor at Tilwezembe date back many years. The BBC ran an episode of its documentary series *Panorama* on April 15, 2012, that focused on Glencore's role in child labor at Tilwezembe.[5] Both Glencore and the Congolese government dismissed the story as an exaggeration. The truth, however, is that the system of artisanal mining at the site has evolved into a sophisticated economy that appears to include two of the largest artisanal mining cooperatives in Lualaba Province, as well as officials working for SAEMAPE. I had to rely on testimonies regarding the conditions at Tilwezembe, as I was denied entry to the mine on two occasions by FARDC soldiers. The first time, I did not even make it past the head of the dirt road in Mupanja. I made a second attempt after documenting the cases of numerous individuals who were injured while working at the site, and that time I made it much closer.

One of the most informative interviews I conducted was with a soft-spoken, sixteen-year-old boy named Phelix. Phelix began digging at Tilwezembe in 2015. He was the second oldest of seven children and one of three siblings who dug at the mine. His father died when he was eleven, leaving his mother to raise all seven children on her own. Phelix had a thick scar down the right side of his head over which his hair was missing. He said that the scar was caused when a large rock fell on his head while he was working at Tilwezembe. After recovering at home, he returned to work because the family needed every dollar the children could earn. Phelix said he left home to work at Tilwezembe at dawn every morning and typically returned home by sunset. He reported chronic exhaustion and suffered from a nagging cough. Two of the fingers on his left hand were broken and permanently crooked at the middle knuckles. This was how Phelix described the system at the mine:

> What you must understand is that CMKK and COMIKU control most of the *creuseurs* at Tilwezembe. The cooperatives control different parts of the concession. I work in the CMKK area. There are also independent bosses who pay CMKK or COMIKU to exploit other parts of the concession.
>
> I am not registered with CMKK because to get the *carte d'enregistrement* [registration card] you must be eighteen years old. The *creuseurs* like me who are not registered must pay a fee each day of CF 200 [about $0.11] to the cooperatives to dig at Tilwezembe.
>
> There are officials from SAESSCAM who come to the site. Whenever we see them, we become anxious because we know they will find some way to take money from us.
>
> We work in groups in different areas of the mine. I am in a group of twenty boys. The younger boys dig in the pits. The older boys dig in the tunnels . . . Everything we dig we sell to the bosses. The bosses are Chi-

nese and also Congolese and Lebanese . . . My boss controls my work at the mine. He tells us where to dig, and he pays us. If we do not listen to the boss, he will tell the soldiers to punish us.

No matter how much we dig, we never earn more than CF 4,000 [about $2.20]. After my boss buys the cobalt, he sells it to CMKK. They have a truck on the concession. We load the sacks on this truck.

CMKK and COMIKU are the two largest artisanal mining cooperatives in Lualaba Province. COMIKU is owned by Yves Muyej, one of the sons of the first governor of Lualaba Province, Richard Muyej. The Muyejes are loyal allies of Joseph Kabila and, like him, have strong ties to Chinese mining companies. CMKK is owned by officials in Joseph Kabila's inner circle and was initially set up by a now-deceased Colonel Ilunga. Copper-cobalt ore sold up the chain by CMKK and COMIKU is supposed to include assurances that artisanal miners are paid reasonable wages, provided safety equipment, and offered medical care if injured. The ore is also supposed to come with assurances that there were no children involved in the mining and that only registered artisanal miners approved by CMKK and COMIKU work at the site.

Several artisanal miners I interviewed confirmed Phelix's statement that many of the diggers at Tilwezembe were not registered with either CMKK or COMIKU even though they worked at the mine, and that their bosses sold the ore they excavated to the cooperatives. They also confirmed the presence of SAEMAPE officials, and they stated that there were between one and two thousand children digging at Tilwezembe on any given day. They reported that children were typically paid roughly two dollars a day regardless of production and that they received little to no assistance when they suffered injuries. The diggers at Tilwezembe described hazardous conditions and harsh reprisals if they did not obey their bosses. Some were locked inside a shipping container called a *cachot* ("dungeon") without food or water for up to two days.

From a range of testimonies, the economics of the artisanal mining system at Tilwezembe appeared to work in the following way: If a boss paid the children who worked for him about $1.10 per sack of heterogenite that weighed thirty kilograms, he would sell each sack to the cooperatives for $7 or $8, earning him roughly $6 or $7 in profit per sack. From this point forward the value chain became murky, as there was very little transparency as to the pricing of cobalt up the chain until it reached the London Metal Exchange (LME), which sets the global market price for fully refined cobalt. What I was able to piece together is that most mining cooperatives (and depots) on average sold ore with a 2 or 3 percent grade of cobalt to industrial mining companies in the DRC for a price that was roughly 15–20 percent of the price of refined cobalt on the LME. Hence, if a kilogram of refined cobalt on the LME sold for $60, then cooperatives would sell cobalt-containing ore for $9–$12 per kilogram. Bearing in mind that they probably bought thirty kilograms of said ore for $8, the cooperatives emerged from the system as massive profit-generating businesses. These profits largely went into the pockets of their owners, who tended to be business leaders or government officials.

Colleagues in Kolwezi, as well as the artisanal miners I interviewed who worked at Tilwezembe, agreed that the major buyers of cobalt from Tilwezembe included the following mining companies: Congo Dong-Fang Mining (Huayou Cobalt), Kamoto Copper Company (Glencore), COMMUS (Zijin Mining), and CHEMAF (Shalina Resources). These four companies were described locally as buyers of heterogenite *à-tout-venant* ("from all sellers"), which suggested that they did not discriminate as to how and from whom they purchased ore. It was challenging to verify these reports through on-the-ground supply chain tracing. Waiting within eyeshot of the entrance of Tilwezembe for trucks to load and depart was not possible due to the presence of armed FARDC soldiers. For the same reason, hovering too close or too long near the head of the dirt road that led to the mine near Mupanja proved impossible. I was, however, able to determine that the cooperatives loaded the ore into trucks inside the site and transported it to the mining companies or their processing facilities.

Of all the artisanal miners I met in the mining provinces of the DRC, those who worked at Tilwezembe were among the most reluctant to speak. The mere suggestion of discussing the mine caused trepidation in most of the people I approached. Tilwezembe's secrets were not to be revealed. I was told more than once that I was probably a spy working on behalf of the cooperatives to ascertain who would speak. Others suggested that I was a foreign journalist who would expose them for speaking out, which would result in violent reprisals. "The Republican Guard watches everything in Lualaba Province," I was told by a colleague in Kolwezi. "They monitor the villages, and they intimidate anyone who tries to speak. When I say that, what I mean to tell you is if someone who works at Tilwezembe or Lac Malo or Kasulo speaks to someone like you, they will be shot in the night, and their body will be left on the street to instruct anyone else on the consequences of opening their mouths."

Campaigns of violence and intimidation work up to a point, and the point at which they no longer work is the moment a person feels they have nothing left to lose. For those from whom everything has already been taken, even the harshest penalty means little compared to the power of speaking . . . or for speaking on behalf of those who can no longer speak. Coordinating with a local team that was familiar with the communities that worked in Tilwezembe, I was able to identify seventeen people, including Phelix, from a handful of villages who were willing to discuss their work at the mine. We made careful arrangements to protect the identities of the informants—we transported them from their villages before dawn, arranged a safe location to meet beyond prying eyes, kept them in that location until late at night or early the next morning, then returned them home. The interviews were held in a guesthouse several kilometers outside of Kolwezi. The owner was known and trusted by my colleagues.

The interview room at the guesthouse consisted of a small wooden table with white plastic chairs. A fifteen-year-old boy named Muteba arrived first, accompanied by his mother, Delphine. He struggled into the room with the assistance of crutches. Two mangled legs dangled from his narrow waist. He wore a faded red shirt and a pair of frayed black trousers, and he was barefoot. His face was scrunched in an expression of distaste, as if something sour was stuck in his mouth. Muteba sat on one of the plastic chairs across the table. I offered a second chair on which he could prop his infirm legs. Words emerged from his mouth in short bursts and erratic puffs of air.

"I went to school until the fourth year. At that time, my family could not pay the fees. My older brother, Beko, was already working at Tilwezembe. It was in January of 2016 when I started working there. I worked for Boss Chu. Every morning, I said his name to the soldiers at the entrance, and they permitted me into the mine. Boss Chu would give us tags with numbers that tell us which pit to dig in."

I asked Muteba how many people worked for Boss Chu.

"At least forty."

"Were they all children?"

"Yes."

Muteba said that most of the children working for Boss Chu were between the ages of ten and thirteen. They were not yet strong enough to dig tunnels, so they dug at the surface in different areas each day. Muteba said he typically earned around one dollar a day.

"Boss Chu paid us based on the purity of the ore. Some days, if the purity was not good, he did not pay us anything."

"Who decided the purity was not good?"

"Boss Chu."

The night of May 6, 2019, Muteba did not sleep well. There was an ailing dog in the village that howled loudly. The other members of his family slept through the disturbance, but Muteba was a light sleeper, and something about the whimpering animal distressed him. He rose from his hut and went outside into the darkness to search for the dog. He found it huddled meekly next to some bushes at the outskirts of the village.

"Something attacked that dog. Its leg and face were bleeding. It looked at me very sadly. I think it wanted me to end its suffering, but I was afraid."

The next morning, Muteba went to work at Tilwezembe as usual. As he described the events of that day, he turned inward and spoke softly. "I was digging inside a pit with my brother, Beko. There were three other groups digging in that same pit. I heard something like a rumble sound. When I looked up, the pit [wall] collapsed around us . . ."

Muteba stopped speaking, and his eyes moistened. His voice cracked, and he struggled to continue. "I was buried under the stones. I could not move. I tried to scream, but I could hardly breathe. I thought I would choke. In my chest, I could feel my heart was going to explode." After another pause, Muteba added, "After some minutes, I heard shouting. I thank God someone found me. I remember seeing his eyes. They were so big. Some people pulled me out. When I saw my legs, the bones were sticking out of my skin."

At this point, Muteba stared at the peeling plaster on the wall. He wiped his eyes and steadied his breathing.

"After the accident, some men from SAESSCAM took me to the Gé-camines hospital in Kolwezi. The bones in my legs were crushed. The doctors tried to make the bones straight. They did a surgery and put a metal bar in both my legs," Muteba said.

I asked Muteba's mother how they afforded the surgical procedure.

"SAESSCAM paid for this, but after one week, they said they could not pay for more treatment," Delphine replied.

I asked Muteba what happened to his brother.

"Beko was killed. Everyone else was killed when the wall collapsed. I was the only one who survived."

Delphine said that when Beko died in the accident at Tilwezembe, his eighteen-year-old wife was pregnant with their first child. A few months later, she gave birth to a baby girl. With Beko gone and Muteba unable to work, the family was struggling to make it from one day to the next.

"Now I know what that dog felt like," Muteba said. "I wish I had been brave enough to kill it."

The cases of the other artisanal miners who came to speak about their work at Tilwezembe were eerily similar to Muteba's. They were also consistent in how they described the system at the mine. They reported that up to ten thousand people toiled at Tilwezembe on any given day. They also de-scribed a well-honed system that involved bosses, cooperatives, FARDC, and foreign mining companies—each snatching their chunk of value as they pushed cobalt up the chain. Underneath this massive empire, something dark emerged . . . something I had scarcely heard of before. It did not exist at Kipushi. I managed only a scant glance at the village Arthur showed me. A few artisanal miners mentioned it in passing at Tenke Fungurume. I saw glimpses of it at Shabara. However, at Tilwezembe it was the norm:

Tunnels.

Hundreds of tunnels, perhaps over a thousand. At this last stop before Kolwezi, the richest deposits of cobalt were located deeper underground, like the raisins in the cake Dr. Murray Hitzman described, and they could only be accessed by digging tunnels. The bleak consequences of tunnel digging were revealed to me by a child named Kosongo and his mother, Hugotte.

Kosongo started digging at Tilwezembe in 2015 at age eleven. He dug at the surface in a group of six boys around the same age. A man named Chief Banza was in charge of the group. Kosongo said that he worked in an area of the mine controlled by the CMKK cooperative. Chief Banza directed the children where to dig, and he paid them around one dollar a day. According to the children, Chief Banza sold their production to CMKK. In November 2018, Chief Banza told Kosongo's group that they were strong enough to start digging tunnels. Kosongo was fourteen at the time. The move to tunnel digging came with a shift in the relationship between Chief Banza and the children. Kosongo explained:

The best cobalt is maybe twenty or thirty meters under the ground . . . The ground is very hard at Tilwezembe, so it takes a long time to dig [tunnels] . . . It required two months for us to find the cobalt. By that time, the tunnel was twenty meters deep.

As we were digging this tunnel, we did not earn any money because there was no cobalt. Chief Banza gave us food and CF 2,000 [about $1.10] each day while we were digging. Once we found the cobalt, he said we must pay him back from the cobalt we removed from the tunnel. If we did not agree, we were not allowed to work at Tilwezembe.

As an additional threat, Chief Banza told the children that if they tried to work anywhere else, he would send soldiers to their homes and take the money they owed to him from their families. Kosongo said that Chief Banza was known to be a dangerous man, so he felt he had no choice but to work for him under this new arrangement. Some days, Kosongo was paid around a dollar; some days, he was paid nothing.

The children in Kosongo's group had no bargaining power in their arrangement with Chief Banza, nor did they have any alternative sources of income to support their families. They had accrued a large debt to Banza and toiled under the menace of a penalty that soldiers would extort their families unless they complied with his directives, amounting to a textbook definition of forced labor under international law.[6] To make matters worse, the children said that Chief Banza never offered any sort of accounting of the value of the heterogenite he sold to CMKK, which should have been credited against the debts they owed him. Even though heterogenite deposits deeper underground can have more than five times a higher grade of cobalt as deposits at the surface, Kosongo's income did not change from the time he was a surface digger to the time he was a tunnel digger, presumably because he was repaying the debt he accrued across two months. In addition to forced labor in hazardous conditions, the children were also being exploited in a system of debt bondage—an economic advance was being used to extract forced labor from them, and the debt was not being discharged based on a fair market value of the output of their labor. Threats of violence, eviction from the work site, and the lack of any reasonable alternative kept the children ensnared in the system of bondage. In essence, they were child slaves.

Kosongo drew the shape of the tunnel on a piece of paper. The diameter of the main shaft was about one meter. "We press our hands and feet against the wall to climb down the shaft," he explained. At the bottom of the main shaft, the boys dug out a chamber where they gathered sacks of heterogenite to be pulled to the surface with a rope made from torn raffia sacks. The chamber was about one and a half meters tall and two meters wide. Moving out from the chamber, they dug a tunnel parallel to the surface that followed the heterogenite vein they had discovered.

The tunnel was only tall enough for them to shimmy through on their stomachs. The only source of light was from a small battery-powered flashlight fastened to their heads with a headband. Kosongo said they used pickaxes to knock the heterogenite from the tunnel wall, which they piled into raffia sacks.

"It is very hot in the tunnel. There is a lot of dust. It is difficult to breathe," Kosongo explained.

Once they filled a sack with heterogenite, the children dragged it back to the chamber at the bottom of the main shaft.

"Chief Banza drops a rope. We tie it to the sack, and he pulls it to the top."

Kosongo reported that the children typically remained underground for the full day, after which Chief Banza pulled them up one at a time using the same rope he used to pull up the cobalt sacks.

On March 20, 2019, Kosongo and the children in his group gathered in the chamber at the end of the day to begin their ascent to the surface. Kosongo was at the back of the group, lying on his stomach at the junction of the tunnel and the main chamber: "I heard a sound above my head. When I looked up, there was a crack in the ceiling. I tried to crawl into the chamber, but the ceiling fell on my legs. I thought the entire tunnel would fall and we would die." Kosongo said the other children in the chamber pushed the stones off his legs, and Chief Banza pulled him out. Kosongo reported that two men from SAESSCAM drove him to the Gécamines hospital in Kolwezi. "My legs were like fire," he said. "I became unconscious." The collapse of the side tunnel at the junction of the main chamber caused multiple fractures in both of Kosongo's legs. The legs were beyond repair and had to be amputated above the knees. Hugotte said that after a brief period of care following the surgery at the Gécamines hospital in Kolwezi, they received no further support. I asked her who paid for the surgery, and she said it was SAESSCAM (SAEMAPE). Following the amputation, Kosongo grew increasingly depressed and dejected.

"Why was I the only one injured?" he wondered.

Kosongo pulled up his shorts and showed me the stubs that remained of his legs. His eyes moistened, and his lips began to quiver. He placed his hands atop his thighs, yearning for what was missing.

"I used to play football [soccer] every Sunday. I was very good."

After several days of interviews with those who worked or whose children worked at Tilwezembe, I was sure I had seen every expression of human pain. The most heartbreaking faces belonged to the parents who said they lost a child to the mine. One case stands for many. The father's name is Tshite. He sat across from me, face quaking with tremors of rage, sorrow, and guilt. He told me about Lubo, his firstborn child. Tshite adored Lubo ever since the day he was born. The child was his great gift and hope. He promised Lubo he would do whatever it took to ensure he had a better life than he did. Tshite struggled through painful emotions as he described what happened:

> I worked so hard at Tilwezembe to earn money to send Lubo to school. I told him, "I want you to work with your mind, not with your hands." Every day, I came home from Tilwezembe my body was in pain. My head and my neck hurt so badly. The skin on my feet was bleeding. My hands were covered in blisters. I had blisters inside my mouth. My chest was always burning inside. I was coughing all the time.

Tshite said that no matter how much pain he felt or how sick he became, he never stopped working for even one day. He wanted Lubo to stay in school.

One day, Tshite suffered an accident at Tilwezembe that stopped him from working. His right arm was broken in a pit wall collapse. Tshite did not know what to do. "Lubo came to me and said, 'Do not worry, Papa, I will work.' I told him, 'No! You must stay in school. If you leave school, you will never go back.' I told him we would discover some other way. Lubo said it would make him proud to help me. He said he would go back to school as soon as I could work again."

Tshite laid out the events that followed:

Lubo went to work at Tilwezembe. His boss was a Lebanese man named Arran. Arran had more than two hundred boys working for him. He is the biggest boss at Tilwezembe. He told Lubo he must dig the tunnel. I did not want Lubo to do this because I know what can happen, but Arran said if he did not dig the tunnel he could not work at the mine.

Lubo worked at Tilwezembe digging the tunnel for more than one month. Every day I prayed that he would return home safe. My arm was almost better. I thought in a few days I will be able to work again and Lubo can return to school.

On January 18 [2019], Lubo did not come home from Tilwezembe. I ran to the mine. When I arrived, other parents were already there. Everyone was shouting, "Where is my son? Give me my son!" The soldiers pushed their guns in our faces and forced us to return home. I was going crazy. I wanted to know what happened to Lubo! I walked up and down the road. I went back to the mine and pleaded with the soldiers, "Please let me find my son," but they beat me and kicked me.

I stayed in the trees near the mine all night, and I went back in the morning. All the parents came back. There was so much shouting. The soldiers said they would shoot us. Then an official from CMKK came to the mine in a jeep. He told us to keep quiet and he will explain what happened. He said a tunnel had collapsed the previous day. He said no one survived.

In the coming days, Tshite and his wife heard reports that at least forty children had been underground when the tunnel collapsed at Tilwezembe. Other artisanal miners at the site were given the unbearable task of attempting to dig out some of the bodies. They managed to retrieve seventeen, one of whom was Lubo.

"I held my son's dead body. I begged him to come back," Tshite said.

Tshite reported that SAEMAPE provided a coffin for Lubo and that CMKK gave him money for a funeral. When I met Tshite, he was tormented by feelings of guilt that his broken arm cost Lubo his life. He said that it would have been another week at most before he could have returned to work, and Lubo could have returned to school.

"I miss Lubo so much. He was my best friend."

Tshite was not the only one. Six more parents told me that their sons had been buried alive in tunnel collapses at Tilwezembe. The collapses they described all took place between May 2018 and July 2019. According to the parents, five of the seven children who were buried alive in tunnel collapses at Tilwezembe worked for Arran. Arran is the same man I previously mentioned as being linked to uranium smuggling from Shinkolobwe.

I followed the rumors of uranium smuggling in search of evidence, and for almost two years, I was only able to find more rumors, until the summer of 2021, when I managed to get my hands on a copy of the judgment of the High Court of Lubumbashi relating to the case. Based on the contents of the judgment and the testimonies of a few colleagues in the DRC, it appears that in January of 2016, thirty cargo trucks registered to a Chinese mining company called Dragon International Mining arrived at the border crossing with Zambia at Kasumbalesa, not far from Kipushi. Paperwork on the trucks indicated that they were hauling copper and cobalt to Dar es Salaam for export to China. Border guards at Kasumbalesa were supplied with Geiger counters, which they were supposed to use to check for uranium, but rarely did so. On this day, a diligent border guard felt something was amiss and took his Geiger counter to the trucks. The machine started crackling loudly. Twenty-two of the trucks had hidden compartments filled with raw uranium ore.

U.S. intelligence agencies leaped into action to assist the Congolese government with the investigation. They traced the operation back to a Lebanese smuggler named Arran and determined that the uranium was headed for North Korea. There were also reports of North Korean operatives on the ground in the DRC assisting with the deal.

"From a U.S. perspective, we are concerned about the North Koreans and what they are doing in the Congo," U.S. ambassador Mike Hammer explained. "If there are North Koreans here, one has to be on the lookout for any nefarious activity."

Arran was tried in February of 2016 before the Lubumbashi High Court. He was sentenced to five years in prison and ordered to pay a fine of $1 million. He was also sentenced to be expelled from the DRC after serving his prison sentence. Arran was out of prison after a few months, and he remained in the country.

What is not discussed in the court documents but is accepted as fact by everyone with whom I spoke is that a uranium-smuggling operation between the DRC and North Korea could only have been brokered and authorized by Joseph Kabila and that Kabila handpicked Arran to handle the operation.

"There is no question Kabila knew about it," a Western diplomat advised on condition of anonymity. "It is hard to imagine that Kabila didn't have his fingers all over it or personally benefited from it."

The same diplomat speculated that it was likely that Joseph Kabila had Arran released from prison early and put him back in business, which included running a child slave–mining operation at Tilwezembe that was responsible for the deaths of children like Lubo.

By all accounts, Tilwezembe is perhaps the most dangerous industrial mining site in the Copper Belt and home to more child labor than any formal mine in the Congo. The final tally of my interviews was this— twelve men and boys grievously injured and seven children buried alive at Tilwezembe. These cases represented the scant few who were prepared to speak with me during just one of my research trips. Even with only a fraction of the picture, it seemed evident that Tilwezembe was not just a copper-cobalt mine, it was a killing field.

It is tempting to point the finger at local actors as the agents of the carnage—be it corrupt politicians, exploitative cooperatives, unhinged soldiers, or extortionist bosses. They all played their roles, but they were also symptoms of a more malevolent disease: the global economy run amok in Africa. The depravity and indifference unleashed on the children working at Tilwezembe is a direct consequence of a global economic order that preys on the poverty, vulnerability, and devalued humanity of the people who toil at the bottom of global supply chains. Declarations by multinational corporations that the rights and dignity of every worker in their supply chains are protected and preserved seem more disingenuous than ever.

The translator for my interviews, Augustin, was distraught after several days of trying to find the words in English that captured the grief being described in Swahili. He would at times drop his head and sob before attempting to translate what was said. As we parted ways, Augustin had this to say, "Please tell the people in your country, a child in the Congo dies every day so that they can plug in their phones."

Two years after my interviews with the families who suffered at the hands of Tilwezembe, I made a second attempt to enter the mine. I was guided by a Mupanja local along a route to avoid FARDC detection before joining the dirt path that led to the concession. Even from more than a kilometer away, the titanic walls of the mine were imposing. We walked southward on the path through the village and reached an area where the brick huts were more sparsely laid out. Children played with plastic bags near small trash fires. Clothes hung to dry on sagging strings. A girl in a sunbright yellow dress followed her mother up the path as they balanced plastic containers of water on their heads. Motorbikes mowed up and down the dirt road, each loaded with two or three passengers.

A young mother caught my eye. She was sitting on the ground with an infant tucked in her lap. There was an aqua-blue-painted hair salon behind her. The words TOUT VIENT DE DIEU were painted in red above the entrance. Everything comes from God. The baby wore a cloth diaper, and the mother wore a light purple dress. Her open hair flowed gently down her shoulders. I watched as the mother rocked back and forth with her baby in her arms. Each time she rocked forward, she nuzzled her baby's face, and the infant giggled gleefully. She rocked back, her eyes widened with anticipation, and she rocked forward again to nuzzle the exuberant child. Back and forth they went, mother and child, blissful and aglow.

I continued down the dirt path, past the village, and into a forest. I walked by a small lake, after which the path began to ascend toward the foothills of the mine. A fuel truck motored along a second dirt road that led toward Tilwezembe from the east. Two excavators scraped at the dirt atop one of the hills. Motorbikes raced in both directions. At closer inspection, I saw that the drivers were all wearing neon vests. The passengers heading away from the mine were covered in dirt. I lost count of how many looked like teenage boys.

As the path continued southward, the angle of ascent sharpened. I eventually arrived at the security checkpoint at the entrance of Tilwezembe. From the base of the mine, the colossal pit walls swallowed the sky. The checkpoint consisted of a large shipping container to the east of the path, and an FARDC station with two uniformed soldiers packing Kalishnikovs to the west. The path was blocked by a long metal pole atop a hinge. There was just enough room at the end of the pole for the motorbikes to pass through. I asked the FARDC soldiers if I could enter the mine, but they refused.

One of the motorbike drivers was idling at the entrance. He wore the same neon vest as the others. The number *31* was stitched on the back of his vest. He said his name was John, and he explained that he was an authorized transporter for workers at Tilwezembe. That is what the numbers on the vests meant. He was transporter number 31. I asked him how many runs he made each day. "Maybe twenty," he said.

John headed back to Mupanja to ferry the next batch of diggers. I lingered at the foothills of the mine a little longer, taking in this monument to pain. There was a moment when the motorbikes stopped and all was quiet. In that enormous silence, my thoughts turned to them—the countless children like Lubo buried alive at Tilwezembe, forever crushed in the cold earth on the other side of that pit wall.

Although no one will ever know how many children are buried at Tilwezembe, this much is certain—as of November 1, 2021, Tilwezembe is a fully functioning mine, and hundreds of children can be seen entering it each and every day.

6

"We Work in Our Graves"

Kolwezi

The thirst for money transforms men into assassins . . . All means are good to obtain money or humiliate the human being.
—Archbishop Eugène Kabanga Songasonga of Lubumbashi, 1976

THE ROAD HAS COME to an end. We arrive at last at the beating heart of the world's device-driven economy and EV revolution: Kolwezi. There is no other city like it. Kolwezi is a Wild West frontier, home to roughly one-fourth of the world's cobalt reserves. The city's extraordinary mineral endowment has resulted in considerable environmental destruction due to the rapid expansion of mining operations. Look up Kolwezi on Google Earth and zoom in. See the colossal craters, the behemoth open-pit mines, and the immense swaths of dirt. Small artificial lakes provide water to the mining operations, not to the city's inhabitants. Villages have been flattened. Forests have been razed. The earth has been gouged and gashed. Mines swallow all.

Migrants flock to Kolwezi by the thousands each year. They come from neighboring provinces, nearby countries, and as far away as China and India. The migrants are drawn into a vortex of minerals and money from which there is little escape. There is more misery-for-profit in Kolwezi than perhaps any other city in the world. Official estimates of the population of Kolwezi are around 600,000, but the true number is closer to 1.5 million. The city has been stretched beyond its limits. Ramshackle slums and makeshift villages spread out from the city center into the ever-decreasing habitable space. Mines occupy at least 80 percent of the developed land in Kolwezi. The green is gone. Arable earth is extinct. Time-lapse satellite images of Kolwezi from 2012 to 2022 show that the "brown" around the city spread like a tsunami, devouring everything in its path. Kolwezi is the mangled face of progress in Africa. The hunt for cobalt is all.

The road to Kolwezi enters from the east, past chemical factories and worker compounds, into the city center. The central business district contains a dense concentration of shops, markets, churches, hotels, and guesthouses. Trucks, motorbikes, excavators, heavy haulers, and artisanal miners crowd the potholed streets. Kolwezi is by far the most heavily polluted city in the southeastern provinces. Breathing hurts. Looking burns. Even the old colonial neighborhood is crumbling here. Stand almost anywhere in Kolwezi, and there will be a mine in every direction.

To the north of the city center is a neighborhood called Kasulo. It is one of the largest artisanal mining areas in the Congo and ground zero for tunnel digging. Satellite imagery from 2012 compared to 2022 shows an explosion of thousands of dark circles and pink tarps—each one is a tunnel. The cobalt deposits in Kasulo are so rich that Congo DongFang Mining walled off part of the neighborhood in 2018 to run a model site for artisanal mining. Northeast of Kasulo is the second model site, called Mutoshi, run by CHEMAF, the same mining company that operates the Étoile mine near Lubumbashi. We will visit both "model sites" and put the term to the test.

Southwest of the city center is a neighborhood called Kanina, which is near a large washing area for artisanal cobalt at Lake Golf, as well as an industrial mining site called COMMUS. COMMUS is owned by Zijin Mining and straddles the adjacent neighborhood of Musonoie. Musonoie is home to two Glencore-owned industrial mining complexes: Kamoto East and Kamoto Oliveira and Virgule (KOV). Southwest of these mines are the giants of Kolwezi—the Glencore-owned Kamoto Copper Company (KCC) mine and Mashamba East. In aggregate, Glencore's mines in Kolwezi produced a massive 23,800 tons of cobalt in 2021.[1] There are also a few Chinese-operated sites near the KCC complex, including the SICOMINES mines of Mashamba West and Dikuluwe, and the place where we will end our journey—Kamilombe.

Kolwezi was founded by UMHK in 1937 as the capital of its western division in Katanga Province. Control of the city's mineral riches has been a cause for violence dating back to 1960, when Moise Tshombe announced that Katanga was seceding from the nation eleven days after independence. After Tshombe's forces were defeated with U.S. assistance in 1963, Tshombe fled into neighboring Angola. Unwilling to relinquish his dream of an independent Katanga, Tshombe directed two major military campaigns to regain control of the province, known as the Shaba wars. The first Shaba war began on March 8, 1977, when Tshombe led two thousand soldiers to take control of major mining sites across the province. Hundreds of civilians were killed, and tens of thousands fled. The feeble Zairian military offered little resistance. A desperate Joseph Mobutu portrayed the invaders as communists backed by the Soviet Union to draw Western support. Once again fearing a communist takeover of the Congo's crucial mineral assets, the U.S., Belgium, and France sent military aid to retake control of the province.

Tshombe initiated the second Shaba war the following year. This time, his forces swiftly took control of Kolwezi. Western powers were reluctant to enter the fray a second time. Some say that a frantic Mobutu ordered his troops to kill Europeans in Kolwezi to spark Western intervention. After hundreds of Europeans were killed, French and Belgian paratroopers, with air support from the United States, dropped on Kolwezi. The ensuing battle resulted in the destruction of much of the city and hundreds of civilian casualties before control was finally wrested from the rebels.

Militia skirmishes and ethnic conflict continue to be a way of life across the Copper Belt, especially around Kolwezi. As a result, Kolwezi has the heaviest concentration of soldiers and security forces in the region. Most of the city's major mining sites are secured by FARDC, Republican Guard, or both. In the early years of my research, the mining sites were also under the watchful eyes of the former governor of Lualaba Province and staunch ally of Joseph Kabila, Richard Muyej Mangez Mans.

Richard Muyej became the first governor of Lualaba Province in 2016. As governor, he had the final say on many aspects of mining operations in the province. If a mining company wished to expand or alter its operations, they came to him. If there was a dispute with a local community, they sought his adjudication. Muyej was rumored to be siphoning money from mining deals into personal accounts, not unlike Joseph Kabila, and the allegations of corruption eventually caught up with him. As part of the anti-corruption campaign initiated by President Tshisekedi, Muyej was removed from office on September 10, 2021, on charges of embezzling more than $316 million from mining deals.[2]

On my first visit to Kolwezi in 2018, I went to Governor Muyej's office to seek his permission to explore the city's mining sites. The main entrance was guarded by several men with Kalashnikovs, who offered a military salute as I entered. I was led to a security checkpoint inside the compound, where my mobile phone was confiscated, the contents of my backpack were inspected, and I was patted down before being led to a waiting room that was guarded by several more men with Kalashnikovs. I waited for thirty minutes past my appointment time, after which I was informed that Governor Muyej would not be able to meet with me. Instead, I was taken to meet Mrs. Musenga Mafo, commissioner-general of the government of Lualaba Province in charge of humanitarian and social affairs. Mrs. Mafo lent a fair-minded ear to my explanation of why I wished to explore the mining areas around Kolwezi. She expressed concern over the destructive behavior of foreign mining companies in her country, and she was particularly disturbed by the negative impacts of artisanal mining on women and girls. She explained that female artisanal miners suffered chronic sexual assault, were paid much less than men, and had virtually no options for safety.

After a congenial exchange, Mrs. Mafo provided me with her stamp and signature on my *engagement de prise en charge* documentation. Her stamp acted as a shield from the worst outcomes, just as Director Lukalaba's did in Haut-Katanga Province. It did not, however, mean that gun-toting soldiers guarding many of the artisanal mining areas around Kolwezi were inclined to let me enter.

KAPATA, LAKE MALO, AND MASHAMBA EAST

There are numerous villages and settlements scattered around the periphery of Kolwezi. Some have existed for decades, and others have popped up more recently as migrants flowed into the city. Hundreds of thousands of people live in these areas, and they provide a massive labor force for artisanal mining. It would not be a stretch to suggest that much of the EV revolution rests on the weary shoulders of some of the poorest inhabitants of Kolwezi, yet few of them have the benefit of even the most basic amenities of modern life, such as reliable electricity, clean water and sanitation, medical clinics, and schools for children.

Of all the villages around Kolwezi, perhaps none is more important than Kapata. It was originally founded by Gécamines in the 1970s to house the workers at the KCC mine. Today, it is the gateway to the massive artisanal mining territory located in and around the KCC and Mashamba East concessions. Glencore owns 75 percent of both mines through its 100 percent ownership of Katanga Mining. Katanga Mining acquired rights to the mines soon after the Mining Code was established in 2002. Copper and cobalt from the concessions are processed at the Kamoto Concentrator and Luilu Metallurgical Plant in Kolwezi.

A local activist named Gilbert took me on my first trip to Kapata and the surrounding mining areas. He and his colleagues worked to support artisanal mining families and help keep children out of the mines. We drove down a narrow road heading southwest from the city center that was unpaved for the last few kilometers leading to the village. We were repeatedly run off the dirt road by cargo trucks transporting minerals from the mines near Kapata. We parked near the edge of the village and continued by foot. The village consisted of neatly laid rows of redbrick huts, tucked between the massive KCC concession and Lake Kabulungu. Most of the huts were residential, but some had been transformed into small businesses, such as markets that sold vegetables, sodas, cooking oil, and bread. There was also at least one internet café that I spotted. It had two dusty Dell desktops that looked like they had been teleported in from the 1990s. There were open sewer trenches along the edge of the dirt paths in between the huts. Frayed electrical wires snaked through Kapata and provided intermittent electricity, a rarity in Congolese villages. There were also a few village schools that closed for weeks at a time when teachers went unpaid.

The first person Gilbert wanted me to meet in Kapata was an elderly woman named Lubuya. He said that she knew more than anyone about the history of the area. As we neared her home, a few children scurried past us and shouted, "*Ni hao!*"—the typical greeting in Mandarin. Many Congolese people in the Copper Belt have picked up a rudimentary facility with Mandarin through interactions with Chinese depot agents or other mining personnel. We arrived at Lubuya's home and were invited inside. She was an old soul, with kind eyes and a hardened face. Her hair was wrapped in a proud headdress with a matching blouse and skirt decorated with red and orange crescents. She was sixty-nine years old, the oldest person I ever interviewed in the Congo. We sat on plastic chairs inside Lubuya's two-room hut, which she shared with three grandchildren, two boys and one girl. The children dug for cobalt at nearby Lake Malo. Lubuya's husband had died fourteen years ago. The grandchildren's mother, Lubuya's daughter, had died of an illness six years ago. Their father had left soon after, leaving Lubuya to raise her grandchildren on her own.

Lubuya said she first came to Kapata in 1977. She described Kolwezi as a quieter city in those days. People had space to live and food to eat. The air and water were clean. The villagers were poor, but they managed:

We have a system called *kazi*. This means you take a job with a company and they pay you a salary and give you food rations. They give you a home to live in and school for the children. That is how we came to Kapata so my husband could work for Gécamines.

Our lives were good at that time. Our needs were met. The troubles began when Gécamines stopped paying the workers in 1992. People were hungry and angry. That is when the men started to go to the mine to dig for themselves.

There were no *comptoirs* like there are today, so the men took a bus to Lubumbashi to sell the stones in the marketplace. It was a very difficult situation, but that was the only possibility.

When the foreign mining companies came to Kolwezi, the foreign traders came with them. They built *comptoirs* in this area. The families dig in the mines because they can sell to the *comptoirs* and walk home with money in their hands.

People ask, why are the children working in the mines? My grandchildren are there now. Would you rather they starve? Many of the children lost their parents. Sometimes a woman will marry again and the man chases the children out of the house. What are those children supposed to do? They can only survive by digging.

Lubuya was just getting started. She continued by sharing her concerns about modern-day life in Kolwezi. She said another problem was a substantial increase in the costs of food and housing due to the influx of foreign mining operations. The increases forced many families to chase money in artisanal mining. She also decried the destruction of agricultural land and the pollution of air and water by mining companies. She reserved her harshest commentary, however, for the country's leadership:

We have a saying, *"Mtoto wa nyoka ni nyoka"*—the child of a snake is a snake. Laurent Kabila was the first snake. He invaded Congo with the Rwandans and called himself a liberator . . . His son is also a snake. He sold our country to the Chinese and kept the money to himself.

Let me tell you, people say things were better under Mobutu. They say Mobutu was strong and at that time Congo was proud. Mobutu made himself rich while the people suffered. Our leaders only care for themselves.

After graciously answering my questions on a range of topics, Lubuya was curious to learn more about me and what life was like in America. She could not believe that nearly everyone in the U.S. had electricity or that a smartphone with cobalt in the battery cost up to $1,000.

"People here cannot dream of having so much money," she said.

As I was leaving, Lubuya's face hardened, and she looked at me skeptically.

"Why have you really come here?" she asked.

I had already explained the purpose of my visit when I first sat down with her, so I repeated that my intention was to document the conditions of artisanal cobalt mining.

"Why?" she asked again, as if my reason made no sense.

"If I can describe the conditions accurately, I hope it may inspire people to help improve things here."

Lubuya looked at me as if I were a fool.

"Every day people are dying because of the cobalt. Describing this will not change anything."

From Kapata, I followed a path to Lake Malo through a small forest of eucalyptus trees. The lake was situated adjacent to the sixty-meter-tall dirt walls of the KCC open-pit mine. It was a relatively small lake that swelled during the rainy season to a peak size of roughly three hundred meters across and declined to about one-third that size by the end of the dry season. From the tree line, the scene was remarkable. Thousands of people filled every available patch of dirt around the circumference of the lake. Hundreds of people trudged up and down the gargantuan walls of the KCC mine. Scores lugged large sacks of ore to the depots next to Lake Malo. Even the discovery of high levels of uranium in the dirt at the KCC mine in 2018 did not stop artisanal mining in the area. The diggers and washers who worked in the KCC zone were part of a sophisticated ecosystem that fed cobalt straight into the formal supply chain. To explore the area in more detail, I first had to secure the permission of the main boss at Lake Malo, Chief Djamba.

I found Chief Djamba sitting at a wooden desk inside one of the depots next to Lake Malo. There were seventeen depots in total. Fifteen were run by Chinese agents and two by Congolese. The numbers shifted with each visit, but the depots were always dominated by Chinese buyers. The depots were more formal than the pink-tarp setups I had seen in places like Kipushi, Likasi, or Fungurume. Several of the depots were built inside large metal shipping containers, guarded by plainclothes men with weapons. The armed guards also roamed the lake to ensure that artisanal miners only sold cobalt to the adjacent depots. Most of the depots had a price list at the entrance written in black marker on raffia sacks. The prices ranged from CF 250 [about $0.14] per kilogram for 1 percent grade to CF 3,000 [about $1.67] for 7 percent grade.

Chief Djamba was protected by armed men in black uniforms. I sat on a chair at the entrance of the container while Gilbert requested permission for us to move around Lake Malo and speak to the artisanal miners. He showed Chief Djamba the signature and stamp on my *prise en charge* documentation from Mrs. Mafo, which did not appear to make much of an impression. As Gilbert made our case, the chief stared directly at me and took long drags from a cigarette. This scenario continued for several minutes—Gilbert speaking anxiously to Chief Djamba, and Chief Djamba staring at me as he smoked. Eventually, Chief Djamba said something in Swahili to Gilbert in a raspy voice.

"We can go," Gilbert said. "But you must leave your phone and backpack here."

We approached Lake Malo from the east. The dirt walls of the KCC mine rose beyond the lake to the north and west. Unlike Étoile, MIKAS, Mutanda, Tenke Fungurume, and Tilwezembe, the KCC mine was not walled, fenced, or otherwise secured until the summer of 2021. Anyone could walk up the hill into the mine, dig, and walk back down with a sack stuffed with ore. Even after Glencore built a short concrete fence atop the hill, artisanal miners simply climbed over it.

As we neared the lake, the din of voices grew louder and more frenzied. Amorphous shapes sharpened into a swarm of women and children. Gilbert described how the system worked:

> The people dig around the lake and fill sacks with stones. Children climb to the KCC pit to dig. They bring the sacks to the lake where the women and girls wash the stones. After the stones are clean, they place them in a pile. They fill a sack with these stones and take the sacks to the *comptoirs*.

I asked Gilbert what happened to the ore after it was purchased at the depots.

"They take the ore from Lake Malo in trucks to Luilu. Those were the trucks we passed on the road to Kapata, if you remember."

I asked if the ore was taken anywhere else besides the Luilu facility.

"Some is also taken to the CDM processing facility in Lubumbashi."

"So all the cobalt is taken either to KCC or to CDM?"

"We can say almost all of it. There is a small amount that is sold to other mining companies."

On the following day, I followed cargo trucks filled with heterogenite from the depots near Lake Malo to the security gate of the Luilu facility in Kolwezi. The cargo trucks continued through the gate and into the facility. I also saw one red-colored cargo truck loading sacks of ore from the Chinese-manned depots. I was told the truck belonged to CDM, although it was not possible to follow the truck all the way to Lubumbashi to determine if it was indeed heading to the CDM processing facility there, assuming that was its destination.

Not far south of the lake, Gilbert spotted a group of boys he knew—three brothers between the ages of nine and thirteen. Gilbert patted the youngest child on the back, and dust flew off his shirt like from an old sofa. The brothers lived in Kapata and dug each day around Lake Malo. None of them had ever attended a day of school. The eldest, Tambwe, said he had recently climbed down from the KCC pit with a sack of ore and was about to head back up. To this point, I had still not looked up close into an industrial open-pit copper-cobalt mine in the Congo, so I asked Tambwe if we could join him. He agreed and said he knew a safe path up the hill.

I followed Tambwe away from Lake Malo back along the eucalyptus forest toward the base of the western section of the wall. It was a mountain of gravel and dirt at least forty meters high, inclined at a forty-five-degree angle. Several children were climbing up the hill with empty sacks, and several more were climbing down with sacks stuffed with stones draped over their shoulders. Tambwe pointed to the path up the hill that he trusted, and we started our climb. As we ascended, each step felt unsteady. The gravel shifted under my feet, causing me to slip on a few occasions. I had to keep every muscle engaged to maintain balance, which was exhausting. During the ascent, we passed by numerous groups of children who were digging inside holes in the wall of the mine that were two or three meters deep. We also passed by several tunnels dug into the side of the mountain. Most of them were marked by pink tarps so that people did not fall into them. It seemed that every conceivable source of cobalt was being excavated.

We arrived at the top of the hill, walked along a chewed-up field of dirt and up another slight incline when I saw it at last—the horrible beauty of an open-pit copper-cobalt mine. It was an enormous rectangle roughly 450 meters by 200 meters in size and at least 120 meters deep. The pit had been excavated in benches to prevent collapse. Imagine taking one of the step pyramids from Egypt, turning it upside down, and smashing it into the earth. When you picked it up, you would have an open-pit copper-cobalt mine such as the one at KCC. The symmetry of the terraces was elegant, almost Zen-like, despite the destruction I knew it represented. There were hundreds of people scattered across the mine scrounging for stones with no respite from the blistering sun, except inside the numerous tunnel openings I could see.

Tambwe bid me farewell and ventured off to gather another sack of stones. I walked back to the edge of the wall and cast my eyes across the horizon. Atop this horrid hill, I could survey the full measure of violence that assailed the people of Kolwezi as they dug for cobalt for a few dollars a day. The land was a hellscape of craters and tunnels, patrolled by maniacs with guns. An obscuring pallor hung thick above the terrain, as if the earth itself could not bear to be seen. I had just about taken in the bleak surroundings when a hot breeze whipped across the mine, scattering grit into my eyes and mouth. I coughed several times, and since my water bottle was in my backpack with Chief Djamba, I had to spit into my handkerchief to create enough moisture to clear the grime from my eyes. The message was clear—I did not belong here.

The return journey down the hill proved more difficult than the way up, even without a sack of cobalt on my shoulders. Gravity pulled me forward, and the ground gave way under the force of each step. I turned my feet sideways and stayed low to the ground to keep from tumbling to the bottom. All around me, children were clambering up and down the hill in bare feet or, if they were lucky, in plastic flip-flops. One child passed by on his way down the hill, deftly navigating the same treacherous terrain under the weight of a raffia sack stuffed with stones. I marveled at his adroit movements, but I could not help but wonder what kind of damage was being done to his ankles, knees, back, and neck . . . assuming he lived long enough for the consequences to make themselves known.

I reached the bottom of the hill and walked with Gilbert back over to Lake Malo. Close up, the water appeared like a brackish cloud of scum. Women and girls stood knee-deep in the lake and jerked sieves up and down to separate dirt from stones. I asked Gilbert how polluted the water might be. "Why don't we ask them," he replied. He approached a woman bent over in the water at a perfect right angle and posed the question. She responded in a shrill tirade. Other women added their opinions and gesticulated excitedly. Gilbert knew the answer to my question, but he wanted me to see the emotions unleashed by it.

"The mama says the lake is poison," he reported. "She said, 'It kills the babies inside us. Mosquitoes do not drink the blood of the people who work here.'"

We spoke to several more women washing stones in the lake. Most of them expressed anxiety about the toxicity of the water and had complaints of burning skin and upset stomachs. Some of the women complained of physical assault by the soldiers who patrolled the area. They all said working in the lake was the only way they could earn money, although the depots invariably shortchanged them.

"We are never paid more than two percent purity even when we can see with our eyes that the sample is greater," one woman said.

Most of the women and girls washing stones in Lake Malo worked as part of family units, although some washed stones for other diggers, and some washed stones that they dug themselves. Despite working ten-hour days in toxic conditions under the hellish sun, the incomes of most women and girls who worked at Lake Malo was barely more than one dollar per day.

Although I was able to speak casually with many of the people working in and around Lake Malo, the more detailed interviews I conducted took place inside homes in Kapata or other secure settings where people felt it was safer to talk. One such interview was with a fifteen-year-old boy, Archange. He sat in a red wheelchair with his arms folded tightly over his chest. He was bone thin and anxious, and he clenched his jaw rapidly throughout the interview. Archange said that he went to school until the fifth year. His favorite subject was French. When the family could no longer afford the school fees, he had to drop out and started digging for cobalt in the KCC pit in the summer of 2018.

"When I woke every morning, I wanted to cry because I had to go to the mine," he said. "My entire body hurt every day, my head hurt, my neck hurt. Sometimes even my eyes hurt."

Fighting through painful memories, Archange described the day he was injured. He woke on September 14, 2018, covered in dust. It was the last month of the dry season, and Kapata's water supply was down to a trickle. Bathing this late in the season was only for Sundays, and then only just a wet rag over face, legs, and arms. Archange felt feverish and had been suffering from a hacking cough for several days. This is what he said happened:

I went to Lake Malo later that day because I was not feeling well. I climbed to the KCC mine to dig. I filled the first sack, and I was walking down the hill. Maybe I was feeling weak or a little dizzy. When I walked down, the ground slipped under my feet. I fell all the way to the bottom. When I stopped falling, I felt like the world was spinning around me. I could not move any part of my body. Some people called my parents. They took me to the hospital.

At the hospital in Kolwezi, Archange learned that his spine had been fractured in three places. As a result of his injuries, he was paralyzed below the waist. The doctors could do nothing for him except provide a wheelchair.

I would meet three more boys who had suffered debilitating leg or spine damage falling down the wall of the KCC mine. The entire proposition was an accident waiting to happen. I barely managed to walk up and down the wall myself, without having to carry a cobalt sack and not being malnourished and exhausted. There would no doubt be many more boys who had suffered similar falls than just the ones I met. The cobalt excavated from the KCC mine by children like Archange made its way safely up the chain into our phones and cars, while the risks associated with scrounging it out of the pit were borne solely by the residents of Kapata. Without the income from Archange's work, his family was struggling. He felt guilty that he had become a burden to his parents and admitted that he had suicidal thoughts.

"I sit in this wheelchair while my family works so hard. I wish I could help them, but I cannot do anything. I cannot even dress myself. I cannot bear living anymore."

Not long after my first visit to Lake Malo, I was asked to meet at the bar of the Moon Palace hotel in Kolwezi with a senior Gécamines executive who was in town from Kinshasa, named Aristote. Aristote had a refined presence and disarming manner, although I could feel that he was scrutinizing me intently to determine whether I was a friend or foe. We met at the bar next to an outdoor swimming pool, and Aristote wasted no time asking me about the purpose of my research and my plans after I left the DRC. He listened patiently as I described my intentions. When he finally shared his thoughts, the agenda became clear.

"I am sure you know that many foreign NGOs attack Gécamines and the Congolese mining sector," Aristote said.

I asked why they would do so, and he replied that it helped the NGOs with fundraising. He contended that foreign NGOs used the mining sector to enrich themselves, and as such, their allegations should not be believed. He further stated that some foreign NGOs had fabricated claims that money went missing from Gécamines accounts, which they then used as evidence of supposed misdealing. According to Aristote, it was Gécamines that was being shortchanged by foreign mining companies.

Aristote argued that the Mining Code in 2002 was forced on the DRC by the World Bank in exchange for much-needed loans. The country was reeling from years of war and violence dating back to the Rwandan genocide and was in desperate need of financial support. Aristote contended that the World Bank offered its support primarily with the ambition of opening the DRC's mining concessions to its stakeholders so that they could get rich. Once the foreign mining companies got a foothold in the country, Aristote suggested that they used questionable practices to cheat the Congolese government on tax payments. As an example, he said that mining companies claimed higher capital expenditures and operating expenses than they originally projected in their feasibility studies. Based on these elevated expenses, the mining companies then asserted that they had not made any profit and therefore did not need to pay taxes or dividends to Gécamines.

"They use accounting tricks to cheat us. But the NGOs only accuse the Congolese of being corrupt because they believe all Congolese are corrupt," Aristote said.

Aristote's claims that NGOs made false statements about Gécamines and the Congolese government to raise funds for themselves seemed far-fetched. In my experience, only a small number of NGOs had been found to use catastrophes for profit. Or, as King Leopold did with the

AIC, they may cloak their avarice in claims of humanitarian intentions. During all my time in the Congo, I only encountered one case of the kind of questionable dealings by an NGO that Aristote described, and it was at the CHEMAF model mining site near Kolwezi. Every other NGO I interacted with was staffed by dedicated and principled people who put themselves at considerable risk while working on shoestring budgets to assist some of the poorest and most exploited people in the world.

Aristote's other assertion—that foreign mining companies were using accounting tricks to shortchange Gécamines on their tax payments—proved to have merit. When I mentioned Aristote's claims to colleagues, they confirmed that foreign mining companies were suspected to use accounting loopholes to minimize their tax payments to the Congolese government. This was one of the reasons cited by the Congolese government for the trebling of tax rates on cobalt and the implementation of the supertax in 2018. Sylvestre, the same senior member of President Tshisekedi's administration who spoke to me about anti-corruption efforts with Chinese mining contracts, pointed his finger directly at Chinese mining companies with regard to accounting irregularities:

The Chinese companies have a negative impact on the Congo through tax evasion and revenue evasion. How did we discover this? We discovered that most Chinese mining companies have two accounts: one account that they prepare for us that understates production, and another account that they show to the Chinese government and state-run banks that is higher than what they declare to us. This is because once they start production, they have to repay their loans. The second issue is the separation of minerals. Copper always comes with a percentage of cobalt. After they separate the metals, a Chinese company will declare the cobalt to us, but not the copper. They know we do not have the capacity to monitor this, so it is another way they evade their payments to us.

The tax and revenue irregularities raised by Aristote and confirmed by Sylvestre led me to probe the matter further with a visit to the Lualaba Provincial Ministry of Mines. The ministry oversees the collection of taxes, royalties, and other payments from the joint ventures between Gécamines and foreign mining companies. A clerical employee, Charles, explained that the ministry did not actually have a single resource of reliable data on tax collections. I assumed that he said this because any records they might have were not to be shared with outsiders, so I asked instead if he could please explain more about how the tax system was supposed to work.

"The province collects revenues from the mining companies based on the tonnage and type of ore extracted," Charles explained. "The revenues are remitted to the central government in Kinshasa. The central government redistributes a portion of these revenues back to each province based on their population."

Setting aside the fact that the country's last census was conducted in 1984 and population estimates in each province were vague estimates at best, the system Charles described seemed to be an equitable way of allocating financial resources across the country. Charles did not agree.

"The problem we have is that Lualaba and Haut-Katanga by themselves provide maybe half the revenues to the central government, but we do not receive an adequate share in return," Charles said.

It was the age-old tension of the Congo—Katanga's riches should be for Katangans. Populist politicians continue to call for the secession of Katanga from the DRC, and their desire to keep Katanga's riches at home have led to numerous schemes to minimize tax payments to Kinshasa. One of the primary schemes utilized is known as "one-third, one-third, one-third," in which only one-third of the actual mining payments due are sent to Kinshasa, one-third is kept by a provincial official(s) as a bribe for fudging the books, and one-third is kept by the mining company as a kickback in the financial evasion scheme.

My visit to the Lualaba Provincial Ministry of Mines left me with more questions than answers. How were mining revenues being accounted for, and where was the money going? I recalled that in 2018, Glencore alone was responsible for $1.08 billion in tax and royalty payments to the central government, equaling 18.3 percent of the national budget that year. It was not a surprise then when Charles suggested that Lualaba and

Haut-Katanga Provinces contributed up to half the revenues for the national budget. However, when I reviewed the DRC's budget for 2021, called the Projet de Loi de Finances de L'Exercice,[3] I was surprised to uncover the following two pieces of information: 1) taxes, royalties, and other revenues collected from the mining sector did not appear anywhere in the $6.9 billion national budget, and 2) Lualaba Province was listed as contributing only 4.1 percent of revenues to the central government's total budget. I checked 2018, and again, Lualaba Province was listed as contributing only 4.1 percent of revenues to the national budget, the same year that Glencore alone was responsible for 18.3 percent. The years 2019 and 2020 also showed Lualaba Province contributing 4.1 percent. Were these just made-up numbers? Where were all the revenues from the mining sector going? To this day, I have been unable to find any answers to these questions.

As murky as the accounting practices in the formal mining sector seemed to be, it was even less clear how revenues from artisanal production were being accounted for. The artisanal mining cooperatives that managed the official ZEAs were supposed to keep track of their production to determine tax payments to the provincial government, but no one audited their books, so they could easily fudge the numbers and pocket the difference. What about the hundreds of informal artisanal sites outside of the formal ZEAs, in villages, hills, forests, and other remote areas? Was any of the production from these sites being accounted for by the state, and even if it were being captured at some point along the chain, where did the money go? Every missing dollar could be used to invest in the welfare of the Congolese people. Just a fraction of the funds siphoned at various junctures by *négociants* and depots could easily pay for all the teachers' salaries, books, and supplies needed to ensure that the children in the mining provinces could remain in school full-time. These funds would also likely be sufficient to expand public health infrastructure, sanitation, and electrification across the Copper Belt. Graft seemed to infect almost every level of governance in the DRC, quite apart from the financial trickery allegedly used by foreign mining companies to shortchange the Congolese government.

Every possible claw was clutching at the value being created by the artisanal miners of the Congo. Theirs was the accounting that most deserved clarity, and the next dismal entry in the ledger came from a mine called Mashamba East.

Glencore's Mashamba East mine is located just west of the main pit at KCC along the northern edge of Kapata. The first time I ventured from Kolwezi to explore Mashamba East, I was slowed by a road-repair project that stretched for more than a kilometer. As we crawled through the construction zone, I noticed that all the workers were Chinese.

"The Chinese companies bring their workers from China because they do not trust African people," Gilbert explained. "They think we will cheat them, yet they are in our country making money for themselves."

I asked why Congolese construction companies weren't doing the road work instead of the Chinese.

"Chinese companies make a bid lower than anyone else to get the contract. They will pay their workers small wages to complete the project. The Chinese have no constraints on human rights, so other companies cannot compete with them."

Gilbert's comments were echoed by Asad Khan, CEO of Big Boss Congo:

The Chinese companies have an unfair advantage over every other company operating in the Congo, including my own. First, although they claim they are private companies, they all receive funding from the government of China. Basically, this means they receive free money and have almost no cost of capital. You cannot compete on this basis. It is an extremely difficult environment to succeed . . . The Chinese mining contracts signed by the Kabila government are lopsided and benefit the DRC state and the population very little.

I arrived at the periphery of Mashamba East and walked up to the main security entrance. It was a white concrete wall topped by barbed wire, guarded by FARDC. I tried to gain entry by showing my stamp and signature from Mrs. Mafo as evidence of governmental support, but I was turned away. Fortunately, it was a rather simple matter to walk east of the main entrance and hike up the dirt wall of the mine, where I was able to see scores of men and boys digging in trenches. Children were digging for cobalt inside the wall of the mine as well, just like they did at KCC. There was even one very large tunnel that had been excavated inside the wall of Mashamba East no more than a hundred meters east of the security entrance.

Although I never managed to enter Mashamba East, I learned a great deal about the conditions inside the mine from interviews with several children who said they dug inside it. The first interview was with a spirited fourteen-year-old boy named Kabola. He told me something I had not heard before: "I was recruited by soldiers to dig at the concession." Kabola explained:

> The FARDC recruit children from Kapata, and also from other villages near Kolwezi. They tell us to come to the mine to dig. One soldier will control five or six boys in one group. The soldier I worked for is Zeus. What he said is if I did not want to be poor and stupid, he can help me make money. He said I can use this money to pay the school fees.
>
> I did the digging for Zeus . . . He paid me CF 2,000 [about $1.10] each day. My family needed this money, so I had to keep digging. How could I ever go to school?

I asked Kabola what happened to the ore he dug for Zeus. Kabola said that Zeus sold the ore to the depots near Lake Malo, as did most of the other FARDC soldiers that ran child labor groups at Mashamba East. Kabola realized that he could probably make much more money if he sold the ore to the depots directly, so one day, he decided to take his sack of cobalt to the depots near Lake Malo.

"Zeus saw me walking out with my cobalt, and he shouted at me. I did not turn around. I kept walking. Then I heard a bang . . . I could not breathe. I fell to the ground. I thought I was going to die," Kabola said.

Zeus shot Kabola under his left shoulder. He was twelve years old at the time. He was rushed to a hospital in Kolwezi where the bullet was removed, after which he recovered for a few days before returning home. He suffered bone and nerve damage down his left arm because of the bullet wound. He cannot make a fist and experiences shooting pains in his arm. He is unlikely ever to go to school due to the family's financial constraints, and he will most certainly struggle to find work given the limitations caused by his injury. Even if he wanted to dig for cobalt at some other site, Zeus paid his father a visit and told him that if he tried to dig at Lake Malo, Kamilombe, or anywhere else near Kolwezi, he would "shoot Kabola in the head, not the back."

I spoke with five more boys between the ages of twelve and fifteen who said they worked at Mashamba East within the previous six months and had suffered injuries. Three suffered broken bones in a single pit wall collapse, one was severely beaten by an FARDC soldier for reasons he did not understand, and the fifth lost his footing while climbing down a tunnel shaft and suffered a broken leg. The children reported earning a little more than one dollar per day. They all said they were recruited by FARDC soldiers, and they all reported that they were compelled to sell their production to the soldier who controlled their work at the mine. To the best of their knowledge, the soldiers sold the ore to the depots next to Lake Malo. Two of the children said that they heard some of the FARDC soldiers transported the ore to a marketplace called Musompo instead. The soldiers appeared to pocket the difference between the dollar-a-day wages they paid the children and the sales prices they received at the depots. Based on an average cobalt grade of 2 percent in the ore at Mashamba East and an average daily production of roughly thirty kilograms of ore per child, the soldiers were probably making up to fifty dollars per day, which was as much as fifty times the average daily wage of the children who worked for them.

The realities of the working conditions for artisanal miners across the broader KCC and Mashamba East mining concessions proved to be much worse than I anticipated. Child labor, subhuman working conditions, toxic and potentially radioactive exposure, wages that rarely exceeded two dollars per day, and an untold rash of injuries were the norm. Astonishingly, the appalling conditions at the mines remained almost entirely invisible to the outside world. Mining accidents were rarely reported, and families were forced to face the consequences of injured loved ones on their own. Across all the interviews I conducted, I received testimonies of seven tunnel collapses at KCC and Mashamba East that took place between June 2018 and November 2021, but only one of these catastrophes was ever reported in the media—the collapse of a tunnel inside the KCC mine on June 27, 2019, that killed forty-one people. In response to the tragedy, Glencore issued a public statement that more than two thousand artisanal miners illegally entered its mining sites each day and that "KCC urges all illegal miners to cease from putting their lives at risk by trespassing on a major industrial site."[4]

Naming KCC as the agent of the message, as if it were some entity disconnected from Glencore, is another example of how companies at the top of the chain eschew full accountability for the artisanal miners at the bottom. Consumer-facing tech and EV companies, mining companies, and other stakeholders in the cobalt chain invariably point their fingers downstream, even at their own subsidiaries, as if doing so somehow severs their responsibility for what is happening in the cobalt mines of the Congo. Although these companies consistently proclaim their commitments to international human rights norms, the implementation of these commitments seems to be nonexistent in the DRC. Everyone from the FARDC soldiers to the Chinese mineral traders, the Congolese government, multinational mining companies, and mega-cap tech and EV companies plays their part in preying upon those who dig for cobalt out of every crater, pit wall, and tunnel at KCC, Mashamba East, and other mines near Kapata. The global economy presses like a dead weight on the artisanal miners, crushing them into the very earth upon which they scrounge.

If there was one face of this misery, one child debased by piracy cloaked as commerce, it was Elodie. I met her toward the end of my first visit to the KCC mining area. She was fifteen years old, foraging in the dirt near the periphery of Lake Malo in a faded orange sarong with purple birds dancing on it. She was scarcely more than bones and sinew. Her raw-boned face was crusted with mucus, her hair knotted in clumps of dirt. She suffered from a rib-cracking cough. Her feeble two-month-old son was wrapped tightly in a frayed cloth around her back. His tiny head flopped side to side each time she hacked at the ground with a piece of rebar. I'd seen enough to know what the late stages of an HIV infection looked like, and it looked like Elodie. Although she moved over the earth with the shape and semblance of a child, she was the nullity of the word.

Elodie was orphaned by cobalt mining. She said her father died in a tunnel collapse at the KCC site in August 2017. I could not find any public reports of the collapse, although others in Kapata remembered it. Elodie's mother had died around a year before her father. She washed stones at Lake Malo, and as best as Elodie could recall, her mother contracted an infection from which she was unable to recover. After the loss of her parents, Elodie said she turned to prostitution to survive. Soldiers and artisanal miners purchased her regularly.

"The men in Congo hate women," she said. "They beat us and laugh."

Elodie became pregnant. After her son was born, she started digging at Lake Malo. She said that prostitution and digging for cobalt were the same—"*Muango yangu njoo soko.*" My body is my marketplace. Elodie slept in an abandoned, half-finished brick hut near the southern edge of Kapata with a group of orphaned children. The children were known as *shegués,* a word derived from "Schengen area," which indicates that they are vagabonds without families. There are thousands of *shegués* across the Copper Belt, and they survive by any means necessary, be it scrounging for cobalt, doing petty jobs, or being purchased for sex. Elodie said she typically earned about CF 1,000 (about $0.55) a day at Lake Malo, which was not enough to meet even the most rudimentary needs. She was forced to let soldiers do "unnatural things" to her in order to survive.

Elodie was one of the most brutalized children I met in the DRC. She had been thrown to a pack of wolves by a system of such merciless calculation that it somehow managed to transform her degradation into shiny gadgets and cars sold around the world. The consumers of these devices, were they to stand next to Elodie, would appear like aliens from another dimension. Nothing in form or circumstance would bind them to the same planet, aside from the cobalt that flowed from one to the other.

Elodie soon grew weary of my presence. I was just another unwelcome burden. I moved along the abysmal landscape at Lake Malo and watched her from a distance—her labored movements, her jolting coughs, the way her wiry muscles tightened and released with each stab of the rebar. She was the latest entry in an ancient chronicle of torment that stretched back generations in the heart of Africa. I could imagine Elodie's great-great-great-grandmother losing a hand to the Force Publique after her great-great-great-grandfather failed to meet his rubber quota that day. Perhaps their children suffered slavery on a palm tree plantation leased by the Belgians to the Lever brothers. Perhaps the next generation endured forced labor at a copper mine in Katanga owned by UMHK, and perhaps Elodie's grandparents were butchered for diamonds in the Kasai during Africa's Great War. Her parents, we know, were killed by cobalt mining near Kolwezi, leaving behind Elodie. This succession of torment, hypothetical though it may be, could also not be more real. It is the tragic inheritance of all who enter the world in the Congo. The ailing infant on Elodie's back will inherit it all.

KANINA, LAKE GOLF, AND COMMUS

The neighborhood of Kanina is located about nine kilometers northeast of Kapata, next to a massive industrial copper-cobalt mine, COMMUS, as well as a large cobalt washing area at Lake Golf. The system at Lake Golf is similar to Lake Malo. Artisanal miners dig for heterogenite in a nearby site called Tshipuki, which they carry in sacks over to Lake Golf to be washed by women and children. An earnest and articulate teenage boy named Geany explained, "I go in the morning after breakfast, and I dig . . . Once or twice in the day, we carry the ores to Lake Golf. My mother and my sisters are washing there." Geany said that after the co-balt was washed *négociants* and soldiers at Lake Golf who bought the ore. According to Geany, they took the sacks of cobalt to sell to depots at the Musompo marketplace. He added that in the last year, a few of the soldiers at Lake Golf asked him to help them transport sacks of co-balt to the marketplace from time to time. He loaded sacks into a truck and unloaded them at Musompo. According to Geany, the soldiers sold all their sacks of cobalt only to Depot 555.

Although Lake Golf was heavily secured by FARDC soldiers, I en-deavored to visit the area. I arrived at a security checkpoint that included at least a dozen soldiers who reported to a commander stationed in an operating center built into a big metal shipping container, like some of the depots near Lake Malo. The soldiers guarding Lake Golf were not as aggressive as the ones at Mashamba East, but they still refused entry. It took almost an hour of discussion before the soldiers finally let me through with an armed chaperone. We walked from the security check-point for about ten minutes and arrived at the periphery of Lake Golf. It was much bigger than Lake Malo and similarly packed with women and children washing and sorting heterogenite stones. Several FARDC soldiers were patrolling the area. There were numerous bicycles, motor-bikes, and two pickup trucks parked near the lake waiting to transport the ore. Several piles of heterogenite lined the edge of the lake, some of which were more than a meter tall.

Hundreds of women and children stood knee-deep in the water, bent sharply as they hand-washed one heterogenite stone at a time. The wa-ter of the lake was a clouded khaki color from the shoreline to about five meters into the lake, after which it turned gray out to deeper water. The muddy shore was littered with stray raffia sacks, crushed plastic bottles, and discarded candy wrappers. Several children carted plastic buckets filled with water in plastic bags to sell to thirsty workers. A boy, perhaps seven or eight, wearing black shorts and a ripped, lime-color T-shirt, yelped in the dirt as he tried to pull something sharp out of his right in-dex finger. His twiggish limbs were streaked in mud. Two girls caked in mud up to their waists dragged a sopping raffia sack stuffed with stones across the ground, using all their strength to budge it just a few inches at a time. They looked no older than ten.

With the FARDC chaperone monitoring my movements, it was not possible to conduct interviews at Lake Golf. I was nevertheless able to have a few casual conversations with some of the women and children who were rinsing stones. They said they cleaned the heterogenite pebbles for seven or eight hours a day and that "the men" bought the heterogenite from them, which I took to mean the *négociants* and FARDC soldiers hovering nearby. The women confirmed that they mostly worked in family units and that it was their brothers and husbands who did most of the digging over at Tshipuki. Although it proved difficult to get more than a few sentences into a conversation with any one person, given all the talking, shouting, and sloshing going on, I was nevertheless able to get a good sense of how the system worked.

Then there was Aimée. I found her sitting alone in the mud near the shoreline, rinsing and stacking stones atop an orange raffia sack. She was perhaps eight or nine years old, had no hair, and wore leggings with red and tan stripes and a pink T-shirt with a light brown cartoon puppy on the front. Like so many of the children I met in Kolwezi, Aimée was an orphan. I introduced myself and asked her about the puppy on her shirt. She said his name was Alphonse. I started to speak with her about her work as a group of women gathered around in a protective formation. I had just about managed to learn that Aimée's parents were dead and that she lived with an aunt in Kanina when she suddenly began to scream at the top of her lungs. The women shouted angrily at me and moved to console the child. The commotion escalated, and FARDC soldiers rushed over. My translator tried to calm the situation, but Aimée would not stop screaming. I did not understand what I had done to upset her. Was my presence the cause of her panic? Did I ever stop to think that I might represent a form of violence to a child like her, a forced confrontation with pain? For some, talking can be catharsis. For others, it makes the hell all too real. My approach had profoundly unsettled her, and my regret came too late.

As I left Lake Golf amid a storm of protest, I thought I would never hear such howls again . . . until the day I reached Kamilombe.

It was around this time that I decided I would try to meet Arran. I kept hearing his name in villages around Kolwezi from the parents of children who worked or had worked for him at Tilwezembe. These parents reinforced the image of a callous operative who preyed on children to enrich himself, although he was hardly alone in this regard. I asked Gilbert to help me arrange a meeting, but he felt very strongly that it was not a good idea. "Arran is very dangerous. It is best if he does not know your face," Gilbert advised. He suggested that if he were to even try to set up a meeting, it could lead to serious blowback for him, his colleagues, and his family. Arran was said to have the protection of Lebanese organized crime, Governor Muyej, and perhaps even Joseph Kabila himself. I was told that since his release from prison, Arran had expanded his business interests to include a fleet of transportation trucks, several properties in the Copper Belt, and partial ownership in an artisanal mining cooperative. It did not seem like there was any economic necessity for him to exploit children. So why did he do it?

Although I was never able to ask Arran this question directly, I managed to meet another Lebanese cobalt trader named Hani. We met at the open-air restaurant in a quaint courtyard inside L'Hôtel Hacienda in Kolwezi. He was thin, in his midforties, and wore black sneakers, black jeans, a gray shirt, and a gray scarf. Not long after Hani arrived, the electricity at the hotel went out, so we spoke by candlelight.

"The Lebanese people have been in the Congo a long time," Hani said. "We migrated as traders during the colonial time. Most Lebanese people went to the Kasai to trade diamonds. The diamond trade was good for us because we had links to markets in the Middle Eastern countries."

Hani said that Lebanese people lived in their own communities in Lubumbashi and Kolwezi. They often gathered in restaurants and bars, which was where he had seen Arran a few times.

"I go to Lubumbashi when I can," Hani said. "There is more to do there. We meet at the Mykonos restaurant. Arran is there sometimes. We watch the football [soccer] matches and share news from Lebanon."

Hani echoed the warnings I had received that Arran was too dangerous to trifle with. He suggested that Arran was one of the leaders of Lebanese criminal activity in the Congo and that he was involved in laundering money for "criminal groups."

"What do you mean by criminal groups?" I asked.

"Hezbollah," he replied. Hani listed other groups as well, including Nigerian organized crime and Somali pirates. "Congo is the easiest place for these groups to clean their money."

When I investigated the matter further, it appeared that Hani's assertions relating to Lebanese money laundering for terrorist groups had merit. At low levels, it seemed that dirty money was laundered through the Lebanese mineral and diamond trading network, then deposited into banks and even cryptocurrency wallets. At higher levels, there were big companies involved, chief among them a commodity-trading firm based in Kinshasa called Congo Futur, which was run by a Lebanese ally of Arran named Kassim Tajideen. Tajideen happened to be a prominent financial supporter of Hezbollah. The U.S. Treasury Department put Congo Futur under targeted sanctions in 2010, alleging that the firm was part of a network of businesses in the DRC that was laundering millions of dollars for Hezbollah using accounts in the BGFIBank, the same bank used by Joseph Kabila to facilitate crooked transactions with Chinese mining companies.[5]

According to U.S. ambassador Mike Hammer, the U.S. government is well aware of Lebanese money-laundering networks in the DRC and links to terrorist groups like Hezbollah: "I would say that the U.S. government is concerned about [terrorist] links to specific Lebanese here. It is something we track and follow. Clearly, there are linkages and bad actors. We approach the Congolese government when we become aware of issues, and we have sanctioned Congolese businesses when we become aware of support of Hezbollah."

As I continued speaking with Hani about Arran's activities, the restaurant began to fill with patrons who looked like they might be government officials. Hani grew uncomfortable talking any further about Arran, so we switched to discussing his background. Hani explained that he moved to the DRC in 2014 after a cousin who was already in the country persuaded him that there was money to be made.

"We have no kind of life in Lebanon. Lebanon is a failed country. Here a person can make a business for themselves."

Hani made his business operating a copper-cobalt depot on the highway east of Kolwezi. He bought cobalt from anyone who came to sell it—artisanal miners, *négociants,* and FARDC soldiers. He said Chinese mining companies were the primary buyers from his depot. I asked how he knew they were the buyers.

"I know their trucks. We all know which trucks are from which company."

I asked Hani how he managed to secure a depot for himself since they were supposed to be owned and operated by Congolese nationals.

"I paid one thousand dollars for the permit."

"That's all you had to do?"

"Yes."

Hani said he usually bought around three to four hundred kilograms of copper-cobalt ore each day and that he sold the ore for two to three times the purchase price, depending on grade and time of year. Hani's only operating expenses were monthly fees of a few hundred dollars to someone in the provincial government—he did not want to specify whom—and salary of fifty dollars a day each for two guards at the depot, as well as transportation costs. Hani said he generally made a profit of around $3,000 per month during the rainy season and $5,000 per month during the dry season.

I asked Hani if he ever made any inquiries as to the source of the cobalt ore he purchased.

"What do you mean?" he asked.

"I mean, do you try to determine if the ore came from child labor like Arran uses or some other kind of abuse?"

He laughed and lit a cigarette in the candle at our dining table.

"One does not ask such questions here," he said.

"Why not?"

"There would be no cobalt left to buy."

Standing at the edge of Kanina, the hills of the open-pit mine at COM-MUS swallow the landscape. China-based Zijin Mining owns 72 percent of the mine in a joint venture with Gécamines. Zijin bought Huayou Cobalt's share in the mine in 2014 for $77.9 million. The two companies remain strategic partners, and COMMUS ships much of its cobalt supply to Huayou for refining, which amounted to about 1,400 tons in 2021.[6] The main gate to COMMUS is secured by guards who would not allow me to enter despite repeated attempts. Fortunately, much of what I wanted to learn about COMMUS took place right outside the concession.

Like Kapata, the homes in Kanina are mostly redbrick with sheet metal roofs. There are similarly a few quasi-functional schools that children attend on and off based on their ability to pay the fees. Electricity is inconsistent, and there is no sanitation system in the neighborhood. I spoke with numerous residents of Kanina, and they all complained of persistent and troublesome pollution from the COMMUS concession.

"There are explosions at the mine," one resident complained. "Dirt falls over our homes. Everything is dirty. Our houses shake in the night, and we cannot sleep."

"Clouds of yellow gas float over our homes and fall in our food and water," another resident said.

COMMUS has its own processing facility, just like China Molybdenum has at Tenke Fungurume. Like the residents of Tenke, the residents of Kanina often find themselves, their food, their animals, their belongings, and their children covered in mustard-colored dust.

"COMMUS is supposed to contain their activities to the mine . . . We protest, but the government will not listen. COMMUS will not listen. No one can stop them," said a third resident.

Pollution was not the only problem being caused by the COMMUS mining site. It was also the scene of considerable child labor. Hundreds of children from Kanina worked every day just outside the concession picking stones. They were known as *trieurs,* people who sorted stones by hand. Why would children be handpicking stones outside a giant, Chinese-owned copper-cobalt concession? The best way to understand the situation is to examine the difference between industrial and artisanal mining.

Industrial mining is like doing surgery with a shovel artisanal mining is like doing it with a scalpel. During industrial excavation, tons of dirt, stone, and ore are gathered indiscriminately with large machinery, crushed down to pebbles, and processed to extract minerals of value. It is by design a blunt-force, low-yield, high-volume business. Artisanal miners, on the other hand, can use more precise tools to dig or tunnel for high-grade deposits of ore, extract only the ore, and leave the valueless dirt and stones behind. Or, like the children sorting through rubble outside COMMUS, they can simply handpick the stones of value and discard the rest. Artisanal mining techniques can yield up to ten or fifteen times a higher grade of cobalt per ton than industrial mining can. This is the primary reason that many industrial copper-cobalt mines in the DRC informally allow artisanal mining to take place on their concessions, and it is also why they tend to supplement industrial production by purchasing high-grade artisanal ore from depots. COMMUS appeared to have figured out a third option—dump tons of indiscriminate stone and dirt outside their concession and let children handpick the valuable ore.

I walked along the periphery of the COMMUS mine in clear view of the security guards, and I saw several mountains of rubble up to five meters tall piled next to the road. Hundreds of children were sitting, kneeling, and crouching on the stones, picking out bits of cobalt-containing ore. Almost all the children were residents of Kanina. Their families needed money to meet basic needs, so they were easily drawn into stone-picking outside the COMMUS site. An eight-year-old boy named Emmanuel explained, "We throw the cobalt stones to one side and the other stones to another side. We fill the sacks with the cobalt and carry it to the *comptoirs* over there by the road." Several children said they worked in the same way as Emmanuel described. They told me that they typically started picking stones by midmorning and worked for five or six hours. Aside from breathing in a good deal of dust and suffering minor cuts and injuries, the children had a relatively safer working environment than those who worked at places like Tilwezembe, Mashamba East, and Lake Malo.

I visited the depots to which the children said they sold ore. They were located on the road just outside the COMMUS concession. They were little more than tables and did not even go to the trouble of hanging tarps with their names painted on them. The agents operating the depots were all Chinese. They made a cursory inspection of the contents of each sack and paid a set amount to the children per sack of $0.40–$0.50. Most children managed to fill one or two sacks per day. There were a few guards near the depots wearing the same gray uniforms as the security guards at the front gate of the COMMUS mine. I lingered in the area just long enough to watch some of the ore from the depots being loaded into trucks and transported directly into the COMMUS concession. There did not appear to be much more to the system beyond what I saw during the day of my visit. I was bizarrely relieved that it seemed to be a relatively safer form of child labor in the Congo's artisanal mining sector, given the brutal and dangerous conditions I had witnessed.

It turned out that I had severely misconstrued the potential for harm to the children who picked stones dumped by COMMUS next to their site. On October 26, 2020, I received a mobile phone video via WhatsApp from a colleague in Kolwezi. The video opened on a screaming crowd of Kanina residents. Two white jeeps raced through the front gate of the COMMUS concession as stones and bottles flew at the vehicles. An excavator was engulfed in flames just behind the main gate. The person taking the video walked slowly toward the entrance of the mine. Another jeep raced into the concession. More stones and bottles flew.

The videographer arrived near the entrance of the mine and pointed the phone to the ground. In the dirt lay the bloodstained body of a dead boy. He was barefoot, arms resting by his side. His yellow shirt was soaked in blood over his right shoulder. The back of his head was also drenched in blood. The child's mother was kneeling next to him, howling with grief. She pulled down the boy's shirt to reveal a bullet wound on the right side of his chest. The camera moved to a second body lying in the dirt about two meters away. He was also barefoot, wearing gray trousers rolled up to his knees. His blue shirt was soaked in blood over his left shoulder. His mother too wailed by his side. Residents shouted into the camera, demanding justice for the murder of their children.

The colleague who sent the video told me that the two boys, ages thirteen and fourteen, started walking with their sacks of cobalt stones in the opposite direction of the COMMUS depots to try to earn more than the pittance they were being paid by the depot agents. The COMMUS security guards promptly gunned them down.

As the months passed, I received more testimonies of violence at COMMUS. Beatings and riots seemed to be repeated occurrences, similar to the situation between the residents of Fungurume and TFM. The last video I received was sent by a nun on July 22, 2021. In the footage, COMMUS security guards can be seen using thick ropes to viciously whip Congolese workers lying in the dirt. The workers scream with each lash, in a scene reminiscent of King Leopold's slaves being whipped with *chicottes* 120 years earlier. Three Chinese men wearing black COMMUS uniforms with orange hard hats watch as the punishment is meted out. One of them appears to instruct the guards to whip harder.

MUSOMPO

Like minor tributaries that merge into the Congo River, artisanally mined cobalt merges from hundreds of different sources into the global cobalt supply chain. The primary mode of entry is the depots. Some depots are formal complexes like those next to Lake Malo; others are roadside tables like those set up outside COMMUS. Artisanally mined cobalt is funneled through this untraceable system of traders who ask no questions as to the conditions under which the cobalt is produced. Were women and girls being slowly poisoned in toxic water as they rinsed the stones? Were

boys losing legs in pit wall collapses? Were children inhaling toxic particulates hacking at the dirt? Were people being paid anything akin to a
decent wage? Were children being shot? No one asked, no one cared—not
even at the largest copper-cobalt buying market in the DRC: Musompo.

The Musompo marketplace is located on the highway about fifteen
kilometers east of Kolwezi. There are usually somewhere between fifty to
sixty depots operating at the complex. Most of the depots are run by Chinese buyers. The depots are a mix of brick, metal, and cement structures.
Many have metal fencing as a barrier between buyers and sellers. Several
have armed guards. The names of the depots are typically spray-painted
on a wall at the front. Some of the depot names include Andre, Jeef, Gi-
rafe, Mukubwaken, Panda, Sarah, Big Show, Lucien, Song, Tshomeka,
Yanick, Soin, Manga, Star, Kaloni, Baraka, Shuang, and so on. There
are also a couple of dozen depots named simply by number: 1818, 1217,
1208, 5555, 008, 888, 999, 111, 414, 555, and so on. Each depot is run
by a "boss." There is a constant flow into Musompo of pickup trucks,
cars, and motorbikes laden with sacks of cobalt ore. These are the sellers,
and they are almost all *négociants*. Only a small number of artisanal
miners can bicycle their loads to Musompo from nearby sites. The buyers
arrive in large cargo trucks that they load with cobalt sacks purchased
from the depots. These large cargo trucks invariably belong to industrial mining companies.

I started with a stroll through the market. Most of the depots had
one or two young Chinese men sitting at small tables covered with cut-
open raffia sacks or plastic sheets. Congolese guards sat nearby on plastic chairs. Some of the depots were stuffed with sacks of cobalt three or
four meters high. There must have been several thousand sacks of cobalt between all the depots at Musompo. Most of the depots had graffiti
painted on the walls and price sheets posted at the front. The price sheets
went to a remarkable 20 percent grade and included phrases like *Karibu
Kwetu* ("Welcome to Our Place") and *Teneur ya Bien* ("Good Terms").

In time, I would gather price data from depots across Haut-Katanga
and Lualaba Provinces. The prices at Musompo proved to be highest of
all. They were 20–25 percent greater than in the Kasulo neighborhood

of Kolwezi, up to 35 percent greater than Kamilombe, Kanina, and Lake Malo, up to 50 percent greater than Fungurume, Kambove, and Likasi, and up to 60 percent greater than the depots near Kipushi. By all accounts, heterogenite should fetch a similar price for the same grade regardless of where it was sold, so there were clearly other market forces behind the variance in prices. Perhaps being forced by soldiers to sell cobalt at the depots at Lake Malo pushed prices downward in that area. Perhaps open competition at Musompo pushed prices upward. Perhaps the inability to access markets except via *négociants* explained why prices near Kipushi were so low. Whatever the reasons, the variability of pricing at depots, along with the lack of bargaining power and access to markets, represented considerable disadvantages for artisanal miners. It bears repeating that removing the layers of intermediaries and allowing artisanal miners to sell production at standardized prices directly to mining companies would be much more advantageous for them—either that, or paying them fixed, livable wages. But even with that reform, there still would be no accountability for mining companies and their upstream customers for the conditions under which the cobalt was being mined. The system was opaque and untraceable by design.

I stopped near Depot 1818 to observe a transaction. A Congolese *négociant* brought two sacks of heterogenite on his motorbike for sale to Boss Peng, who ran the depot. The *négociant* untied the string fastened at the top of each sack to reveal the contents. Boss Peng pointed a Metorex at the stones, which returned a reading of 3.1 percent grade. Boss Peng's handwritten price sheet listed a rate of CF 1,800 (about $1.00) per kilogram of cobalt with 3 percent grade. The *négociant* haggled. I could not ascertain if the discussion was over price or grade. It was an animated exchange, but never adversarial. The two traders came to an agreement, and Boss Peng weighed the sacks on a flat metal scale. The sacks totaled 71.6 kilograms. Boss Peng punched numbers into an oversize calculator with fat plastic buttons and showed the *négociant* the result. The *négociant* nodded, and Boss Peng unlocked a padlock on a metal box and counted out a giant stack of crumpled 500 Congolese franc notes. The *négociant* resealed the sacks with strings, took his money, and wheeled his motorbike over to a group of *négociants* who were taking a smoke break. Boss Peng's guards carted the sacks behind the metal fencing at the depot and stacked them on top of an existing collection of nineteen sacks. In a matter of minutes, cobalt from somewhere near Kolwezi and mined in unknown conditions had entered the chain.

I walked over to the group of *négociants* to strike up a conversation. They were young men in their twenties and thirties, wearing jeans, sneakers, and light jackets even though it was quite hot outside. One of them had a T-shirt under his jacket with the red-tailed hawk mascot for the University of Utah on the front. I asked the *négociants* about the source of the heterogenite they sold to the depots. They replied that the source was the Kasulo neighborhood of Kolwezi.

"The prices at the depots in Kasulo are not as good as Musompo," one of the *négociants*, Razi, said. "Some *creuseurs* arrange with us to sell the cobalt here."

I asked why the artisanal miners didn't just bring the cobalt to Musompo themselves.

"They don't have motorbikes!" one of the other *négociants* replied.

When I asked if they could tell me more about their arrangements with the artisanal miners, they said that they split the sale price of the cobalt 50–50 with them.

Similar to the system at Kipushi, possession of a motorbike earned the *négociants* the same daily income as the *group* of artisanal miners who produced the cobalt they sold at Musompo. Razi, who had just transacted with Boss Peng, made about thirty-six dollars on the two sacks of cobalt. The other thirty-six dollars would ostensibly be split between the artisanal miners who produced the supply at Kasulo. Despite the split, and depending on the number of people in the group, this income was considerably greater than most artisanal areas I had documented. There was a simple explanation. The heterogenite deposits under Kasulo had perhaps the highest grade of cobalt anywhere in the Copper Belt. Still, something did not add up. Prices at the depots in Kasulo were on average 20–25 percent less than Musompo, so why would an artisanal miner part with half his income to a *négociant* in exchange for at most a 25 percent increase in sales price? The answer came when I visited Kasulo—soldiers often extorted artisanal miners in the neighborhood after they sold their ore to the depots.

The *négociants* at Musompo turned out to be the best source of information on how the marketplace worked, so I spoke to as many of them as I could. Some told me that they sold heterogenite to whichever depot offered the best price; others had arrangements to sell only to certain depots. I learned that not all *négociants* took half the income; some took one-third, and some took one-fourth. There was no logic that I could ascertain behind these differences, other than the share the artisanal miners were able to negotiate. I asked numerous *négociants* what happened to the cobalt purchased at Musompo, and I was told that the main buyers of heterogenite sold at Musompo were CDM, COMMUS, SICOMINES, CHEMAF, and KCC.

Before leaving Musompo, I tracked down Depot 555, the one that Geany mentioned as the buyer of most of the cobalt from Tshipuki. It was located about forty meters east of Depot 1818. I stood at a distance for a time and observed as four sets of *négociants* came to the depot—three on motorbikes, and one pair in a pickup truck loaded with so much cobalt that the tires were flattened to the ground. The *négociants* transacted quickly with Boss Chen, who remained behind the fencing. After loading their sacks, they drove east down the highway in the direction of Lubumbashi. The fifth arrival was a distinctive, red-painted cargo truck. I would see many more that looked just like it inside the main CDM concession in Kasulo. I watched as two Congolese men wearing light gray jumpsuits exited the truck and spoke with Boss Chen at Depot 555. They subsequently loaded more than two dozen cobalt sacks from the depot into the truck, which then drove off down the highway.

After the CDM cargo truck departed, it was growing late, and activity at Musompo was slowing down. Depot 555 remained empty for a time except for Boss Chen and his guards. I walked over to see if I could start up a conversation. Chen was wearing cargo pants, sneakers with no socks, and a plain blue shirt, with his legs propped on a wooden table as he tapped on his smartphone. Unlike many of the Chinese depot agents

I approached, Chen was quite affable and happy to talk. He said that he was originally from Fujian and had been working at Depot 555 for two years. He said he earned a good salary and was glad he came to the DRC for work, but he missed his family and was only able to see them once a year when he returned to China for Chūn Jié, the lunar new year festival. I asked Chen what the draw was to venture all the way to the Congo and spend one year at a time away from his wife and children.

"China is too competitive. Someone like me cannot advance in China. Africa is a big place. It is not so competitive. We can find opportunities here," Chen said.

Chen lived in a flat in a walled Chinese enclave in Kolwezi, where many of the Chinese expatriates in the area resided. The enclave included a Chinese grocery store and private restaurant. They also had a private Chinese medical clinic nearby.

"It is less crowded here than China. It is less polluted. I will try to bring my family here. We can have a better life," Chen said.

I noticed that Depot 555 did not have a price sheet listed anywhere. Chen explained, "The *négociants* argue on the price, so I check the price on the London Metal Exchange on my phone and show it to them. I offer a percent of this price based on the purity. Then they do not argue."

I was curious to understand how Chen set up his depot, since they were only supposed to be owned and operated by Congolese nationals.

"CDM arranged the depot," he said.

When I asked him if he knew how CDM set up a depot, we had the following exchange:

CHEN: Here anyone can do business if they pay the correct price.
ME: You mean a bribe?
CHEN: Yes. It is a good system.
ME: You are saying bribery is good?
CHEN: In China, not even a bribe can work unless you are in the elite
    circles. Here, money makes you elite. That is why so many Chinese
    come to Africa.
ME: I see.

I made three trips to Musompo across the years, and based on everything I saw and heard during those visits, it appeared that some of the biggest mining companies in the Congo were supplementing their production with cobalt ore that was excavated by artisanal miners and sold by *négociants* to the marketplace. From Musompo forward, there was no way to determine the source of the cobalt—all the sacks were dumped together in the same transport trucks and dropped off for processing at the same facilities. Musompo's function seemed to be little more than a massive, centralized laundering mechanism for artisanally mined cobalt into the formal supply chain.

There were two buyers of cobalt at Musompo that were of particular interest to me—CDM and CHEMAF. These were the two companies that operated the two model sites for artisanal mining in Lualaba Province. Being a model mine was supposed to mean safe working conditions for artisanal miners, no child labor, fair wages, no dangerous tunnel digging, and above all, ironclad assurances that cobalt mined from the sites was *never* mixed with cobalt from any other source. These declarations were meant to assure the buyers of their cobalt that their supply chains were untainted by child labor or other abuses. Boss Chen was neither the first nor the last person to assert that CDM and CHEMAF shopped openly for artisanal cobalt from other markets.

It was time to pay the model sites a visit.

THE CHEMAF MODEL SITE

The CHEMAF model site for artisanal mining was located north of Kolwezi in a mine called Mutoshi near the village of Mukoma. CHEMAF acquired the rights to the concession in a joint venture with Gécamines in 2016. I had high hopes for the model site because I was told it had been designed in coordination with a Washington, D.C.–based nongovernmental organization called Pact. Pact is a well-regarded NGO that works in more than forty countries on issues ranging from women's empowerment to sustainability, health and social services, and artisanal mining.

The CHEMAF model site was launched in 2017. I met in Kolwezi with a few members of the DRC-based team for Pact in September 2019 prior to visiting the Mutoshi site. They asked to speak anonymously for fear of negative reactions by Pact headquarters. I asked why there would be any negative reactions for speaking with me, and they said that they were not supposed to speak with outsiders about the Mutoshi site. They explained that the organization had received several million dollars in support from Apple, Microsoft, Google, Dell, and a commodity trading company called Trafigura to set up the model site in Mutoshi, and a certain image had to be maintained. The purpose of the site was to provide a clean source of cobalt for CHEMAF customers, which included the donors. Most of the mineral supply from CHEMAF was sent to Trafigura, which was also the primary corporate partner of the model site.

The Pact team in Kolwezi described some of the policies that had been implemented at the Mutoshi model site: only adult workers registered with the COMIAKOL artisanal mining cooperative were allowed to work at the mine; the concession was surrounded by an impenetrable, electrified fence to keep unregistered workers from entering; all workers were given uniforms and personal protective equipment; no alcohol or pregnant women were allowed on the concession; a CHEMAF radiation officer conducted testing every month to ensure artisanal miners were not being exposed to unsafe levels of uranium in the heterogenite; all ore mined at the site was tagged in bags that were kept isolated from any other cobalt supply during transport to CHEMAF's processing facility in Lubumbashi; and the tagged cobalt hydroxide from the processing facility was shipped directly to Trafigura. The Pact team also said that they conducted regular audits at the site to ensure that all procedures were being maintained. Finally, the team told me that a portion of the millions of dollars they received from donors for the model site was to support efforts to remove at least 2,000 children from artisanal mines around Kolwezi and place them in schools until they completed their primary education.

I posed a few questions to the Pact staff about the CHEMAF supply chain, starting with whether their drivers purchased cobalt from market-places like Musompo. They responded that the drivers were not supposed to purchase cobalt from other sources under the policy they had designed; however, they conceded that this had become an issue in recent months due to lower production at the model site, which resulted in the need to fill the trucks with more cobalt from Musompo on the way to the processing facility in Lubumbashi. The Pact staff stressed that this should not be considered an issue, because the cobalt supply from the model site at Mutoshi was tagged and kept separate at all times. They added that the artisanal cobalt from Mutoshi was processed in separate batches at the facility, then re-bagged and retagged. Since all the tagged and untagged cobalt was exported primarily to Trafigura, I asked whether the company also kept the tagged cobalt from Mutoshi separate from cobalt that arrived from other sources. The Pact staff could not say, although they conceded it was unlikely. Tagging the bags served little purpose if the practice was not maintained all the way up the chain. I asked the Pact staff whether they could arrange a tour of the model site in Mutoshi so I could take a closer look, but they said it was not possible.

A few days later, I managed to arrange a visit to the Mutoshi mine through one of the leaders of the COMIAKOL cooperative. As I neared the site, I was expecting to see the impenetrable metal fence that the Pact staff had described, but it turned out to be a spaghetti-wire fence that consisted of thin metal strings draped eighteen or so inches apart held up by metal poles, like a clothesline turned on its side. The spaghetti wire had been yanked down in numerous places, creating just enough space for a person to pass through. The fence was not electrified.

I approached the entrance of the concession and saw three signs, the largest with the following text written in French and English: OUR VALUES—TRANSPARENT, DYNAMIC, RESPECTFUL, ACCOUNTABLE, SOCIALLY RESPONSIBLE. OUR VISION—BUILDING A RESPONSIBLE AND VALUE DRIVEN MINING COMPANY. SAFETY IS OUR NUMBER ONE PRIORITY. The second sign was a drawing of a pregnant woman inside a red circle with a line crossed over her. The third sign had two drawings—one of a bottle inside a red circle with a line crossed over it, and another of two children inside a red circle with a line crossed over them. There was a security checkpoint next to the signs with separate entrances for males and females. CHEMAF staff checked the badges of workers registered with the COMIAKOL cooperative before allowing them to enter. To register with COMIAKOL, an individual had to produce his or her voter registration card that showed they were more than eighteen years of age. CHEMAF staff later conceded that voter registration cards were often forged to show that fifteen- and sixteen-year-old children were eighteen, thereby allowing them to work at the site.

A stern-faced armed guard in sunglasses opened the front gate and directed me to the CHEMAF offices, which were located about twenty meters into the site behind a second spaghetti-wire fence that also was not electrified. The offices were built into metal shipping containers. One container housed the management team, a second container was for support staff, and a third container was fashioned into a medical clinic to treat injured workers. The COMIAKOL official who had arranged my visit, Sylvain, greeted me warmly, accompanied by three of his colleagues.

After I passed a Breathalyzer test, the COMIAKOL team provided an oral presentation about the mine that consisted of a statement of the vision and mission described on the sign at the front gate, a review of the statistics on injuries in the workplace at Mutoshi, and a description of CHEMAF's other mines and processing facilities. Sylvain said that CO-MIAKOL managed all the artisanal miners at the site, for which they were paid a fixed monthly fee by CHEMAF as well as a percent of production. He made a special point of discussing the importance of artisanal mining to the overall mining industry: "The artisanal cobalt has a higher grade than cobalt mined mechanically, so it is necessary for the mining industry to have artisanal mining. Here we are trying to improve the conditions for the artisanal miners, as you will see for yourself." I asked Sylvain how many artisanal miners worked at Mutoshi. He said that there were around five thousand artisanal miners registered with COMIAKOL; however, in recent months, only around eight to nine hundred artisanal miners came to the concession each day. He attributed the drop-off to the collapse in cobalt prices during 2019, which had caused delays in payments to the artisanal miners. Sylvain added that many artisanal miners had been taking their cobalt sacks out of the site to sell to nearby depots and be paid more quickly.

Sylvain next showed me a map with the layout of the mine. It contained a large open-pit digging area behind the main offices, a small washing pool near the front gate, a much larger washing pool behind the main pit, a few other digging areas, and a handful of waste-rock dumping zones behind the main washing pool. Sylvain was proud of the prohibition on alcohol and pregnant women at the mine. When I probed, he conceded that the prohibition on pregnancy only involved women who were visibly pregnant and that prior to that time, toxic exposure to cobalt and uranium could have harmful effects on a developing fetus. After the presentation was completed, I was given an orange neon vest and a yellow hard hat to wear as we toured the mine. I was instructed not to take pictures, and I was told I would only be permitted to see the open pit nearest to the front gate.

The open pit was about thirty meters behind the main office. On the walk over, Sylvain described the different categories of workers at the concession. He said that men divided into groups based on task. One group dug trenches in the main pit. Another group extracted the ore from the trenches. A third collected the ore in sacks and transported it to the washing basins, which was where women cleaned the stones. Some of the men also worked as *salakate,* which meant they did odd tasks around the mine. Sylvain said that each working area had on-site toilets and clean drinking water to promote good sanitation and prevent waterborne illness. He also stressed that the site did not allow any tunnel digging, which I was very relieved to hear.

We arrived at the open pit, which was about 120 meters in diameter and not very deep. The dirt in the pit was grayer in hue than the copper color I was accustomed to seeing at other mining sites around Kolwezi. At the time of my visit, about a hundred artisanal miners were digging in small trenches and shallow shafts in various areas of the pit. The diggers all wore indigo uniforms that had patches on the arms, knees, and chests made up of three stripes, two neon green and one gray in the middle. All the workers wore hard hats. Some, but not all, wore thick work gloves. None of the workers wore masks or goggles. Some looked to be boys around fifteen or sixteen years old. I asked if I could speak to some of the diggers, but I was not given permission.

I asked Sylvain what happened to the cobalt after it was excavated and washed. He replied that COMIAKOL transported the sacks in their trucks to a depot in an area called Kimwehulu. At the depot, the ore was crushed and a sample was analyzed for grade, a process that could sometimes take more than a day. After the sample was analyzed, the artisanal miners were paid based on the grade. Sylvain said that CHEMAF did not buy anything below 2 percent grade, in which case COMIAKOL had the option to sell the ore to another depot. According to Sylvain, the average daily wages for the artisanal miners varied based on production but were roughly two to three dollars for diggers and one dollar for washers.

I asked whether CHEMAF had considered offering the artisanal miners fixed wages as opposed to piece-rate wages. I suggested that doing so might provide workers with greater stability and a sense of security and that it might also prevent the artisanal miners from selling cobalt to external depots where they could be paid more, or more quickly. Sylvain responded that a fixed wage was not possible because of the fluctuations in the price of cobalt, a reasoning that I did not accept. Employees of industrial mines were paid fixed salaries that did not fluctuate based on the price of the underlying commodity, so why should artisanal miners be any different? Piece-rate wage systems by nature shifted market risks from mining companies to workers. Doing so placed substantial pressure on artisanal miners to dig themselves to the bone, take more risks, and bring their children into the mines to boost incomes.

Following our discussion of fixed versus piece-rate wages, Sylvain offered the following information unsolicited: "Because the cobalt here is lower grade, many of the *creuseurs* here buy cobalt from people who dig outside the concession where the ore has a higher grade. They include this in their production to increase their earnings."

"How do they bring that ore onto the site?" I asked.

"Children bring it through the fence."

"Do children sell cobalt that they dig themselves?"

"Yes, this happens."

We continued the tour at a nearby washing pool. Several young women were kneeling in a brackish, cruddy pool of water rinsing stones that varied in size from pebbles to twice the size of a fist. This was not the main washing basin behind the open pit, which I was not allowed to see. The women in the smaller washing pool did not have any safety equipment to protect their hands or legs from whatever toxic substances had accumulated in the water. I watched as some of the women filled raffia sacks with the stones they had washed, and I asked Sylvain at which point the bags of ore were tagged, as the Pact personnel had described.

"We do not tag bags at all," he replied.

I was surprised by the answer and followed up by asking whether ore from other sources was added to the CHEMAF trucks during transport to their processing facility in Lubumbashi. Sylvain said that drivers were instructed to purchase cobalt from depots on the way to get the maximum load for transport.

"Depots like the ones at Musompo?" I asked.

"Yes."

The tour ended, and Sylvain led me back to the main office. Along the way, I asked him about the radiation officer who was supposed to check radiation levels at the site. He could not say when the officer had last done so. The final question I asked was whether Pact staff conducted regular audits on working conditions at the site, as they had told me they did.

"Pact staff never come here. They only advised us in the beginning on accounting and financial management," Sylvain replied.

Although I had been prevented from interviewing artisanal miners working at the CHEMAF site during my visit, I had little trouble conducting interviews off-site. The conversations offered valuable insights into the operations at the Mutoshi mine. An artisanal miner who worked at Mutoshi named Kalenga had this to say:

Most of the *creuseurs* at Mutoshi stopped working because of problems with our payment. CHEMAF says it is because cobalt prices are low. They say they lost profit so they must cut our payment. Sometimes we are not paid for three or four weeks. For this reason, most of the *creuseurs* left Mutoshi. We can earn more outside the CHEMAF concession, and we are paid on the same day.

An artisanal miner named Mashala added:

Of course we have to buy cobalt outside the concession. The purity in the concession is very low, and now we have to spend more of our time clearing the dirt and transporting it to the dump, whereas CHEMAF used to do this with the excavator, but now they say they must reduce their petrol expense. This work takes two hours each day, so we have less time to dig, and we earn less. This is why we must buy cobalt to support our wages.

By contrast, a washer named Julie was outspoken about the improvements she had experienced:

The women do not suffer the same harassment from the men at Mutoshi. When I worked at other places, the men would always harass us. The SAESSCAM officers and the mining police would harass us. This does not happen at Mutoshi. We feel safe there.

Another benefit Julie noted was the improved sanitation standards:

This is much better for us. All the time I was sick when I was working at other mines. Now I am not so sick. Because of this, we save money on medicines. I use this money to keep my children in school.

A second washer named Maombi added:

Yes, we suffer less harassment, this is true. I do not mind that we earn less, because there is no chance a man can attack me while I am on the CHEMAF concession. I am very grateful for this.

Based on everything I saw and heard during my tour of the Mutoshi mine, as well as my subsequent interviews with artisanal miners who worked at the site, the conditions at the CHEMAF model site did not match what I had been told by some of the Pact staff in Kolwezi. Specifically, there appeared to be child-mined cobalt entering Mutoshi through the spaghetti-wire fence. Teenagers worked at the site with fake voter registration cards. The radiation officer was not regularly checking radiation levels. Bags of cobalt were not tagged, and cobalt from unknown origins was purchased from external depots and mixed at CHEMAF's refining facility in Lubumbashi. Crucially, reduced or delayed wage payments appeared to be a major disincentive for many artisanal miners and was compromising the viability of the entire operation. The purported supply chain transparency and traceability turned out to be a fiction.

Setting aside these deficiencies, there were several improvements at the Mutoshi mine compared to other artisanal mining sites in the DRC, especially for female workers. Women endured constant harassment and sexual assault at most of the sites I documented. They received pitiful wages for their work and were still expected to run their households and manage children. Even if they were earning anemic wages at CHEMAF, the reduction in sexual assault was a considerable improvement in their lives. Supplying clean water, toilets, and at least some protective gear also helped mitigate illness and toxic exposure. The mine was not crawling with children or (visibly) pregnant women. There also did not appear to be any sort of tunnel digging, which prevented the worst tragedies from occurring.

After my visit to the Mutoshi model site, there was one remaining matter I wanted to verify, so I met with the Pact team in Kolwezi one more time. I asked them exactly how many of the 2,000 children they had placed in schools under the program, which at that time had been operating for two full years. I was told that 219 children had been enrolled in school.

"Enrolled . . . but how many are still in school?" I asked.

They could not say.

Despite its shortcomings, the CHEMAF site demonstrated that it was possible to organize artisanal mining in a safer and more dignified manner. Even the problems I uncovered at the mine could be repaired were there the will to do so. Unfortunately, CHEMAF and its partners appeared to take the opposite approach. I received word from colleagues in Kolwezi a few months after my visit that CHEMAF had ended its association with Pact and shut down the artisanal mine.

THE CDM MODEL SITE

The second model mine in Kolwezi belongs to CDM. It is located in the heart of a neighborhood called Kasulo. There is no place like Kasulo anywhere in the world. It is the frenzied apex of the mad scramble for cobalt. The best way to understand what happened in Kasulo is to look back to the fabled California gold rush.

On January 24, 1848, a sawmill operator in Coloma, California, named James Marshall spotted a nugget of gold in a riverbed. News spread quickly, and treasure seekers from across the country flocked to California in search of riches. They ripped up hills, chopped down trees, dammed rivers, and burrowed thousands of mine shafts into the Sierra Nevada mountains. Hydraulic mining was the technique of the day, involving the use of high-powered water jets that ripped away entire hillsides. The environmental and humanitarian damage caused by the gold rush was substantial. California's agricultural sector was hard hit by dammed rivers and mining runoff. Indigenous people were evicted from land upon which they had lived for generations wherever gold deposits were found. Violence between locals and prospectors flared. The land became a lawless frontier of crime and bedlam.

No one could quite tell me who the "Mr. Marshall" of Kasulo was, but the story goes that in 2014, a local resident was digging a well next to his home when he found a hunk of heterogenite that turned out to have a staggering 20 percent grade of cobalt, higher than anywhere else in the world. The inhabitants of Kasulo promptly took hold of every shovel, spade, and piece of rebar they could find and started digging tunnels all over the neighborhood. People flocked en masse to Kasulo to join the scramble for blue gold. Locals were displaced, the earth was despoiled, and conflict erupted. There are no precise figures as to how many tunnels there are in Kasulo, but locals estimate over two thousand.

In April 2017, Governor Muyej awarded a purchasing monopoly to Congo DongFang Mining for all the cobalt in Kasulo in exchange for a payment of $12 million. CDM was also awarded rights to set up an artisanal mining zone inside the neighborhood in coordination with the artisanal mining cooperative COMIKU. COMIKU is owned by Yves Muyej, one of Governor Muyej's sons. As part of the deal, CDM was obliged to pay resettlement compensation to the households living in the concession zone. The man in charge of the process, Mr. Yav Katshung, was director of the office of the governor of Lualaba province, as well as chief counsel in the DRC for CDM, which was a clear conflict of interests. A total of 554 households were identified as being inside the future concession. The inhabitants were given two options by Mr. Katshung—receive a fixed payment of between $400 and $2,000 depending on the value of their homes, or move into one of the new homes being built in a village called Samukinda, located about twenty kilometers from Kasulo.

I spoke with several families who used to live in the CDM concession area more than a year after they were displaced. They reported that to their knowledge only a few payments to the 554 households had been made and that the payments were less than promised. Very few families elected to move to Samukinda, because it was too far from sources of income. In addition, the new homes built in Samukinda for the displaced residents of Kasulo were small, slipshod, and unfinished. The families with whom I spoke ended up cramming into nearby villages and were struggling to make ends meet. Whether in villages like Kamatanda, towns like Fungurume, or cities like Kolwezi, the consequences of displacement due to mining operations were always the same—exacerbated poverty, increased hardship, and growing desperation. None of this, however, stopped CDM from moving quickly to wall off their prized concession and set up an artisanal mining model site, at which annual cobalt production has been as high as 8,100 tons.[7]

I arrived at the entrance of the CDM concession in Kasulo, where I was greeted by Republican Guard soldiers. They were expecting me, as I had been given authorization by Governor Muyej's office to tour the heavily secured site. The entrance to the CDM mine had a similar system of control as CHEMAF had at the Mutoshi mine. It included separate entrances for males and females and verification by the security guards for COMIKU identification badges before allowing entry. The front gate did not broadcast a pithy mission statement as the CHEMAF one did, but it did show the same figures of a pregnant woman, children, and a bottle of alcohol inside red circles with lines crossed over them.

Unlike most of the formal mining concessions that I visited, CDM did not bother asking me to take a Breathalyzer test. I passed through the security gate after a thorough search of my possessions, and I was led into the main CDM office situated immediately to the right of the entrance, next to a small medical clinic. There were about five or six CDM managers in the main office who handled day-to-day operations. About a dozen of the same red cargo trucks that I saw at Musompo were parked to the left of the main entrance. There were also thirteen depots across from the trucks, built under three hangar-like structures. The depots were operated by CDM staff. A hundred or so meters farther into the site there was a large open-air pit mine.

I took a seat at a conference table inside the CDM office. The director of the site, Mr. Li, sat at a nearby desk, smoking a cigarette and speaking into his smartphone in Mandarin. He looked over at me from time to time, but otherwise ignored me. After a few minutes, I was joined at the conference table by high-ranking members of COMIKU. Even though I had been granted permission to tour the site, they wanted to discuss my intentions.

Tensions were high in the area, as a few journalists had recently managed to expose some of the realities inside Kasulo. In response, CDM built a concrete wall in early 2018 around the entire neighborhood, and security guards were posted to prevent entry of outsiders without authorization. I reassured the COMIKU staff that it was not my intention to make any trouble. Like the COMIAKOL team at CHEMAF, the COMIKU team offered an oral presentation about the CDM mine. They started by focusing on the importance of artisanal mining cooperatives.

"The mining cooperatives ensure formality and safety to artisanal mining," one of the COMIKU leaders explained.

I was told that COMIKU registered all the workers, monitored onsite excavation, maintained safe working conditions, and ensured that there were no children at the site. In exchange, COMIKU received a fixed management fee each month from CDM as well as a small share of production.

"When the artisanal miners dig on their own, they take too many risks. They also put their children in the mines. We try to educate families that children should be in school," a COMIKU official said.

I asked what happened if a family could not afford the school fees.

"The schools should not have fees," I was told, as if saying so would solve the problem.

The COMIKU team took exception to foreigners who told "wild stories" about the harms of artisanal mining without knowing the local context. They assured me that the mine adhered to international standards on hazardous work; however, they asserted that the international community also had to appreciate that in the Congo, a fifteen-year-old boy would consider himself to be a grown man. Europeans and Americans were not in a position to determine what constituted adulthood in the Congo. A fifteen-year-old already had to provide for his family as an adult would, I was told.

It was a fair point. The norms of wealthy countries could not simply be imposed upon the poor. What makes eighteen the magic number for adulthood? A strong, thoughtful, fifteen-year-old male in the Congo who wants to provide for his family may be every bit an adult as an eighteen-year-old high schooler in the West. The problem, however, is that if lines are not drawn somewhere, vulnerable children will invariably be exploited, and it is impossible to go case by case for every teenager in poor nations to determine who is adequately mature to make "adult" decisions and perform "adult" work. The fact that families across the DRC are faced with the non-choice of putting a child in school or putting them to work so that the family can survive means that those families have been abandoned by the Congolese state just as much as they have been abandoned by the global economy.

After my meeting with the COMIKU officials, it was time for the tour. I was instructed not to take any photos and told that one of the COMIKU officials, Jean-Paul, was to accompany me. We were given orange-and-yellow vests to wear, along with an olive-colored hard hat. During our walk to the pit, Jean-Paul explained that there were more than fourteen thousand artisanal miners who were registered to work at the site and that they usually had ten thousand people working inside the concession on any given day. The artisanal miners were encouraged to organize themselves in groups to dig tunnels in and around the main pit to gather heterogenite. Therein, I noted the first difference between this model site and CHEMAF's—CDM allowed tunnel digging.

The open pit at the CDM model site was roughly two hundred meters in diameter and about thirty meters deep. The dirt in and around the pit was a rich copper color, deeper in hue than I had seen at other mines. At the base of the pit, there were more than 150 tunnel openings laid out in lines about three meters apart. I saw around one hundred artisanal miners working at the surface. There must have been several times this number of people in the tunnels below. Piles of heterogenite were scattered across the pit. Unlike the CHEMAF site, none of the artisanal miners I saw at the CDM site wore uniforms or had any sort of protective equipment. I did not see any visibly pregnant women or alcohol bottles during my visit.

We walked into the pit and met with a group of diggers emerging from a tunnel. Two men stood astride a plank of wood over the tunnel and pulled the men up one at a time with a rope. Nine individuals exited the tunnel; two of them looked to be under eighteen years old. The leader of the group was a young man named Fiston. He was thin and muscular, wearing brown shorts, plastic flip-flops, and an orange shirt. He had a small hunk of muscle missing from his right thigh. Fiston described what it was like working at the CDM site: "We were digging in Kasulo before we registered to work here. When we started working here, they paid us a wage each week while we were digging the tunnel. It took us more than one month to find the heterogenite vein."

After Fiston's group found the vein of heterogenite, they had to start repaying the advance of $25 per week that they had received. Fiston said they also had to repay the cost of their registration cards with COMIKU, which was $150. They were only permitted to sell the heterogenite they dug out of the tunnel to the CDM depots inside the concession. Half of what they earned was deducted for debt repayment, and the other half they kept as income. Fiston and his team members were not sure how much of their debts remained, but they said that COMIKU and the CDM bosses kept a tally, and it would be shown to them if they requested.

I asked Fiston how deep their tunnel was, and he said they eventually dug to a depth of forty meters. That was deeper than any tunnel I had yet encountered. Fiston said that some of the tunnels in the CDM concession were as deep as sixty meters and that some of them connected underground. I asked how they managed to breathe so deep underground, and Fiston said that CDM had about twenty air pumps that they provided to some of the groups, which helped to ventilate the tunnels. Fiston also said that CDM provided axes that they could use to chop branches from trees on the concession to use as supports in the tunnels. I asked if there had been any tunnel collapses at the CDM site. Fiston looked to Jean-Paul, back at me, and said no. With Jean-Paul monitoring the conversations, it was not possible to probe sensitive areas such as tunnel collapses or injuries. I spoke to two more groups in the open-pit area, and they relayed similar information as Fiston's group.

We rounded the back of the pockmarked pit and climbed up a slope to level ground, at which point I managed to make out that there were more open pits behind a patch of trees, even though I had been led to believe there was only one. I asked Jean-Paul if we could visit the other pits. He seemed reluctant but said he would discuss the matter with his fellow COMIKU officials. We returned to the main office, and after a good deal of back-and-forth, COMIKU agreed to allow me to look around the other open pits, but they said I was not allowed to speak with any more artisanal miners.

I walked with Jean-Paul past the main pit, turned left, and arrived at a surface-level digging area at least twice the size of the first pit. There must have been around three hundred tunnel openings in this digging area, many of which had pink tarps over them. Working clockwise around the concession through various patches of trees, I encountered four more open pits, each of which had hundreds of tunnels. There was no way to know how many people might be digging underground, but it was likely to be several thousand. The two pits at the back of the concession were the least developed with the fewest number of tunnels. In total, I estimate there to be at least 1,100 tunnels in the CDM concession in Kasulo. It was impossible that they were all adequately ventilated by twenty air pumps, nor could they possibly all have adequate supports using tree branches.

The final stop on my tour of the CDM model site was the depots in the hangar-like structures near the front of the concession. The scene was chaotic—hundreds of artisanal miners had gathered next to stacks of orange- and white-colored raffia sacks stuffed with heterogenite. The thirteen depots were lined up at the back of the hangars, with names like Boss Van and Boss Liu. The depots were wooden booths with metal fencing. In addition to the bosses, there were Congolese men inside the depots who were using giant two-handed metal mallets to crush the large heterogenite stones down to rubble. Backpacks and other personal effects hung on nails against the walls. The price lists were handwritten in black marker and posted at the front of each depot. Even though the heterogenite under the CDM site in Kasulo was known to have the highest grade in the Congo at upward of 20 percent, the price lists were capped at 10 percent. The per-kilogram prices offered at the depots inside the CDM concession were also 20–25 percent lower than the prices offered at depots across the street in the broader Kasulo neighborhood, including those operated by CDM agents. This price disparity meant that the artisanal miners who worked inside the CDM model site were repaying their up-front wage advances and equipment expenses at submarket rates, which amounted to a system of debt bondage, just like the system Kosongo worked under at Tilwezembe.

After the stones were crushed to pebble size, they were stuffed into raffia sacks that the artisanal miners loaded into the cargo trucks near the front gate. The trucks ran at idle, spitting out foul gray smoke on everyone in the area. Seven of the CDM cargo trucks were loaded with sacks of crushed heterogenite parked near the main entrance on the day of my visit. A SAEMAPE official wrote down the weight of each truck to determine CDM's royalty payment. The weight was also used to determine the value of the production fee paid to COMIKU by CDM. As the trucks started to depart, several of the COMIKU officials walked over to see me off. They also made a request that sounded more like an instruction—the main cooperatives operating in Lualaba Province had asked for a meeting. I was given a piece of paper with the details of time and place.

The CDM model site failed the term more severely than the CHEMAF one did. I saw at least two dozen teenage boys working at the concession. There was a complete lack of personal protective equipment for the workers. Tunnel digging was taking place all over the concession, which meant that the artisanal miners were crouched underground for hours at a time, breathing air suffused with toxic particulates without masks. Although no one at the CDM site said that tunnels collapsed, it was certainly possible that some had. The system of debt bondage was yet another mode of exploitation, along with the inability of the artisanal miners to negotiate prices or seek alternate markets. In essence, the CDM model site placed a thin veneer of formality over a highly dangerous and exploitative system that seemed designed to maximize production and minimize worker well-being, safety, and income. Even the paltry expense of uniforms and safety equipment was eschewed. Why then were there more than fourteen thousand artisanal miners registered to work at the CDM concession?

I interviewed seven artisanal miners who worked at the CDM model site outside of the concession to explore this question further. The first answer I received was that it was very difficult to find places to dig in the broader Kasulo neighborhood. Almost all the land and digging sites were accounted for. Some of the interviewees were inhabitants of Kasulo, but they said they did not have a plot of land on which to dig or had not been successful at joining a team of diggers at a current site. "People only dig with their families or people they have known for a long time," I was told. The artisanal miners knew that the prices at the depots inside the concession were lower than the prices across the street in the neighborhood, but they saw this as part of the deal of having a reliable place to dig. All the people I interviewed felt that working at the CDM model site with all its hazards was still safer than digging in Kasulo. In particular, the fact that at least some of the tunnels had supports made the proposition seem less risky. I asked about tunnel collapses inside the CDM concession, and the artisanal miners recalled two in the previous fifteen months. They said that as far as they knew, they had been partial collapses of the main shafts. They did not know how many people had been injured or killed.

My meeting with three of the largest artisanal mining cooperatives in Lualaba Province took place two days after my visit to the CDM model site at a sports bar that catered to wealthy locals and expats called Taverne La Bavière. The bar had several TV screens showing soccer matches and a few billiards tables, and it was decorated with flags from around the world. I was greeted by three high-ranking officials—Peter (CMKK), François (COMIKU), and Leon (COMIAKOL). They were aware of my visits to artisanal mining areas around Kolwezi and said that they had requested the meeting to be sure that I had an accurate understanding of the role that cooperatives played in the artisanal mining sector. I had already been given a good deal of messaging on the matter, but it seemed unavoidable that I would have to sit through another session.

Working steadily through bottles of Primus beer, the officials explained that cooperatives were integral to improving working conditions in the artisanal mining sector.

"Without the cooperatives, the artisanal miners would have no protection from exploitation," Peter said. He added that he objected to the term *creuseur* because "it is a disparaging word. It suggests that the artisanal miner is like a machine that can only dig."

Although much of the conversation consisted of old information on the importance of mining cooperatives, the discussion eventually moved to a critique of the negative aspects of Chinese operations in the Congo. François complained that Chinese mining companies had come to the Congo to become rich on its resources while the people of the Congo remained poor. I had no disagreement on this point, but solely blaming the Chinese seemed too convenient. The Chinese, for instance, were not responsible for all the money that went missing from taxes and royalty payments to the Congolese government or for the government's failure to equitably distribute revenues from the mining sector to the poorest people of the Copper Belt. I took the risk of suggesting that the Congolese government could be considered equally guilty of the same offense as the Chinese—absconding with mining riches while its people languished. Much to my surprise, the officials agreed.

"It is true that money from the sale of concessions is not shared properly with the people," Leon said.

"Also the royalty payments," François added.

"That is why the cooperatives are important. We ensure the maximum wages for the artisanal miners. We protect their interests," Leon said.

I did not take the risk of pointing out that scores of artisanal miners I interviewed described cooperatives as the central agents of their exploitation. Perhaps some cooperatives operated as these three officials described, but from everything I had learned, CMKK, COMIKU, and

COMIAKOL seemed to serve little function other than to enrich their powerful owners while allowing everyone up the chain to claim that the cobalt from their operations was produced without child labor or hazardous working conditions. I pushed the officials on the issue of child labor, and as expected, they assured me that there were no children working at the sites they managed, which did not match with my investigations. They also asserted that most people working at artisanal mining ZEAs were registered with mining cooperatives, which again did not match with my investigations. On the contrary, I had been told that many cooperatives at formal ZEAs and even at massive sites like Tilwezembe took daily fees from diggers, including children, to allow them to work on the sites. The officials did, however, note fairly that there were simply not enough ZEAs to accommodate hundreds of thousands of artisanal miners in Haut-Katanga and Lualaba Provinces. The officials also conceded that because many ZEAs were located right next to villages, it made it more likely that children would end up digging at the sites as opposed to going to school. I asked the officials if they could explain why schools in the Congo were inadequately funded even though education up to eighteen years of age was supposed to be free. They did not have an answer. No one anywhere did.

The lack of government support of public education in the DRC is an inexplicable failure that severely exacerbates levels of poverty and child labor in the country. At just five or six dollars a month, the fees per child required to keep schools functional are so small that even a modest amount of funding could help solve the problem. Put another way, the monthly fees per child required to keep Congolese children in school and out of mines was equal to two Primus beers at Taverne La Bavière.

As I left, the officials ordered a third round.

UNDERWORLD

Of all the European explorers of Africa, perhaps none gave their hearts more to the people of the continent than David Livingstone. It was only fitting, then, that after Livingstone passed away in eastern Zambia on May 1, 1873, his loyal companions Susi and Chuma buried his heart under a mpundu tree. They embalmed his body, wrapped him in a tatted sailcloth, and carried him 2,400 kilometers to Zanzibar so that his remains could be shipped to England. Almost a year after he passed, Livingstone received a state burial at Westminster Abbey. Upon the stone that marks his final resting place are inscribed the last words he wrote in his journal, "All I can add in my solitude, is, may Heaven's rich blessing come down on everyone, American, English, or Turk, who will help to heal this open sore in the world." Livingstone dreamed that commerce and Christianity would eradicate "the desolating slave trade" that ravaged eastern Africa. Fate spared him the tragic truth—his efforts to open the interior of Africa to commerce and Christianity led to immeasurable suffering of the people he so loved. In no place has that suffering been greater than in the Congo.

Kasulo is the new sore in the heart of Africa. The neighborhood is a manic hive of tunnels that swarm with desperate and intoxicated diggers who stare death in the face each day. Everyone who digs in Kasulo lives in mortal fear of being buried alive. It is a neighborhood of concentrated hazard and the distillation of the entire system of cobalt mining in the Congo—all the madness, violence, and indignity culminate here. Kasulo is also the face of everything that is wrong with the global economy. Nothing matters here but the resource; people and environment are disposable. Every element of civilization has been abandoned. It is an unrestrained frenzy without moral boundary. The people of Kasulo are left—encouraged—to fend, fight, and die for themselves in a Hobbesian state of war, persevering each day "in continual fear and danger of violent death." Kasulo brings us to the razor's edge of a terrible truth. We will find within this place the dark secret that the leviathans atop the cobalt supply chain do not want us to see. The neighborhood is the inconvenient rumor that they hope will remain forever buried alongside the people who live here. Kasulo was walled off for precisely this reason—no one must uncover the truth. Republican Guard and FARDC patrol the wall in a hot and dusty version of 1960s Berlin, but like every wall that has ever been built since the dawn of wall building, this one has cracks. My adroit guide, Claude, was a resident of Kasulo, and he knew its secrets well. He took me to the eastern fringe near a defunct rail line, where we found an unguarded gap in the barrier and made our way in.

"Kasulo is a cemetery," Claude told me with the eyes of a priest who has lost faith in God. "No one knows how many people are buried here."

The essence of Kasulo is a devil's gamble: tunnel diggers risk their lives for the prospects of riches. Mind you, the "richest" income I documented in Kasulo was an average take-home pay of $7 per day. There are spikes to $12 or even $15 when a particularly rich vein of heterogenite is found. That is the lotto ticket everyone is after. The most fortunate tunnel diggers in Kasulo earn around $3,000 per year. By way of comparison, the CEOs of the technology and car companies that buy the cobalt mined from Kasulo earn $3,000 in an hour, and they do so without having to put their lives at risk each day that they go to work.

I entered Kasulo midmorning on a Friday and was soon greeted by two young boys and five drunk men. Most of the adult artisanal miners I met in the neighborhood drank a bootleg alcohol made from manioc, called *lotoko*. Being intoxicated was how most of the diggers in the neighborhood dulled the dread of descending into the tunnels. The five men led me to a pink tarp held up like a tent by wooden sticks. The two boys scampered behind the tarp and stole shy glances. Their father, Ikolo, explained that the tunnel was next to his house, which included a tiny plot of land. His eyes were bloodshot, and he slurred as he spoke. Ikolo's team had slept for a few hours that morning and was preparing to climb back down the tunnel. Another group of men had been underground for much of the night. Ikolo showed me the entrance to the tunnel shaft. There was a plank of wood laid across the opening. Ikolo said that the diggers climbed down the shaft by pressing their arms and legs against the walls and working their way down:

This tunnel is thirty meters to the bottom. That is where we found the heterogenite vein. The vein is like a snake under the ground. When we find the snake, we follow it as far as we can. It requires experience to know which direction to go and how far to follow it. We use this [rebar] to knock the stone from the wall.

Ikolo explained that after they filled enough sacks with heterogenite, one of the members of the group would climb up the tunnel shaft to pull up the sacks using a rope tied to the plank of wood over the opening. The sacks were stored inside Ikolo's house until they were ready to sell. "We have an arrangement with a *négociant*," Ikolo explained. "He brings his truck near the train tracks, and we place the sacks in his truck."

"Where does the *négociant* sell the cobalt?" I asked.

"Musompo," he replied.

I asked Ikolo about his arrangement with the *négociant,* and he said that the *négociant* gave them half the money from the sale of ore at Musompo. According to Ikolo, this amount was still more than he would earn at depots in Kasulo, because soldiers extorted money from them.

The hazardous existence of tunnel digging was not the life Ikolo had planned for himself. He was originally from Fungurume, where he owned an auto repair shop. He got married in 2012, and he and his wife decided to move to Kolwezi. At that time, Kasulo was a quieter neighborhood where he was able to afford a home and small plot. He had intentions of opening a repair shop on the main road to Kolwezi, but everything changed in 2014 when that man digging a well in Kasulo found cobalt. Initially, Ikolo resisted the rush to start digging, but the neighborhood was soon overwhelmed by prospectors and a flurry of small businesses to support the burgeoning population. Overnight, it became too expensive and too competitive to try to run his own business. Ikolo did the odd repair work to make ends meet, trying everything to avoid the dangers of tunnel digging despite the potential windfalls. His two sons were born, and with the added expenses, his family could no longer make ends meet.

"We could only eat once each day. My sons were hungry and sick. I had no other choice," Ikolo said.

In early 2018, Ikolo rounded up a group of relations and started digging the tunnel on his plot. His goal was to earn enough to ensure that his children received a full education.

"I never went to school. I do not want my sons to live this way."

Ikolo knelt to the ground and drew the shape of the tunnel in the dirt with his finger. The main shaft went straight down, then bent around bedrock that they were unable to tunnel through, then continued down to the vein, which they followed in an L shape from the base of the main shaft. They had been working at the tunnel for five months. It did not have any supports, and they did not have an air pump.

"It is very difficult to breathe in the tunnel," Ikolo said. "It is hot, and we sweat."

I asked Ikolo what it felt like when he was underground hacking at the heterogenite vein.

"All the men must stay calm. We know the tunnel might collapse. We are not stupid. We pray before we go down. We focus on our work. It is in God's hands if we live."

Ikolo estimated that a tunnel collapsed every month in Kasulo. He said everyone knew when it happened: "We hear the news the same day. We console the families as we hope they will console ours."

Ikolo said that during the rainy months, tunnels in Kasulo collapsed more often and can also flood very quickly. If diggers are underground when a storm breaks, they are likely to drown.

The entire operation seemed like a death sentence, be it from suffocation, drowning, or collapse. I asked Ikolo if it was worth the risk. He went silent for a moment before offering a response.

"There is no other work here. Cobalt is the only possibility. We go down the tunnel. If we make it back with enough cobalt, our worries are finished for one day."

Ikolo looked somberly at his two boys, ages four and five.

"Every time I go in the tunnel, I wonder if I will see my sons again."

Ikolo kissed his boys and climbed down the tunnel. Light clung to him as long as it could, and then he was gone. I looked at his children and wondered whether they understood where their father was going. Did they realize that might have been the last time they ever saw him? Would they remember him if it was? Ikolo understood. It was impossible to imagine the anxiety he endured each moment that he was crouched underground beneath tons of merciless earth, wondering if the next whack against the tunnel wall might be his last. Ikolo hoped to live long enough to educate his sons and provide them a better life, but that aspiration could be buried with him today, tomorrow, or the next day. If the worst did happen, his sons would one day face the same devil's bargain their father did—risk their lives in the underworld, just to survive.

I walked from Ikolo's tunnel farther into the heart of Kasulo. All around me, the grim circus unfolded. The place reeked of fever and violence. The earth was upturned and spoiled. There were hills and chasms in every direction. Space was compressed by a horde of huts, digging supply shops, food and alcohol markets, hair salons, mobile phone top-up kiosks, motorbikes, bicycles, piles of rubble, stacks of raffia sacks, and copper-cobalt depots. Big black speakers blared pop music in a head-wringing mash-up of tones. Hammers, mallets, and rebar were strewn along the ground. Dirt paths were littered with smashed boxes, plastic bags, and empty liquor bottles. Children scampered through the maze of disarray. Teenagers hauled sacks of heterogenite along dirt paths on rusty bicycles. There were tunnels and tarps in every direction. The people whose ancestors were once forced to measure their lives in kilos of rubber were now forced to measure their lives in kilos of cobalt.

A fight broke out between several men near a shack-brothel. A madam stood at the front entrance, decked in a vibrant indigo, azure, and gold-trim *pagne*. She handled the money, and she preferred to be paid in U.S. dollars. She was willing to let me look around the brothel for a fee of ten dollars, but I was not allowed to speak to any of the women or girls, some of whom looked to be as young as fourteen. The brothel consisted of small, brick-wall *chambres* ("rooms") with no roofs and dusty mattresses on the ground. There were stray cigarette butts, liquor bottles, and other trash scattered in the dirt. Some of the walls had pinups of half-naked women. In one of the *chambres* toward the back, there was a young girl wearing a deep violet dress, with her hair tied in pigtails. Her childlike radiance was a jarring contrast to the sordid surroundings. The madam followed behind as I looked around, staying close enough that I could feel her hot breath on the back of my neck. Eventually, she grew impatient and directed me back outside. I asked if she knew how many brothels there were in Kasulo. She shrugged, clicked her lips, and said, "Maybe ten. I don't know." She explained that the diggers came to her on the days they were paid. "They want to celebrate. They want to feel alive," she said. Soldiers, on the other hand, took women without paying.

I spent the remainder of the day meeting with a few groups of tunnel diggers throughout Kasulo. As I listened to their stories, a semblance of order emerged beneath the chaos. There was a well-established system that included a micro-economy of sponsors, diggers, sellers, buyers, and enforcers. The group that most helped me understand the cobalt ecosystem was located at a digging site close to the center of the neighborhood. The four men and two teenagers, ages fourteen to twenty-five, were part of a larger troop of more than thirty men and boys who were excavating a tunnel complex located next to a four-room brick home.

The oldest member of the subgroup, Mutombo, invited me to look around the tunnel area. He wore dark brown sweatpants and a green Heineken T-shirt. He was muscular and vibrant, with the confidence of a New York City street hustler. Mutombo explained that his group of diggers were brothers and cousins. They were not digging in a home they owned or that was owned by anyone else in the other groups. The owner of the home, Jacques, lived in Lubumbashi. His brother, Régis, lived nearby in Kasulo and managed the thirty diggers at the home. Jacques and Régis were "pit owners" who sponsored the artisanal miners who were digging at the home. The sponsorship system worked the same as it did inside the CDM model site. Mutombo explained:

When we start to dig the tunnel, the sponsors give us a wage each week. They also give us the tools for digging, a water pump, two air pumps, and headlamps . . . People come from many villages to dig on the properties of the people who live here. Everyone comes to Kasulo to find cobalt. *Fuata nyuki ule asali* ["Follow the bees in order to eat honey"].

Mutombo said that it took them three months to find a vein of heterogenite, and that they had been exploiting that vein for around a month. The heterogenite that they excavated from the tunnel was then sold by Régis at a depot not far from the home. The share in income was 60–40 in favor of Régis. On the best days, Mutombo said he walked home with ten dollars. I asked what would happen after the diggers repaid the sponsorship, and Mutombo said that he believed the system would change to a 50–50 split at that time, although he was not certain. Crucially, the artisanal miners were not allowed to go to the depot with Régis. They had to accept that he faithfully represented the price for which he sold the ore.

"We climb down, we dig, we climb up. We wash the dust away. This is our life. We can only move forward," Mutombo said.

Mutombo lit a cigarette and breathed the smoke out wistfully. We talked more about his background and what brought him to Kasulo.

"I was born in Likasi. Can you believe I have seven older brothers? My mother wanted a girl, so she kept trying, and when I was born, she said to my father, 'You must be a witch! Take four of these boys and exchange them for one girl!'"

Mutombo laughed with abandon. It was the first time I heard an artisanal miner laugh. Mutombo left school in the eighth year and started digging for cobalt at artisanal mines near Likasi, including Tocotens, where Patoke was a digger.

"I know you will say education is important, but I wanted to help my parents. I wanted to buy things for myself," Mutombo said.

Three of Mutombo's older brothers were already artisanal miners, and one had moved to Zambia to work at a cement-manufacturing company in Ndola. The others worked in Likasi and Lubumbashi.

"I have a plan. I will not dig forever. I am saving money. When I have enough, I will start a business to sell cigarettes and beer in Kasulo. Every *creuseur* needs cigarettes and beer!"

There are few people in the world who tempt providence more brashly than a tunnel-digging artisanal miner who dares to have a dream. Every day that Mutombo climbed down the tunnel increased the probability that he might suffer a horrid demise. Why did he do it? The absence of a reliable alternative provided part of the answer, but not all of it. There was still the "get rich quick" impulse that drove artisanal miners to Kasulo. It was a massive and oftentimes tragic gamble. As with all casinos, the house eventually won. Tunnel diggers like Mutombo only shared in a fraction of the lowest rung of the value chain. Almost all the value of their labor was siphoned away and distributed upstream. Mutombo was nevertheless able to secure a comparably generous income relative to his peers in the mining provinces. Each member of his team produced roughly ten kilograms of heterogenite per day. Assuming an average 4 percent grade and price of roughly $1.30 per kilogram, the team members earned an average of about $5.20 per day after a 60–40 percent split with their sponsor, which would increase to $6.50 per day once the split moved to 50–50. This is the highest average income of any artisanal cobalt miners I documented in the DRC.

These numbers also suggest that the aggregate cobalt production from Kasulo is massive. If each digger produced roughly 250 kilograms of heterogenite per month and there were 18,000 tunnel diggers in Kasulo, then the neighborhood would produce approximately 54,000 *tons* of heterogenite per year. There are thought to be somewhere between 600,000 and 800,000 tons of heterogenite under Kasulo, so at best, the scramble has another ten or fifteen years to run. A lot of money (by Congolese standards) will be made by Kasulo's tunnel diggers during that time. Countless lives will be lost. When the cobalt finally runs dry, the world will carry on and leave Kasulo behind, just like a lion that has finished gorging. That is the "disaster" that Gloria, the student in Lubumbashi, warned about. Once the resources have been looted, the Congolese people will be left with nothing but worthless dirt and empty stomachs. In the interim, the prospect of earning five or ten dollars a day beckoned thousands of diggers like Mutombo into the tunnels. The global economy depended on it. Mutombo's daily descent created value denoted in the billions of dollars for everyone up the chain, yet only he and those like him assumed all the risk. The system was all upside for everyone but Mutombo, and the riches he created were stacked to the sky atop his earnest shoulders.

Mutombo's team members began their descent. I peered down the shaft as the first young man pressed his feet and hands against the walls of the tunnel and disappeared into the abyss. I asked Mutombo whether the tunnel had any supports. It did not. Neither did any of the other tunnels in Kasulo as far as he was aware. As the second man made his way down the shaft, Mutombo described the tunnel-digging process in more detail. The first step was called *kufanya découverte,* a mash-up of Swahili and French that meant "to do the discovery." This was the phase during which the artisanal miners used shovels to dig the shaft straight down until they discovered a vein of heterogenite. Once the ore was discovered, the *attaquant* ("attacker") led the digging team by determining the best way to follow the vein, a process called *kufwata filon.*

Mutombo said that he was the *attaquant* for his team. It was a job he took very seriously.

"It requires experience to know how deep to pursue the cobalt," Mutombo explained. "When we follow the vein, this is the time we are most anxious. Each meter we dig, the risk that the tunnel will collapse is greater."

Mutombo pointed to two wires plugged into a diesel generator next to the home that snaked down the tunnel shaft. He said they were for the air pumps, which helped them breathe when they stayed underground for an entire night.

"We may sleep for some time in the chamber at the bottom of the main shaft, or sometimes we sleep deeper inside the tunnel. That machine keeps us from suffocating."

I asked Mutombo why he didn't return to the surface for a nap, rather than spend any more time underground than necessary.

"God has already determined our fate. If we are supposed to die in the tunnel, that is where we will die."

Mutombo yelled down the tunnel shaft and dropped a long rope made of torn-up raffia sacks tied together.

"Let me show you," he said with a smile, as if offering a glimpse of a great treasure.

Mutombo looped one end of the raffia rope around his left wrist and took a wide stance on the plank of wood over the tunnel opening. Someone shouted from below. Mutombo started pulling the rope up in brisk, powerful motions. Every muscle in his body was taut as he pulled, breathed, pulled. I thought for sure the bag would be near the top, but he kept pulling and pulling until it finally emerged—a raffia sack filled with at least thirty kilograms of high-grade heterogenite. Mutombo dropped the sack next to the tunnel and caught his breath. Beads of sweat slipped down his forehead onto the bridge of his nose. The back of his shirt was drenched. He stepped off the plank and unlooped the rope from his wrist. He untied the sack, opened the top, and smiled ear to ear.

"Cobalt."

I reached into the sack and picked up a fist-size chunk of heterogenite. It looked similar to that first chunk I held in Kipushi—a beguiling mix of teal and azure, speckles of silver, splashed with orange and reddish patches. The colors in this specimen were deeper and richer. This was some of the highest-grade cobalt ore in the world, and it was everywhere under Kasulo, waiting to be discovered like raisins in a cake.

Mutombo was the last member of his team to venture into the python's belly. Like all the diggers in Kasulo, he clung tightly to dreams of a better life. To achieve his goals, he had to live like a shadow trapped between two worlds—the surface and the tunnel, the living and the dead. Unlike most of the artisanal miners in Kasulo, Mutombo did not drink alcohol. He faced the dread head-on. I believe he understood that he was living on borrowed time. Each day he repaid his debt to Jacques and Régis, his debt to the dead grew. One day, they might settle the account. He was compelled nevertheless to delve underground in search of blue gold.

Money and death were served together in Kasulo; the diggers could not have one without the other.

Mutombo grasped my hands tightly before he descended. Our eyes locked in a moment of shared understanding. Although I would never see him again, we were forever linked by the flow of stones from his world to mine.

I watched Mutombo creep down the tunnel. Just before the shadows took him, he looked up at me and smiled, like the moment light first fell upon the earth.

The heterogenite excavated by Mutombo and his team began its journey up the chain at a depot located not far from the digging site. I walked over to it to investigate, but the depot was patrolled by soldiers. From a distance, I could see that the metal shack had handwritten prices posted at the front based on grades from 1 to 20 percent. I never found an artisanal miner in Kasulo who said they knew anyone who was paid for more than 10 percent. A Chinese man was sitting inside the depot on a plastic chair, framed by towering sacks of heterogenite. With the soldiers present, it was not possible to speak with him. I faced similar restrictions at several other depots in Kasulo. Even those that were unmonitored by soldiers yielded only brief exchanges. Claude said he knew the manager of Depot 88, Boss Xi, and he was able to arrange a meeting with Xi one evening outside of Kasulo.

I went with Claude on the arranged evening to a roadside chicken café near the outskirts of Kolwezi. Cars and motorbikes passed by in a ghostly haze of fumes and dust. While we waited for Xi, Claude talked more about the tensions between the Chinese and Congolese communities. He explained that as the Congolese people saw their land being despoiled and resources extracted with little to no benefit to their communities, resentments grew and occasionally boiled over. The riots described by Promesse and Asad at Tenke Fungurume and the heartbreaking video of the riot at COMMUS after children were gunned down were a few examples. I found Claude to be very thoughtful on the dynamics between the Chinese and Congolese communities, and he even expressed a desire to visit China one day, "to see where they all came from." He was also one of the only Congolese people I met who was on amicable terms with a few members of the Chinese community, including Boss Xi. The prevailing reality, however, was that Congolese people did not form friendships with the Chinese.

"The relationship we have with the Chinese is only by the transaction," Claude said.

Claude suggested that the lack of social interaction between the Chinese and Congolese communities caused suspicions to fester.

"There are many biases in both directions," he explained.

I asked if he could give some examples.

"Congolese people feel that the Chinese treat us like animals. Or they think that we are dirty. They will not eat any food touched by a Congolese person. This is why they only eat in their private restaurants."

As for attitudes in the other direction—"The Chinese do not have emotions. They are like robots. How else can they stay away from their families for one year at a time?"

Perhaps the biggest complaint the Congolese had about the Chinese was this: "They burn their bodies!" Cremation was a shocking practice to most Congolese. Claude related a story about a Chinese construction worker who was killed in an accident at a work site near Kolwezi. It was not possible to return the body to China, so the family asked that he be cremated in the Congo.

"They arranged a ceremony in their community. They burned the body. I could not believe it. How can he join his ancestors if he is ashes?!"

I told Claude that as Indians we had the same tradition. He shrugged politely. It simply did not compute.

Despite the cultural differences, Claude said that many Congolese people had a begrudging respect for the Chinese: "They work collectively to reach their goals. Congolese people only work for themselves. Because of this, China is an advanced country and Congo is poor. Many Congolese are envious of this."

Boss Xi arrived and greeted Claude amicably. They had been acquaintances for a little over a year, although they did not socialize with each other. They met when Claude saw Xi in Depot 88 looking very sick with a bad cough.

"He brought me medicine and was kind to me," Xi said.

As Claude predicted, Xi did not eat anything at the chicken café. Claude ordered a bowl of chicken *mwambe* (chicken stew), and I had a soda. Xi said that he would eat at the restaurant in the Chinese compound in Kolwezi later that night.

"The restaurant has a satellite, so we can see our programs from China," he said. Xi also enjoyed watching streaming shows on his mobile phone. His favorite show was a fantasy crime serial called *Guardian,* about alien races that live with humans on another planet and fight over limited resources.

Claude told Xi more about who I was and the research I was doing into cobalt mining.

"It is good we can talk here," Xi said. "In Kasulo, the soldiers will harass us."

Xi was thirty-two years old and was originally from Wuhan. Our meeting turned out to be about a year before the COVID-19 pandemic emerged from his home city and spread across the globe. Xi had been in the Congo for almost two years when we met. His first post was working at the CDM processing facility in Lubumbashi, after which he was sent to help man a depot in Musompo, and finally to operate Depot 88 in Kasulo. Xi said he worked at the depot six days a week, usually from about ten in the morning until six in the evening. He bought heterogenite from the artisanal miners or pit bosses, recorded the transactions, and occasionally had arguments over price and grade. He said that he kept his money in a locked box that he delivered to his boss at the CDM mine at the end of the day. The heterogenite that he purchased was transported from the depot by diggers who worked at the CDM site to a point where it could be loaded into a pickup truck and driven into the concession. I asked how a fellow from Wuhan ended up working at a depot in Kasulo.

Xi said he saw a job posting online for a manager position at CDM. Xi went for an interview and was shown photos of comfortable apartments that he would live in. He accepted the position, and CDM arranged his visa and flight. After Xi arrived in Kolwezi, he said the conditions were not as represented.

"The flats are not very nice, and I have to share with three other employees from CDM. I was paid only half the amount they promised. This job is not what I expected," Xi said.

I asked Xi if he ever thought about returning home to find another job, but he said his contract was for five years. If he broke the contract, word would get out, and he would find it very difficult to find alternate employment. He added that if he left the CDM job, it would also be challenging for him to get paperwork to return home.

"I know many Chinese who left Congo and went to South Africa," Xi said. "It will be very difficult for them to get documents to return to China. They do not have families like I do, so I cannot take that risk."

Xi's wife and a son were back in Wuhan. He had been reluctant to leave them behind for a job thousands of miles away, but he felt that there were no good jobs in China, and the posting in the Congo was the only option he could find after more than a year of searching. It was proving especially difficult for Xi during his second year in the Congo to remain away from his family.

"I can only see their faces on WeChat," he explained. "When I came here, my son was two. Now he is four. I wonder if he understands who I am."

Xi's salary for manning the depot worked out to roughly $1,300 per month. Although this was half the sum he was promised, it was still almost eight times the average wage of tunnel diggers in Kasulo and more than twenty times the average wage of artisanal miners across the mining provinces.

It was difficult not to feel empathy for Xi. He was stuck far from home, isolated, and mired in monotony. He persevered through the challenging conditions so that he could provide for his family, not unlike Ikolo, albeit one (much safer) rung higher on the cobalt chain. Before Xi left, he said this: "Maybe you can speak to the CDM bosses in Lubumbashi. They have a good life. They live in private homes and travel to China often. Please ask them why our life in Kolwezi must be so bad."

I didn't bother telling Xi that the only CDM official willing to speak with me was too busy complaining about how Africans were lazy and ignorant to be worried about the quality of life of depot managers like him.

With each visit to Kasulo, the madness only seemed to grow. The air was hot with the scramble for cobalt. The full spectrum of human emotion burst forth from every tunnel: hope, dread, greed, fear, anger, envy, and above all—torment. The mothers of Kasulo endured the greatest torment of all. Most of them did not wish to speak with me. There is grief, and then there is soul-wrenching misery. There is loss, and then there is life-destroying calamity. One encounters the limits of what human hearts can endure all too often in the Congo. The land is filled with monsters, and the beast that dwells beneath Kasulo is a thousand-headed hydra, mouths agape at the surface, waiting for its prey to enter.

I met a young mother named Jolie on my second visit to Kasulo. She said she wanted to speak about an accident, but the moment I entered her small home of cracked brick walls and rusted roofing, it felt as if she already regretted my presence. Grief pressed hard against her slender frame. Her wide eyes were sunk deep within her face. The bones in her wrists seemed to stand up above the flesh. Her teeth were clenched like a skeleton's. The skin on her neck had striated discolorations that appeared like ribbons. She breathed with a raspy cadence, but the voice that emerged was somehow reminiscent of the soft song of a nightingale.

Jolie said that she had not slept through a night in months. Most nights, she stared at the shapes of the rust stains on the metal roof. Stray light entered the narrow space between brick and metal. Shadows played tricks on her mind. As she drifted from consciousness to slumber, forms appeared. She could not see the faces, but she knew who they were. She tried to scream, but nothing emerged. She tried to get up, but she could not budge. She wanted to take hold, but she could not lift her arms. She gnashed her teeth with such force that she felt they would crack loose from her gums. Eventually, she jolted awake in a panic. For a few minutes, she could not tell what was real and what was a dream.

Jolie lived each day fearing any reminder of the moment she received the news that her husband, Crispin, and sixteen-year-old son, Prosper, had been caught in a tunnel collapse in Kasulo.

"My life ended that day. *Mimi ni mzimu* [I am a ghost]."

Jolie remembered rushing to the scene of the collapse in a state of terror. She declined to discuss any details of the event beyond that. She eventually returned home to the dead silence. The clothes hanging to dry still smelled of her husband and son. The bowls from which they ate morning stew were the last things they had touched. Everything in this suffocating space reminded her of them. Her home was pain. Stepping outside was even worse.

"The tunnel is only ten meters from here. I walk by that place every day. I look down at the ground. Crispin and Prosper are still there. They are under my feet."

When a tunnel collapses in Kasulo, most bodies are never recovered. The family members are unable to give their loved ones a proper funeral. They are compelled instead to walk each day upon their dead. That is the reality that no one up the chain wants us to see. That is the truth that is meant to be forever buried here. The cruel design of a tunnel collapse makes sure of it, and everyone knows it. Perhaps they count on it—the impenetrable silence that obscures the vast tally of severed lives upon which great fortunes are built. Amid the tragedies, there are a scant few who by flukes of fate survived the brutal efficiency of a tunnel collapse. They were somehow just close enough to the surface and managed to cling to life just long enough for someone to dig them out. One such survivor was seventeen-year-old Lucien in Kasulo.

Lucien sat morosely on the ground of his two-room hut. His mother, Alexandrine, and his father, Josué, sat next to him. Josué made it clear that he was not happy with my presence.

"What are you doing here? What are you doing here?" he kept asking.

I told him I had come to understand what happened to his son.

"Look at him! You can see what happened."

"Yes, but could you please explain how he was injured?"

"What good will it do?"

"If people outside the Congo learn how children like Lucien are injured while they dig for cobalt, it may help improve the conditions here."

"This will not help my son."

"No . . . but maybe it will help someone else's."

Josué scoffed, but he eventually agreed to let me speak with Lucien about the accident.

Lucien was tall and lean with piercing eyes. Both of his legs were shattered, feebly held together by metal rods. He seemed to be in a heightened state of agitation. Blood pumped in quick pulses through a bulging vein on his forehead. He clenched his jaw rapidly as his eyes darted across the space in front of him, as if searching for something to focus on to still his mind. Lucien started to speak a few times, but quickly pulled back. With his mother's gentle encouragement, he managed to recount the ordeal.

When Lucien was fifteen, he started working with Josué at the site of an ambitious tunnel complex in Kasulo. There were more than fifty men and teenage boys working in several groups to excavate the complex. At more than sixty meters, the main tunnel shaft was one of the deepest anyone ever described to me. The main chamber at the base of the shaft was large enough for all fifty diggers to gather. They dug three additional tunnels that branched off from the main chamber, following various veins of heterogenite. They had air pumps and water pumps for each tunnel. Every artisanal miner was outfitted with a headband light and a pickax. Lucien was a hard worker and managed to earn five or six dollars a day. He felt proud that the income helped pay for school fees for his three younger siblings. The family had food to eat, including chicken once a week, and they were able to buy new clothes from time to time.

The morning of the accident, Lucien left home after breakfast with his pickax to dig at the complex. Josué stayed behind, as he was recovering from a cough and fever. In low tones and without a gesture, Lucien described what happened next:

> At the end of the day, a group of us gathered in the chamber to organize our exit from the tunnel. We had a rope tied to a tree that we used to climb up. I was near the front with my friend Kally. He took the rope first. I was beneath him. We only climbed a few minutes when the entire tunnel fell around us. It happened so fast. It was like the ground swallowed me. I could not move. I could hardly breathe. My heart was burning inside.
>
> By God's mercy, some people started to dig for us. Kally and I were close to the top. The people pulled us out.

According to Lucien, there were close to fifty artisanal miners in the tunnel complex at the time of the collapse. He said that only he and Kally survived. It is not clear whether the main shaft alone collapsed or also the chamber at the base of the shaft and the other three tunnels.

"No one knows what happened to the others. If all the tunnels collapsed at one time, they would die quickly. But if only the main tunnel collapsed, they would be trapped. Maybe after a day, the air would finish."

Although Lucien survived the collapse, he suffered multiple fractures in his legs. His parents could only afford one surgery at the hospital in Kolwezi, out of at least two or three that the doctors said he needed. His three younger siblings were forced to leave school, as the family could no longer afford the fees. Lucien's wounds had not healed fully when I met him several months after his surgery. He appeared pale and feeble, and the condition of the bones in his legs was unknown. Lucien received no postoperative care or physical therapy. It was entirely possible that his bones had not re-fused properly, or at all. Looking upon her ailing child, Alexandrine was beside herself. "How can my son live like this? His life is ruined." She said that if her husband had not been sick, he might have died in the tunnel with the others.

Josué remained silent throughout the interview. I understood why he was reluctant for his son to relive this tragedy. Before I left, Josué grabbed my arm and looked at me with the face of a man on fire.

"Now you understand how people like us work?"

"I believe so."

"Tell me."

"You work in horrible conditions and—"

"No! We work in our graves."

7

The Final Truth

Kamilombe

A great melancholy descended on me. Yes, this was the very spot. But there was no shadowy friend to stand by my side in the night of enormous wilderness, no great haunting memory, but only the unholy recollection of a prosaic newspaper "stunt" and the distasteful knowledge of the vilest scramble for loot that ever disfigured the history of human conscience.

—Joseph Conrad, "Geography and Some Explorers," *Last Essays*

HENRY MORTON STANLEY'S STUNT to become famous by finding Dr. Livingstone unleashed catastrophic consequences on the Congo that reverberate to this day. He could not have known when he began his search what was to come, just as Livingstone could not have known that his discovery of quinine and explorations of the African interior would help pave the way for the European colonization of the continent. Nevertheless, by the time Stanley was bullying his way through the upper Congo and swindling natives of their territory on behalf of King Leopold, he surely had a sense of what was in store, but he continued anyway. Did he do it for the money? For fame? To please a king? In the end, the *why* has little meaning, only the consequences matter—a vile scramble for loot that continues to disfigure the Congo 140 years later. The mutation unleashed by Stanley has reproduced across the generations as one treasure after another has been discovered and plundered, culminating today in the pernicious scramble for cobalt. There is no way to calculate the toll taken on the people of the Congo since the time of Stanley's newspaper stunt, and certainly not since Diego Cão first set anchor in Loango Bay in 1482. For centuries, slavery and violence have plagued the Congolese people, and the cobalt crush is the latest menace adding to their misery.

There is one final person we should meet before we arrive at the end of our journey at Kamilombe. Her name is Bisette. I spoke with her on September 22, 2019, just outside of Kolwezi. The day began with a cool breeze flowing down from the hills. The early-morning sky was bleached by white light. I ate a quick breakfast at my guesthouse, consisting of an omelet with onions, boiled potatoes, and instant coffee. I headed east on the highway and arrived at a discreet guesthouse where I would be conducting interviews for the day. Bisette was already there, sitting at a small table with her hands folded neatly in her lap. Her skin was sallow, her face heavy and downcast. A small, ovular discoloration in her skin beneath her right eye appeared like a permanent tear. There was barely any hair left on her head. She did not bother to hide the loss. The word *service* was sewn in tattered stiches on her olive shirt, just above her heart. She had come to tell me about her eldest son, Raphael.

Bisette spoke about her son with pride. "Raphael was a very kind boy. He was very smart. He loved going to school." When Raphael reached the sixth year, the family could no longer afford the school fees. He started digging for cobalt at Mashamba East, the Glencore-owned mine where Kabola was shot. The family made a plan that once Raphael earned enough to pay for the next year of fees, he would return to school to continue his studies.

"He wanted to go to university and be a teacher," Bisette said. "He wanted that all children can learn so they can improve their lives."

As a surface digger at Mashamba East, Raphael only earned around one dollar per day, barely enough to help with basic expenses for him and his five younger siblings. A year passed, then another, and the plan to return to school was eventually abandoned. Once he was strong enough, the tunnels beckoned. Raphael joined a group of more than thirty artisanal miners who were digging a tunnel at Mashamba East.

"He left home every morning and did not return until it was dark. He was so tired every day. Sometimes he would go to sleep without eating."

Raphael's earnings improved as a tunnel digger to around two or three dollars per day.

"I did not want him to dig in the tunnel. But he said he wanted to help the family."

On April 16, 2018, Raphael departed home early in the morning as usual. It was the end of the rainy season, so the big storms had passed. The air was crisp, and water was plentiful.

"I was washing our clothes when my nephew, Numbi, ran into our home screaming. He also worked at Mashamba East. He said a tunnel had collapsed. He said Raphael was inside."

Bisette and her husband rushed from Kapata to Mashamba East. As she ran, she prayed to God, "Please let my son be alive."

When Bisette arrived at the mine, her worst nightmares were realized. No one had survived. Diggers at the site managed to retrieve a few of the bodies, including Raphael's. Although he had been nearer to the surface like Lucien, the rescuers were unable to reach him in time.

"Can you imagine holding your child's dead body in your arms?"

Bisette and her husband took Raphael's body home. They washed their son's lifeless corpse to prepare him for burial rites.

"I kept waiting for his eyes to open."

Raphael's death was too much for Bisette to bear, just like Tshite's loss of Lubo, and Jolie's loss of Prosper. Bisette said that ever since Raphael's demise, she hardly eats, she hardly sleeps, and her hair began falling out.

"When my son died, I died."

Bisette did not wish to answer additional questions about Raphael's death or her family's circumstances afterward. She came only to recount what happened the day her son was killed. After her testimony, she stepped outside and sat quietly on the ground.

I watched Bisette sitting in the heavy silence, and my thoughts drifted toward her son's final moments. Was he in pain under the avalanche of rock and dirt? Did panic take hold in the enormous darkness? Did he cry out to his mother with his last gasp of air? Questions like these must torture Bisette. They must torture every parent whose child was buried alive in a cobalt tunnel.

Bisette returned to the interview room and said she was ready to leave. I had arranged for a colleague to return her to her village, but she said instead that she needed to go to Kamilombe.

My heart collapsed. There could be only one reason to go to Kamilombe that day. It was the same reason I was at the mine the day before.

A change came over Bisette's features that haunts me to this day— she cried out, on behalf of every mother in this heart of darkness, "Our children are dying like dogs."

The previous day, September 21, 2019, I woke before dawn to prepare for a visit to the KCC mining area. I planned for a full day of exploration, including the village of Kapata, Lake Malo, and the pit walls of KCC and Mashamba East. It had been about a year since my previous visit to the area, so I was eager to see what had changed.

I headed southwest toward Kapata. I passed by the crowded neighborhood of Kanina, the giant red pit walls of COMMUS, and the entrance to the rowdy washing zone at Lake Golf. The last stretch of road to Kapata had finally been paved as part of the SICOMINES deal, albeit many years behind schedule. There seemed to be more cargo trucks than ever hauling copper-cobalt ore up and down the narrow road. I arrived at the eastern edge of Kapata and entered the village on foot. It seemed much the same as before. Toddlers played in the dirt between the rows of huts. Young girls lugged plastic containers filled with cloudy water. Old women hung clothes to dry on strings between adjacent huts. Boys walked over to the KCC concession carrying tattered raffia sacks and rusty digging tools. The same internet café was still in the village with the same ancient Dell desktops.

I spoke with a few locals and was told that tensions were higher in the village due to an increased presence of FARDC and other armed security at nearby mining areas. Too many outsiders were telling stories about the mines, and the soldiers had been deployed to keep them out. The villagers also reported more pollution and vehicle accidents in the area after the road to the village was paved. Regrettably, child labor seemed to be on the rise. The villagers said that children were leaving schools in larger numbers to dig for cobalt. The reasons appeared to include lower payments for cobalt from depots, increased costs for food and supplies, and the never-ending pressure to feed cobalt up the chain.

After reconnecting with a few familiar faces, there was one remaining person in Kapata I wanted to track down before walking over to Lake Malo: Elodie. I knew it was a long shot, but I still wanted to try. I asked around in the southern edge of the village where Elodie said she lived with other *shegués,* and I was eventually told by three women roasting cassava that Elodie and her baby had been found dead under a thorn tree several months earlier. Mother and infant were buried; the women did not know where. The news struck hard. I had held out hope that some- how, Elodie might still be alive and in the area . . . but hope in the Congo is like a hot coal—take hold, and it will scald you to the bone.

I found a thorn tree near the southern edge of Kapata and sat beneath it to pray. I imagined Elodie lying under the branches to rest at the end of another exhausting day. Did she know it was the end? Was her baby al- ready dead, or did he linger next to his mother's corpse for a time? Was he hungry? Was he frightened? Was she? What thoughts passed through her mind during the final beats of her heart? Was she angry, sad, regret- ful . . . or did she simply whisper to whichever God might be listening, "Please take me home."

I walked with heavy footsteps from Kapata to Lake Malo. News of Elo- die's demise still weighed on my heart. I passed through the eucalyptus forest and onto the broad wasteland that prefaced the lake. Months of scorching heat during the dry season had reduced Lake Malo to a pond.

Trees were withered and the ground was cracked. People lumbered wearily across the burning earth. Although there were fewer people at the lake than during my previous visit, there were still over a thousand women and girls washing stones in the toxic water. I approached the water's edge and identified a group of girls with whom to speak.

It was not long after, perhaps ten minutes, when I heard the first spine-chilling cries from beyond the perimeter of Lake Malo:

Éboulement! Éboulement!

Time stopped. I chased the screams past the lake, down the road toward the adjacent mining site operated by CDM:

Kamilombe.

Word spread quickly. Soldiers had already blockaded the site of the accident before I arrived. Hundreds of villagers rushed from Kapata. This was the nightmare dreaded by all.

Éboulement. Collapse.

My guide warned me to keep back. The situation was too unpredictable. From the periphery, I could barely make out the opening of the tunnel, now a depression in the surface covered by gravel. Villagers crammed the blockade and demanded access to the tunnel, but the soldiers pointed their weapons aggressively to keep them at bay. The shouting and shoving threatened to erupt into all-out bedlam. Madness swirled at the edge of Kamilombe like a tornado. People were suffocating in a collapsed tunnel just in front of their loved ones, and there was nothing they could do about it. The soldiers eventually ordered some of the artisanal miners working inside the concession to dig for survivors. Villagers sang *mimbo ya Mungu,* songs of God.

When the diggers at Kamilombe unearthed the body of the first crushed corpse, such wails went forth as if to signal the final flight of hope from the earth. Two men lifted a child out of the dirt and laid him gently on the ocher gravel. His bloodied face was locked in a macabre expression of terror. His slender frame was stained with a paste of dirt and blood, the color of burnt umber or rusted metal. The boy looked no older than fifteen, a brief life aborted in the most wretched manner imaginable. Hearing secondhand testimonies was one thing, but when I finally saw the tragic consequences of a tunnel collapse with my own eyes, it was utterly devastating.

Sixty-three men and boys were buried alive in a tunnel collapse at Kamilombe on September 21, 2019. Only four of the sixty-three bodies were recovered. The others would remain forever interred in their final poses of horror. No one has ever accepted responsibility for these deaths. The accident has never even been acknowledged.

This was the final truth of cobalt mining in the Congo: the life of a child buried alive while digging for cobalt counted for nothing. All the dead here counted for nothing. The loot is all.

By evening, a daze fell upon the families whose loved ones had just been killed. Some wandered aimlessly; others sat in the dirt and wept. Although I would not meet her until the following morning, Bisette was at Kamilombe that day. Her nephew, Numbi, the one who brought her news of Raphael's death in the tunnel collapse at Mashamba East, was himself buried alive in the collapse at Kamilombe.

That is why she said, "Our children are dying like dogs."

As the sun slipped fiery and red toward the horizon, a wild wind swept across the plains and swirled like a vortex above the graveyard at Kamilombe. Clouds gathered swiftly like an army of beasts. Although the rains were not due to arrive for another month, a deafening crack of thunder split the sky, and howling torrents burst forth as if to wash the world away.

Epilogue

It's the action, not the fruit of the action, that's important. You have to do the right thing. It may not be in your power, may not be in your time, that there'll be any fruit. But that doesn't mean you stop doing the right thing. You may never know what results come from your action. But if you do nothing, there will be no result.

—Mahatma Gandhi

A FEW MONTHS AFTER THE tunnel collapse at Kamilombe, I met with the Congolese ambassador to the United States, François Nkuna Balumuene. Ambassador Balumuene was a broad, kind-faced man who listened patiently as I described my experiences in his country. We found common ground in the belief that foreign companies should share more of the wealth they generated from Congolese cobalt with the people who dug it out of the ground for them. We discussed the importance of ensuring the safety and dignity of the Congo's artisanal miners, as well as the need to protect the environment across the Copper Belt with more sustainable mining practices. For all the views we shared, Ambassador Balumuene made it clear that he did not think a foreigner should be the one to make such a case on behalf of his people. He felt instead that the people of the Congo needed to speak for themselves about what was happening in their country, and he suggested that if I really wanted to help, I should go back and assist local researchers in doing so.

I told the ambassador I would do as he asked. Lasting change is best achieved when the voices of those who are exploited are able to speak for themselves, and are heard when they do so. The first testimony of a former slave published in 1789 by Olaudah Equiano provided indispensable legitimacy to the original antislavery movement in England. Equiano's book would later inspire Frederick Douglass to publish his testimony in 1845, which served a similar role during the American antislavery movement. Advancing the ability of the Congolese people to conduct their own research and *safely* speak for themselves is the first step to solving the calamities taking place in the mining provinces of the DRC. Incorporating their voices in convenings on how to improve their lives should seem obvious, but it rarely happens. I am not aware of any conferences about cobalt mining at the OECD in Paris or at UN headquarters in Geneva and New York that included artisanal miners at the table. For that matter, I doubt that many of the people, if any, who participate in these conferences have ever visited an artisanal mining site in the Congo and spoken to the people who work there. The same goes for the CEOs of major tech and car companies that buy Congolese cobalt. Meaningful solutions cannot be devised if they are devoid of direct input from those the solutions are meant to assist. This is particularly true in the Congo, where the voices on the ground tell a very different, if not antithetical, story to the one told at the top.

After the collapse at Kamilombe, I was unable to return to the Congo until 2021 due to travel restrictions from the COVID-19 pandemic. When I finally returned, it was immediately clear that the pandemic had caused conditions to deteriorate considerably. Most foreign mining companies suspended operations for extended periods during 2020 and 2021 out of safety concerns for their staffs; however, demand for cobalt only increased. Billions of people around the world relied more than ever on rechargeable devices to continue working or attending school from home.

"COVID put pressure on artisanal miners to supply cobalt when the mines closed," explained Dr. Tshihutu at Mwangeni Hospital in Kolwezi, the largest in Lualaba Province. Dr. Tshihutu said the disease spread particularly quickly at artisanal mining sites because the diggers worked in extremely crowded conditions. It was not feasible for them to socially distance while crammed in a trench or tunnel, and even if there were masks available, wearing them while hacking in a tunnel or digging under the baking sun was impossible. Infected artisanal miners subsequently transmitted the virus in their communities.

"Those who went to the artisanal mines contributed to the spread of the disease in their families when they went back home," Dr. Tshihutu said.

To make matters worse, vaccine supplies in the DRC have been scarce. At the end of 2021, not even 1 percent of adults in the country were fully vaccinated, whereas roughly half the adults in high-income countries had received at least two doses of vaccine. Dr. Ngoy at L'Hôpital Général de Référence de Kampemba in Lubumbashi told me that her government-run hospital typically went two or three months without any supply of vaccines. When they did get supplies, it was usually the Sinovac vaccine from China, which the local population did not trust. Testing was not even available for all of 2020 until a separate clinic was set up with the help of Doctors Without Borders in early 2021. At times, Dr. Ngoy said positivity rates at the clinic surpassed 50 percent. Without vaccines, masks, testing, or other protective mechanisms, countless artisanal miners and other inhabitants of the Copper Belt became sick. Most could not afford hospital care and self-treated at home, with fates unknown.

In addition to a rash of illness and death, artisanal miners were faced with a collapse in incomes during the COVID-19 pandemic. The reduction was caused by an evaporation of buyers at the bottom of the cobalt chain. Most depot agents in the mining provinces are Chinese, like Boss Peng in Musompo or Boss Xi in Kasulo. Most of these agents traveled home in January 2020 for the lunar new year festival, never to return. China locked down, and flights were suspended. The few depot agents who remained slashed prices, which meant incomes for artisanal miners plummeted. Profits up the chain were as great as ever as cobalt prices increased throughout 2020 and 2021, but incomes for artisanal miners reached rock bottom. Families could no longer afford food, clothing, and housing. Thousands of children had to leave school to dig for cobalt to help their families survive.

"I can say that the number of children in the mines has increased a lot because of COVID-19," my guide Philippe said. "Most of those children will never return to school. So much progress we made has been lost."

The same nun who sent me the video from the COMMUS mine in Kolwezi showing Congolese workers being whipped like old-world African slaves while their Chinese bosses looked on, estimated that post-COVID, more than two-thirds of the children across the Copper Belt were not in school. According to her, almost all these children were digging in cobalt mines and becoming increasingly "sick, wounded, and orphaned." Considering the worsening catastrophe, she asked a simple and clarifying question:

> How can a sustainable future be built through sacrificing the very bearers of that future, through depriving children's well-being, and worse even, through depriving children the right to be?

Although conditions for the Congo's artisanal miners have worsened during the COVID-19 pandemic, there is a realistic path forward to alleviate most, if not all, of the harms they are suffering. The path begins with accountability. The biggest problem faced by the Congo's artisanal miners is not the gun-toting soldiers, unscrupulous Chinese buyers, exploitative mining cooperatives, or collapsing tunnels. These and other antagonists are but symptoms of a greater menace. The biggest problem faced by the Congo's artisanal miners is that stakeholders up the chain refuse to accept responsibility for them, even though they all profit in one way or another from their work.

Rather than issue vacant statements on zero-tolerance policies and other hollow PR, corporations should do the one simple thing that would truly help: treat the artisanal miners as equal employees to the people who work at corporate headquarters. We would not send the children of Cupertino to scrounge for cobalt in toxic pits, so why is it permissible to send the children of the Congo? We would not accept blanket press statements about how those children were being treated without independently verifying it, so why don't we do it in the Congo?

We would not treat our hometowns like toxic dumping grounds, so why do we allow it in the Congo? If major technology companies, EV manufacturers, and mining companies acknowledged that artisanal miners were an integral part of their cobalt supply chains and treated them with equal humanity as any other employee, most everything that needs to be done to resolve the calamities currently afflicting artisanal miners would be done.

The path forward cannot, however, follow the typical "flash-in-the-pan" model of addressing human rights violations in global supply chains. All too often, attention will run hot for a brief period, new programs will be announced by corporations and governments, and once the eyes of the world shift elsewhere, conditions will revert to business as usual. Cobalt stakeholders will have to do better than facile PR announcements and half-formed solutions. Unfortunately, that is exactly what they have delivered with the two most recent and highly touted initiatives intended to improve conditions for the DRC's artisanal miners.

The first initiative involved the Musompo marketplace outside Kolwezi. Under pressure to increase transparency at the bottom of cobalt supply chains, a plan was hatched to designate the Musompo marketplace as the sole venue where artisanal cobalt could be sold. Prices for artisanal miners would be standardized to improve incomes, and a system would be implemented that required proof from sellers that no child labor was involved in the mining of cobalt. Construction of the new Musompo Trading Centre began in August 2019, and Governor Muyej announced the launch the following summer, "We are continuing with the ambition of reforming the artisanal mining sector through the launching of the Musompo Trading Centre scheduled for the end of August 2020 . . . With the Trading Centre, all depots and underground counters will be closed and destroyed and all transactions will only take place there."[1]

The initiative was hailed up the chain as a win for artisanal miners and supply chain transparency, but no one seemed to mention the obvious problem—artisanal miners had no way of transporting sacks of cobalt to the center without relying on exploitative *négociants,* which defeated the purpose of the entire operation. Maybe an artisanal miner with a bicycle could wheel a sack of cobalt to Musompo from a few kilometers away, but if the new center was meant to be the only marketplace for buying all artisanal cobalt, how exactly was an artisanal miner working at a site near Kapata, Kambove, or Kipushi supposed to cart their cobalt to Musompo? The only option would be to continue selling sacks of cobalt for a fraction of the market rate to *négociants,* who would then sell it at Musompo. Whatever assurances the *négociants* might give about the absence of child labor would be meaningless.

This obvious design flaw was not even the biggest problem with the new Musompo Trading Centre. The biggest problem was that, despite the announced launch, it was never operational. I visited the center on November 3, 2021, and it was a ghost town. There was no one there, except a single armed guard who let me in to walk around the empty complex of a few dozen blue-painted depots. The story outside the Congo was that all artisanal cobalt was passing through the new Musompo Trading Centre, but the place was derelict. I was informed by colleagues in Kolwezi that there still was no indication as to when the center would begin to operate. Even when (if) it did, the inability of probably 99 percent of artisanal miners to sell their production directly at the center rendered pointless any assurances that it was improving their incomes or serving to eliminate child-mined cobalt from the supply chain.

Meanwhile, the original Musompo marketplace was thriving. It had almost doubled in size since my last visit in 2019, stretching for more than a kilometer down the highway. There were at least eighty depots, and they were packed with motorbikes, pickups, cargo trucks—and thousands of sacks of cobalt. Although I did not conduct interviews at any of the depots that day, I am confident that no one was asking questions about child labor or other abuses.

The second high-profile initiative comes from Glencore's mines near Kapata. Under pressure from the human rights community to address injuries and deaths of artisanal miners at the mine, Glencore built a border fence across the top of the pit wall at KCC and Mashamba East. The new fence was supposed to keep artisanal miners out of the mine and protect them from serious accidents. I investigated the KCC concession on November 4, 2021, and there were hundreds of artisanal miners digging for cobalt in scores of trenches and tunnels deep into the pit wall of the mine. Crucially, I saw numerous artisanal miners climbing over the barrier fence into the KCC mine.

"Climbing this [pit] wall is the hard part," one of the artisanal miners told me. "Climbing over the concrete wall is easy."

The following morning, November 5, 2021, I learned that a tunnel had collapsed *inside* the KCC mine the previous day, just as I was on the other side of the wall conducting interviews. Reports were that numerous artisanal miners had been buried alive. I tried to investigate the accident, but FARDC had already blockaded access to the KCC mine, just like they did at Kamilombe. Contacts in Kapata said that five bodies were eventually recovered and more than twenty people were still missing, including children. That evening, the same official from the COMAKAT cooperative who previously took me on a tour of Shabara met me at my hotel and said he had just come from a meeting at the governor's office during which he was asked to arrange the funerals of the five bodies recovered from the tunnel collapse.

A few weeks earlier, a colleague from the *Panorama* team at the BBC (the same program that aired the special on child labor at Tilwezembe in 2012) was working on a story about cobalt mining around Kolwezi. Glencore assured this colleague that ever since the fence was built, there were no artisanal miners *inside* the KCC mine. I told my colleague about the collapse and the deaths. He put the report to Glencore, and the company conceded to the BBC that there had been an "accident" involving artisanal miners inside the KCC concession but that only one person had died. The news was aired by *Panorama* on December 4, 2021. Had an outsider not happened to be on the ground that day, word of the collapse would likely never have been reported, just like the collapse at Kamilombe. How many other tunnel collapses and deaths go unreported? Was there a collapse at KCC the week before my visit? The week after?

What about at Mashamba East, Kasulo, Tilwezembe, or Kamilombe? No one will ever know.

The dead here still don't count.

One final voice calls to us from the Congo. The nation's greatest freedom fighter and first prime minister, Patrice Lumumba, described his dreams for the future of the country in his final missive to his wife, Pauline, just before he was assassinated. One can imagine the letter being addressed equally to the Congo itself. Lumumba's dream was tragically snuffed out by those who would let nothing stand between them and their scramble to loot the country's resources. Such has been the Congo's nightmare for centuries.

My beloved companion,

I write you these words not knowing whether you will receive them, when you will receive them, and whether I will still be alive when you read them. Throughout the struggle for the independence of my country, I have never doubted for a single instant that the sacred cause to which my comrades and I have dedicated our entire lives would triumph in the end. But what we wanted for our country—its right to an honorable life, to perfect dignity, to independence with no restrictions—was never wanted by Belgian colonialism and its Western allies, who found direct and indirect, intentional and unintentional support among certain high officials of the United Nations, that body in which we placed all our trust when we called on it for help.

They have corrupted some of our countrymen; they have bought others; they have done their part to distort the truth and defile our independence. What else can I say? That whether dead or alive, free or in prison by order of the colonialists, it is not my person that is important. What is important is the Congo, our poor people whose independence has been turned into a cage, with people looking at us from outside the bars, sometimes with charitable compassion, sometimes with glee and delight. But my faith will remain unshakable. I know and feel in my very heart of hearts that sooner or later my people will rid themselves of all their enemies, foreign and domestic, that they will rise up as one to say no to the shame and degradation of colonialism and regain their dignity in the pure light of day.

We are not alone. Africa, Asia, and the free and liberated peoples in every corner of the globe will ever remain at the side of the millions of Congolese who will not abandon the struggle until the day when there will be no more colonizers and no more of their mercenaries in our country. I want my children, whom I leave behind and perhaps will never see again, to be told that the future of the Congo is beautiful and that their country expects them, as it expects every Congolese, to fulfill the sacred task of rebuilding our independence, our sovereignty; for without justice there is no dignity and without independence there are no free men.

Neither brutal assaults, nor cruel mistreatment, nor torture have ever led me to beg for mercy, for I prefer to die with my head held high, unshakable faith, and the greatest confidence in the destiny of my country rather than live in slavery and contempt for sacred principles. History will one day have its say; it will not be the history taught in the United Nations, Washington, Paris, or Brussels, however, but the history taught in the countries that have rid themselves of colonialism and its puppets. Africa will write its own history and both north and south of the Sahara it will be a history full of glory and dignity.

Do not weep for me, my companion; I know that my country, now suffering so much, will be able to defend its independence and its freedom. Long live the Congo! Long live Africa![2]

ACKNOWLEDGMENTS

The people most important to this book, those for whom my gratitude cannot be measured, are the ones who cannot be named without putting them and their families at risk. This book would not exist without the assistance of numerous guides and translators who facilitated my investigations deep into the mining areas of the Congolese Copper Belt. I am forever grateful to them.

I am deeply indebted as well to every Congolese person who bravely shared their stories with me—the children, the fathers, the widows, the orphans, and the mothers who beat their chests. I will not forget the promises I made to you.

My wonderful agent, Steve Harris, appreciated the importance of this book the moment we spoke about it, and he worked tirelessly to find the perfect home for it.

I could not have asked for a better editor than George Witte. I felt great relief the moment I knew the manuscript would be in his hands. He and St. Martin's Press have been immensely supportive of every aspect of this book. I am profoundly grateful for their faith in me and for helping me bring the voices of the Congo's artisanal miners to the world.

My dear friend Kate Nace Day provided incisive feedback on drafts of this book. She was also there whenever I needed a compassionate ear. She was even there when I didn't think I did, and those were the times that mattered most.

I received keen guidance on trimming and clarifying the manuscript from a kindred spirit in the anti-slavery field, Jennifer Bryson Clark.

My colleague and friend Peggy Koenig provided crucial comments on the book. She has also been graciously supportive of my efforts in the Congo—from ground research to helping me find my agent—and for that, I am deeply grateful.

Murray Hitzman and Kim Shedd patiently helped me understand the geology of cobalt and the Copper Belt, which was no small feat considering that the starting point was someone who did not know the difference between a mineral, a rock, and an ore.

Traveling repeatedly to the DRC to conduct research took a heavy financial toll on my family. Thankfully, this toll was blunted by the generous support of Humanity United, the British Academy, the Schooner Foundation, Bruce Korman, Peggy Koenig, and John Hayes.

I owe a special debt to Adam Hochschild. I admired him long before we met, and when he kindly responded to a random email from me, I was over the moon with anticipation to meet him. He persuaded me at our first of several sushi lunches in Berkeley that I had to write *this* book, and he suggested the way I needed to tell *this* story. He is a cherished mentor and encouraged me every step of the way.

I feel indescribable admiration for E. D. Morel and Roger Casement. Their courageous and indefatigable campaign for justice in the Congo has been a constant source of inspiration to me. I remain astounded at what they accomplished more than 120 years ago, in a time of such ignorance and darkness.

Above all, my beloved wife, Aditi, carried this heavy burden with me and gracefully absorbed all that it did to me. I was at times heartbroken, angry, and shell-shocked by what I witnessed in the Congo. Her love and strength carried me through every step of this journey. I would never have crawled out of the darkness without her.

NOTES

Out of an abundance of caution, details of the dates and locations of interviews with sources have been excluded so as to avoid information that could be used to identify them, which could put them, their family members, and my ongoing research at risk.

All links in the notes were last accessed on May 4, 2022.

INTRODUCTION

1. Apple statement available at: https://www.apple.com/supplier-responsibility/pdf/Apple-Conflict-Minerals-Report.pdf.
Samsung statement available at: https://images.samsung.com/is/content/samsung/assets/global/our-values/resource/Samsung-Child-Labour-Prohibition-Policy-Ver2.pdf.
Tesla statement available at: https://www.tesla.com/sites/default/files/about/legal/2018-conflict-minerals-report.pdf.
Daimler statement available at: https://www.daimler.com/sustainability/human-rights/.
Glencore statement available at: https://www.glencore.com/dam/jcr:031b5c7d-b69d-4b66-824a-a0d5aff4ec91/2020-Modern-Slavery-Statement.pdf.
2. See: https://globalbattery.org/cobalt-action-partnership/.
3. Data on ASM available at: https://delvedatabase.org.
4. "history of human conscience": "Geography and Some Explorers," Conrad (1926), p. 25; "basis of administration": Joseph Conrad letter to Roger Casement, December 21, 1903, Conrad (1991), p. 271; "vampire growth": Grogan (1990), p. 227; "veritable hell on earth": Casement (1904), p. 110; "destruction of human life": Morel (1968), p. 4.

CHAPTER 1: "UNSPEAKABLE RICHNESS"

1. See: Darton Commodities (2022), pp. 7, 19; and United States Geological Survey (2022), p. 53.
2. Pakenham (1992), p. 12.
3. World Bank (2020), p. 103.
4. SAESSCAM (Service d'Assistance et d'Encadrement du Small-Scale Mining)

was originally created in 1999, when artisanal mining predominantly involved digging for coltan, gold, copper, and diamonds. In 2003, SAESSCAM was transformed into an official government department within the Ministry of Mines, and in 2010, the agency began to focus more on artisanal mining of copper and cobalt in Katanga Province. In April 2017, SAESSCAM was renamed SAEMAPE (Service d'Assistance et d'Encadrement de L'Exploitation Minière Artisanale et de Petit Echelle) and provided a larger budget and more authority to engage with provincial governments in overseeing artisanal mining in the Copper Belt.

5. Darton Commodities (2022), p. 14.

6. Ibid., p. 45.

7. United States Geological Survey (2022), p. 53.

8. Data from: 1) International Energy Agency (2020), and 2) "Electric cars fend off supply challenges to more than double global sales," available at: https://www.iea.org/commentaries/electric-cars-fend-off-supply-challenges-to-more-than-double-global-sales?utm_source=SendGrid&utm_medium=Email&utm_campaign=IEA+newsletters.

9. Data from: "Battery pack prices fall to an average of \$132/kWh, but rising commodity prices start to bite," available at: https://about.bnef.com/blog/battery-pack-prices-fall-to-an-average-of-132-kwh-but-rising-commodity-prices-start-to-bite/.

10. LCO batteries are 60 percent cobalt, L-NMC batteries are 6–20 percent cobalt, and L-NCA batteries are 6–9 percent cobalt.

11. The most common formulations for L-NMC batteries include NMC-111, NMC-532, NMC-622, and NMC-811, in which the numbers represent the ratios of nickel, manganese, and cobalt. There are also multiple compositions of L-NCA batteries, including NCA-111, NCA-811, and NCA-622, in which the numbers represent the ratios of nickel, cobalt, and aluminum.

12. Morel (1968), p. 42.

CHAPTER 2: "HERE IT IS BETTER NOT TO BE BORN"

1. Livingstone (1858), p. 357.

2. Arnot (1889), pp. 238–239.

3. Pakenham (1992), pp. 400, 409–410.

4. Martelli (1962), p. 159.

5. Ibid., p. 194.

6. Ibid., p. 201.

7. Darton Commodities (2022), p. 9.

8. "Biggest African Bank Leak Shows Kabila Allies Looted Funds," available at: https://www.bloomberg.com/news/features/2021-11-28/africa-s-biggest-data-leak-reveals-china-money-role-in-kabila-s-congo-looting.

9. In response to concerns about the conditions under which these minerals were being mined, a portion of the 2010 Dodd-Frank Wall Street Reform and Consumer Protection Act was devoted to addressing the issue of "3TG conflict minerals"—tantalum, tin, tungsten, and gold. Section 1502 of the act requires that publicly listed U.S. companies monitor their supply chains and disclose whether their prod-

ucts contain 3TG minerals from the DRC. If they do, the companies must disclose efforts to locate alternate sources of minerals to ensure that they are not contributing to human rights abuses. Demand for cobalt had not yet taken off when the act was passed, so it was not included.

10. Holoprosencephaly is a disorder caused by the failure of the embryonic forebrain to sufficiently divide into the double lobes of the cerebral hemispheres, resulting in severe skull and facial defects. In most cases, the babies die before birth. Agnathia otocephaly is a lethal birth defect in which the infant is born without a jaw, with ears fused below the chin, and sometimes with only one eye.

CHAPTER 3: THE HILLS HAVE SECRETS

1. Helmreich (1986), chs. 2, 4.
2. "no part in the affair": Morel (1968), p. 37; "enforced by violence": ibid., p. 58.
3. Morel (1902), pp. 347–348.
4. Morel (1968), p. 96.
5. "China Cash Flowed Through Congo Bank to Former President's Cronies," available at: https://www.bloomberg.com/news/features/2021-11-28/africa-s-biggest -data-leak-reveals-china-money-role-in-kabila-s-congo-looting.
6. "Biggest African Bank Leak Shows Kabila Allies Looted Funds," available at: https://www.bloomberg.com/news/articles/2021-11-19/biggest-african-bank -leak-shows-ex-congo-president-s-allies-looted-state.

CHAPTER 4: COLONY TO THE WORLD

1. Sources for "Invasion and the Slave Trade: 1482–1844": Franklin (1985); Hochschild (1998); Jeal (2007); Livingstone (1858) and (1866); Meredith (2005); Nzongola-Ntalaja (2002); Pakenham (1992); and Stanley (1862) and (1878).

Sources for "Colonization: 1885–1960": Casement (1904); CRISP (1961); Hochschild (1998); Inglis (1973); Karl (1983); Meredith (2005); Stanley (1885); Vanthemsche (2018); Van Lierde (1972); and Van Reybrouk (2014).

Sources for "Hope Born and Destroyed: 1958–January 1961": CRISP (1961); Nzongola-Ntalaja (2002); Van Lierde (1972); Van Reybrouk (2014); and Young (1965). Details of the assassination of Patrice Lumumba in this section are drawn from De Witte (2003).

Sources for "Hell on Earth: February 1961–2022": Kelley (1993); Martelli (1962); Meredith (2005); Nzongola-Ntalaja (2002); Stearns (2011); Vanthemsche (2018); Van Reybrouk (2014); and Young (1965).

2. The slave traders had also prevented Verney Lovett Cameron (who wrote about "unspeakable richness" awaiting an "enterprising capitalist") from passing Nyangwe on the Lualaba in 1872.

3. Despite Casement's extraordinary achievements for human rights, his story ends in tragedy. During World War I, Casement supported the Easter Rising for Irish freedom. He was charged under an arcane treason statute and sentenced to hang. The likes of Woodrow Wilson, the archbishop of Canterbury, Oscar Wilde,

Arthur Conan Doyle, and Joseph Conrad urged that he be reprieved. In response, the Crown prosecutors produced Casement's diaries, which revealed that he was gay. Homosexuality was a mortal sin in the United Kingdom, and public opinion swayed against Casement. He was hanged at Pentonville Prison on August 3, 1916, at the age of fifty-one.

4. Van Lierde (1972), pp. 220–224.

5. De Witte (2003), p. 16.

CHAPTER 5: "IF WE DO NOT DIG, WE DO NOT EAT"

1. Darton Commodities (2022), p. 9.

2. "Chinese Company Removed as Operator of Cobalt Mine in Congo," available at: https://www.nytimes.com/2022/02/28/world/congo-cobalt-mining-china.html

3. Data from: "Glencore Full Year 2018 Production Report," p. 10, available at: https://www.glencore.com/dam/jcr:3c1bb66d-e4f6-43f8-9664-b4541396c297/GLEN_2018-Q4_ProductionReport-.pdf.

4. See: 1) "Subpoena from United States Department of Justice," available at: https://www.glencore. com/media-and-insights/news/Subpoena-from-United-States-Department-of-Justice; 2) "Investigation by the Serious Fraud Office," available at: https://www.glencore.com/ media-and-insights/news/investigation-by-the-serious-fraud-office; and 3) "Investigation by the Office of the Attorney General of Switzerland," available at: https://www. glencore.com/media-and-insights/news/investigation-by-the-office-of-the-attorney-general-of-switzerland.

5. "Panorama questions over Glencore mines," available at: https://www.bbc.com/news/17702487.

6. International Labour Organisation Convention No. 29, Article 2(1) defines forced labor as "all work or service which is exacted from any person under the menace of any penalty and for which the said person has not offered himself voluntarily."

CHAPTER 6: "WE WORK IN OUR GRAVES"

1. Data from: "Glencore Full Year 2021 Production Report," p. 11, available at: https://www.glencore.com/dam/jcr:90d4d8f9-a85e-42ec-ad8a-b75b657f55d2/GLEN_2021-full-year_ProductionReport.pdf.

2. "Lualaba: Richard Muyej destitué de ses fonctions," available at: https://cas-info.ca/2021/09/lualaba-richard-muyej-destitue-de-ses-fonctions/.

3. Available at: https://budget.gouv.cd/wp-content/uploads/budget2021/plf2021/doc1_expose_des_motifs_projet_de_loi-de_finances%202021%20et%20ses%20annexes.pdf.

4. "Announcement Regarding Fatalities of Illegal Artisanal Miners at KCC," available at: https://www.glencore.com/media-and-insights/news/announcement-regarding-fatalities-of-illegal-artisanal-miners-at-kcc.

5. "The Terrorists' Treasury: How a Bank Linked to Congo's President Enabled Hezbollah Financiers to Bust U.S. Sanctions," October 2017, available at: https:

//cdn.thesentry.org/wp-content/uploads/2016/09/TerroristsTreasury_TheSentry
_October2017_final.pdf.

6. Darton Commodities (2022), p. 9.

7. Ibid.

EPILOGUE

1. See: "Lualaba: l'inauguration du Centre de négoce de Musompo en août 2020
va mettre fin aux comptoirs clandestins des minerais," available at: https://deskeco
.com/2020/07/13/lualaba-linauguration-du-centre-de-negoce-de-musompo-en-aout
-2020-va-mettre-fin-aux-comptoirs; and "Lualaba: Richard Muyej déterminé à ré-
former le secteur de l'artisanant minier," available at: https://editeur.cd/newsdetails
.php?newsid=41&cat=2&refid=4QZT2VjNt53E8eSIB7yUcvsYHFa0lzCdbMwnK
oq9GmJWuifDPRxgp61hOkLrXA.

2. Van Lierde (1972), pp. 421–422.

BIBLIOGRAPHY

Arnot, Frederick Stanley. (1889). *Garenganze or Seven Years' Pioneer Mission Work in Central Africa*. James E. Hawkins. London.

Cameron, Verney Lovett. (1877). *Across Africa*, 2 vols. Harper & Brothers Publishers. New York.

Casement, Roger. (1904). *The Casement Report*, in Peter Singleton-Gates and Maurice Girodias, *The Black Diaries: An Account of Roger Casement's Life and Times with a Collection of his Diaries and Public Writings* (New York: Grove Press, 1959), pp. 98–190.

Centre de Recherche et d'Information Socio-Politiques (CRISP). (1961). *Documents Belges et Africains*. Brussels.

Conrad, Joseph. (1991). *Heart of Darkness: An Authoritative Text, Background and Sources, Criticism*. Ed. Robert Kimbrough. Norton Critical Edition, 4th ed. W. W. Norton & Co. New York.

——. (1926). *The Last Essays*. J. M. Dent & Sons. London.

Darton Commodities. "Cobalt Market Review 2022." https://www.dartoncommodities .co.uk/market-research/.

De Witte, Ludo. (2003). *The Assassination of Lumumba*. Verso Books. Brooklyn, NY.

Franklin, John Hope. (1985). *George Washington Williams: A Biography*. University of Chicago Press. Chicago.

Grogan, Ewart S. (1900). *From the Cape to Cairo*. Hurst & Blackett. London.

Helmreich, Jonathan. (1986). *Gathering Rare Ores: The Diplomacy of Uranium Acquisition, 1943–1954*. Princeton University Press. Princeton, NJ.

Hitzman, M. W., A. A. Bookstrom, J. F. Slack, and M. L. Zientek. (2017). *Cobalt— Styles of Deposits and the Search for Primary Deposits*. U.S. Geological Survey Open-File Report 2017–1155. https://doi.org/10.3133/ofr20171155.

Hochschild, Adam. (2006). *Bury the Chains*. Houghton Mifflin. New York.

——. (1998). *King Leopold's Ghost*. Houghton Mifflin. New York.

Inglis, Brian. (1973). *Roger Casement*. Hodder and Stoughton. London.

International Energy Agency. (2020). "Global EV Outlook 2020." Paris.

Jeal, Tim. (2007). *Stanley: The Impossible Life of Africa's Greatest Explorer*. Yale University Press. New Haven, CT.

Karl, Frederick, and Laurence Davies, eds. (1983). *The Collected Letters of Joseph Conrad*. Vols. I, II, III. Cambridge University Press. Cambridge.

Kelley, Sean. (1993). *America's Tyrant: The CIA and Mobutu of Zaire*. American University Press. Washington, D.C.

Livingstone, David. (1858). *Missionary Travels and Researches in South Africa:*

Including a Sketch of Sixteen Years' Residence in the Interior of Africa. Harper & Brothers Publishers. New York.

Livingstone, David, and Charles Livingstone. (1866). *Narrative of an Expedition to the Zambesi and Its Tributaries; and of the Discovery of the Lakes Shirwa and Nyassa.* Harper & Brothers Publishers. New York.

Martelli, George. (1962). *Leopold to Lumumba: A History of the Belgian Congo 1877–1960.* Chapman and Hall. London.

Meredith, Martin. (2005). *The Fate of Africa: A History of the Continent Since Independence.* Public Affairs. New York.

Morel, E. D. (1902). Affairs of West Africa. William Heinemann. London.

——. (1968). *E. D. Morel's History of the Congo Reform Movement.* Eds. William Roger Louis and Jean Stengers. Clarendon Press. Oxford.

Nzongola-Ntalaja, Georges. (2002). *The Congo: From Léopold to Kabila: A People's History.* Zed Books. London.

Pakenham, Thomas. (1992). *The Scramble for Africa.* HarperCollins. New York.

Stanley, Henry M. (1885). *The Congo and the Founding of Its Free State: A Story of Work and Exploration,* 2 vols. Harper & Brothers. New York.

——. (1872). *How I Found Livingstone; Travels, Adventures and Discoveries in Central Africa; Including Four Months' Residence with Dr. Livingstone.* Sampson Low, Marston, Low, and Searle. London.

——. (1878). *Through the Dark Continent; or The Sources of the Nile Around the Great Lakes of Equatorial Africa and Down the Livingstone River to the Atlantic Ocean,* 2 vols. Reprinted by Dover Publications. New York.

Stearns, Jason K. (2011). *Dancing in the Glory of Monsters.* Public Affairs. New York.

United States Geological Survey. (2022). "Mineral Commodities Summary 2022." USGS. Reston, VA.

Vanthemsche, Guy. (2018). *Belgium and the Congo: 1885–1980.* Cambridge University Press. Cambridge.

Van Lierde, Jean, ed. (1972). *Lumumba Speaks: The Speeches and Writings of Patrice Lumumba, 1968–1961.* Little, Brown & Co. Boston.

Van Reybrouk, David. (2014). *Congo: The Epic History of a People.* HarperCollins. New York.

World Bank. (2020). "Minerals for Climate Action: The Mineral Intensity of the Clean Energy Transition." Washington, D.C.

Young, Crawford. (1965). *Politics in the Congo: Decolonization and Independence.* Princeton University Press. Princeton, NJ.

INDEX